AMAZING PLACES
— TO GO IN —
NORTH AMERICA

HUNDREDS OF AMAZING SIGHTS AND EVENTS

Eric Peterson

David Lewis

Publications International, Ltd.

Photo Credits

Eric Peterson, a Denver-based freelance writer and Colorado native, has contributed to numerous guidebooks about the western United States. His recent credits include *Frommer's Colorado, Frommer's Texas,* and *Frommer's Yellowstone & Grand Teton National Parks.* He is the author of the books *Ramble: A Field Guide to the U.S.A., Roadside Americana,* and *The Great American Road Trip.*

David Lewis is a Denver-based freelance writer and editor and served for a decade as a reporter and columnist for the *Rocky Mountain News.*

Facts verified by **Marty Strasen.**

Maps courtesy of **Microsoft Streets & Trips 2006.**

Acknowledgments can be found on page 319.

Contents

New England

The Southwest

Mid-Atlantic

The Rocky Mountains

The South

The Pacific

The Midwest

Mexico and Canada

Unlock the Treasures of North America

Have you ever stood at the rim of the Grand Canyon, peering into the chasms as sunlight reveals the vast, multihued sandstone cliffs? Glimpsed the sweeping arch of the Golden Gate Bridge through the rolling fog? Lolled in the afternoon sunshine on the beaches of Los Cabos surrounded by glistening white sand, palm trees, and waves gently touching the shore?

North America is a diverse landscape dotted with stunning sites, remarkable attractions, and festive events. The great explorers only scratched the surface of the wonders held on the continent. Indeed, the snowcapped peak of Denali in Alaska, the mystifying expanse of Arizona's Grand Canyon, and the sultry swamps of Florida's Everglades are amazing natural features. Beyond these natural beauties are the relics of ancient civilizations and modern-day masterpieces of engineering, architecture, and art. It's no accident that the continent's natural allure has been enhanced by the best of humankind's creations. A trip to New York would be incomplete without seeing the Statue of Liberty, a majestic guardian watching over New York Harbor. And can you really say you know how to party without ever witnessing the grand fete of Mardi Gras in New Orleans?

The landscape of the world has been changing since its beginnings, with some of its most astounding features created over millions of years. Our greatest accomplishments seem minor compared with the longevity of their natural counterparts. And whether natural or carefully constructed, these wonders will not last forever—which is as good a reason as any to visit as many of these places as you can. This book illuminates hundreds of the most amazing places in North America, and its inspiration may have you clamoring to leave behind the comforts of home and see some of these inarguably amazing places with your own eyes.

Lush evergreen forests in Grand Teton National Park sprawl out at the base of Mount Moran, reflected in the still, blue waters of Leigh Lake.

Chapter One
New England

When Europeans first stepped on Plymouth Rock in Massachusetts, New England became central to the formation of the United States. New Englanders have proudly kept their culture distinct and alive. A visit to New England mixes historic sites with such serene locales as White Mountain National Forest and Acadia National Park. The region's Revolutionary War history comes alive with a stroll on Boston's Freedom Trail and reenactments during Boston Harborfest every Fourth of July. Secluded destinations such as Walden Pond contrast nicely with the festive community spirit at hallowed Fenway Park.

At sunrise in autumn, vibrant foliage highlights the placid Center Harbor on Lake Winnipesaukee in New Hampshire.

Acadia National Park

Some say the name "Acadia" came from New England's native Abenaki tribe. Others credit explorer Giovanni da Verrazano, who supposedly called Maine and its environs "Arcadia" after a region in ancient Greece known as a rustic place of perfect peace and quiet—a description that ideally suits Acadia National Park.

Situated off the coast of Maine, Acadia National Park covers nearly half of Mount Desert Island. Originally named Isles des Monts Deserts by explorer Samuel de Champlain in 1604, the island also boasts the towns of Bar Harbor, Southwest Harbor, Mount Desert, and Tremont.

From the coastline, you can see the island's barren mountaintops, sheared off by ancient glaciers. Cadillac Mountain, a granite-topped peak rising 1,532 feet, is the highest mountain along the North Atlantic seaboard. Glaciers created other unique features of Acadia. Look at a topographic map of Mount Desert Island, and you will see that it looks as if it had been gouged by giant bear claws—deep ravines, Long Pond, Echo Lake, Jordan Pond, Eagle Lake, and the seven-mile-long Somes Sound (said to be the only true fjord on the East Coast) all run in parallel lines north to south.

For centuries, the Abenakis fished the sylvan shores of Mount Desert Island; and in the 1800s, farming, fishing, and lumbering provided the local economy. But this way of life changed when artists joined the community in the mid-1850s. Great Hudson River School

Acadia National Park provides splendid views of Maine's rugged coast.

painters such as Thomas Cole and Frederic Church started showing their landscapes of Mount Desert Island to patrons and friends. Eventually this led to more "rusticators," city dwellers who flocked to the island for a breath of fresh air. At first Bohemians came, followed by the rich and famous. The Astor, Carnegie, Ford, Morgan, Pulitzer, and Vanderbilt families all owned estates on the island and vacationed there during summer. Perhaps the most prominent was John D. Rockefeller, whose estate's 45-mile spiderweb of carriage roads have helped make Acadia a hiking and mountain-biking mecca. Rockefeller gave 11,000 acres to Acadia, including some of its most spectacular coastline.

By 1880, Bar Harbor had 30 hotels, and one ambitious entrepreneur had even built a hotel

and a cog railway on Cadillac Mountain. Alarmed by the spiraling development, a group of wealthy islanders began acquiring land to put together what became Acadia National Park in 1919. Today, the park contains more than 40,000 acres and is Maine's only national park.

When visiting this sometimes-crowded island paradise, enjoy carriage rides, sailing, camping, canoeing, fishing, ice-fishing, rowing, cliff-climbing, kayaking, hiking, biking, and more on dozens of trails, beaches, coves, and mountain cliffs. Acadia (and all of Maine's coast) is tormented by wicked weather throughout the winter and early spring, but tourists swarm Acadia and the little nearby towns in the blissful summertime.

Panoramas are plentiful throughout the park. One is Thunder Hole, a coastal rock pounded by huge waves. There's Acadia Mountain Trail, with views of Somes Sound, Echo Lake, and the Cranberry Isles. The pristine Sand Beach lies between rugged coastal rocks and mountains made of tiny crushed shells. Eagle Lake, which spans 425 acres, is the largest on the island. Sieur de Monts Spring symbolizes the preservation of Acadia and features the Wild Gardens of Acadia and the Abbe Museum.

It's hard to go wrong in paradise.

(Opposite page) *Built in 1858, Bass Harbor Head Light marks the entrance to Bass Harbor on the southwest side of Mount Desert Island.*

Boothbay Harbor

Boothbay Harbor lies along Maine's mid-coast. It's often called the Boating Capital of New England and hosts a summer festival called "Windjammer Days." The harbor is a great place for watching whales and puffins, canoeing, kayaking, hiking, biking, mackerel fishing, and camping. You can cruise to Monhegan Island or see sites such as the Maine Resources Aquarium, the Maine Maritime Museum, or Burnt Island Light, a lighthouse built in 1821.

Boothbay Harbor was incorporated in 1764. Thereafter, the settlement became known for

Boothbay Harbor celebrates the age of sail each June with Windjammer Days.

its saw and grist mills and for its shipbuilding industry—more than 500 boats and ships up to 180 feet long were built there. Over time, fishing became more important to the community, which helps explain why today the harbor's symbol is a two-masted fishing schooner, or "pinky."

If you can handle some time away from modern luxuries, this rugged area remains one

of Maine's most beautiful destinations. An hour's drive from Brunswick, Boothbay Harbor is a village of about 2,300 with pleasant shops and boutiques. Its picturesque harbor is exactly how many people picture Maine: Fishers haul in lobster traps, and masts gently rock in the distance. The aroma of steamed mussels mixes with the salty ocean air. You can rent cove-side cottages, dine in fine restaurants, and browse quaint waterfront souvenir, antique, and craft shops. It also pays to explore the neighborhoods inland from the harbor.

Penobscot Bay

Penobscot Bay is Maine's real Down East. While the words "Down East" now refer to the coast of Maine and its culture, the term came from ships sailing downwind from Boston to Maine.

If you're looking forward to exploring the real outdoors, you've found your place. Choose among recreational sports such as fishing for trout, smallmouth bass, or landlocked salmon; hunting bear, moose, deer, grouse, or snowshoe hare; or sailing a three-masted schooner on the bounding main.

The region has Down East civilization, too. Should you seek a vacation spot that has been visited by the rich and famous, from actors to presidential candidates, there are the Penobscot Bay towns of Islesboro, North Haven, and Vinalhaven. If you're eager for a taste of authentic Down East cuisine, the bay area has dinners of lobster and lobster cakes, steamed mussels, corn on the cob, and New England clam chowder, and breakfasts of pancakes and waffles, Maine maple syrup, and Maine blueberry jam.

Penobscot Bay lies just southwest of Acadia National Park and borders Isle au Haut, which in 1943 became the last contribution to Acadia. Towns around the bay include Camden, Bar Harbor, and historic Castine, which was settled by the French in 1613. These nearby towns provide convenient lodging, fine dining, charming shops, and local galleries. There's also Fort Point State Historic Site, which has Fort Point Light (a lighthouse built in 1857), miles of hiking trails, and a gorgeous panorama of the bay and the islands surrounding it.

The rocky shoreline of Penobscot Bay harbors quaint Maine towns with an authentic Down East feel.

White Mountain National Forest

New Hampshire's White Mountain National Forest is the heart of the White Mountains. Mount Washington rises fiercely above the dense woodlands. At 6,288 feet it's the highest mountain in the northeastern United States. On a clear day, you can see into New Hampshire, Maine, Vermont, Massachusetts, and Canada from its peak. The strongest wind of all time was recorded there in 1934— 231 miles per hour.

Mount Washington is part of the White Mountains' Presidential Range. The range also included the legendary Old Man of the Mountain—the rock formation remains New Hampshire's state symbol despite the collapse of its famous profile in 2003.

The vast majority of White Mountain National Forest's 800,000 acres are in New Hampshire, with the eastern edge creeping into Maine. The forest is indisputably nature's domain. It may be an easy drive from urban America, but it seems to be a million miles away. Fir, pine, beech, birch, and maple forests are crisscrossed by hiking trails that range from the half-mile Covered Bridge Nature Trail to the Appalachian Trail, which stretches from Maine to Georgia. The forest offers 23 campgrounds. Despite its size, White Mountain National Forest can get crowded, and some advise avoiding it on summer weekends.

Originating in the White Mountains, the Saco River provides prime stretches for canoeing, kayaking, and tubing.

Lake Winnipesaukee

Vibrant autumn foliage brightens the shoreline of Lake Winnipesaukee.

Lake Winnipesaukee is New Hampshire's largest lake. It is 26 miles long and 15 miles across at its widest point. The driving distance around the lake is 97 miles, though the jagged shoreline measures 179 miles around. Dozens of islands scattered like beads throughout the lake's waters add to its scenic splendor.

Like so many of the spectacular natural formations in North America, Lake Winnipesaukee is a glacial phenomenon. It has also become a vacation phenomenon, attract-ing summer visitors for more than a century. Many come from Boston, which is just a two-hour drive away.

Vacationers are always welcome in the communities that surround Lake Winnipesaukee. The largest is Laconia, where Weirs Beach draws a crowd. Another favorite destination is Wolfeboro, which calls itself the oldest summer resort in America. Sir John Wentworth, colonial governor of New Hampshire, built his summer mansion there in 1769. Many years of local hospitality have yielded a friendly resort with plenty of shopping and culture.

Lake Winnipesaukee is ringed by the Ossipee and Sandwich mountain ranges, allowing other diversions such as hiking, snowshoeing, fishing, and scuba diving. Among the lake's other attractions are the Canterbury Shaker Village and Kimball's Castle, an 1895 mansion with a panoramic view of "the broads," where Lake Winnipesaukee is 180 feet deep.

Green Mountains

The Green Mountains of Vermont are full of surprises. The historic mountain range is a great place for caving, hiking, skiing, and gawking—because that's what most visitors do: Whether staring at the snowcapped mountain peaks or Vermont's kaleidoscopic autumn foliage, they gawk, because they must.

The 250-mile-long Green Mountains become the Berkshires to the south, in Massa-

Historic family farms are sprinkled within the dense forest that sheaths the Green Mountains.

chusetts; to the west is Lake Champlain; and to the east are the White Mountains of New Hampshire. The 385,000-acre Green Mountain National Forest is the public's entry to the mountains. The national forest was formed in 1932 after floods and fires exacerbated by excessive logging threatened the region.

Nowadays, people say the Green Mountains boast six seasons—winter, spring, summer, fall,

Quick Fact

A Fighting Spirit

Thanks to Ethan Allen and the Green Mountain Boys, the mountain range's name rings in history. Allen was the guerrilla leader who first fought against the Province of New York and later resisted the British, helping lead Vermont to its brief, 14-year independence starting in 1777. Told by his doctor, "General, I feel the angels are waiting for you," Allen is said to have replied, "Waiting, are they? Well . . . let them wait." If that isn't Vermont spirit, what is?

mud (early spring), and Black Fly (late May to late July). Avoid those last two! Autumn is the Greens' peak season: The fiery-hued foliage is unforgettable.

Vermont Institute of Natural Science

There are hundreds of authentic Vermont vacation towns where you can get away from it all and enjoy what the state has to offer. But if you are in search of the spirit of the Green Mountain State, you might want to visit Woodstock, Vermont. And if you want to learn about the heart and soul of little Woodstock, take a trip a few miles outside of town, past the Quechee Gorge, to the Vermont Institute of Natural Science (VINS).

The VINS Nature Center is the leading New England care center for raptors—owls, falcons, hawks, eagles, and vultures, about 25 species in all—that can no longer survive in the wild. The center receives injured birds from all over the United States and houses them in specially adapted high-ceilinged cages. The Nature Center is artistically designed so that visitors can view the birds and forget that they are in a building at all.

Bald eagles are among the birds of prey cared for at the VINS Nature Center.

(Above) *Visitors to the center can see raptors such as this great gray owl.*

Guests also enjoy bird-watching along the center's nature trails.

Meanwhile, back in Woodstock, don't overlook the Billings Farm & Museum, a working dairy farm since the 1870s. Next door is the Marsh-Billings-Rockefeller National Historical Park. Vermont's first national park offers guided tours of the Marsh-Billings-Rockefeller Mansion and its grounds and gardens.

Lake Champlain

Samuel de Champlain explored so much of New England that it was only fair to name the spectacular Lake Champlain after him. He discovered the lake in 1609 while in the Champlain Valley, which lies between Vermont's Green Mountains and the Adirondack Mountains of New York. Lake Champlain has since served the needs of merchants and mariners, scalawags and soldiers, smugglers and spies, and patriots and traitors. The lake has seen its share of naval conflict, too: Warfare on the lake climaxed in 1814, when troops led by U.S. Commodore Thomas McDonough defeated the British Navy in a fierce fight. During the 19th century, canal boats and steamboats carried coal, timber, iron ore, and grain across the lake. Today, industry has given way to recreation.

Lake Champlain has become a year-round playground featuring boating, hiking, skiing, snowshoeing, snowmobiling, ice climbing, and rock climbing. Bicycling around Lake Champlain is a special favorite, and cyclists take advantage of the Lake Champlain Bikeways' 35 loops and 10- to 60-mile tours.

Sailing is one way to enjoy the pristine waters of Lake Champlain.

Bounded by Vermont, New York, and Quebec, the lake's Alburg Peninsula juts southward from Quebec, making it one of the few places in the United States that can only be reached through Canada. A more familiar north crossing extends through Ticonderoga, New York. Just east of the town is Fort Ticonderoga, a sterling 18th-century fort with a museum and guided tours.

Harvard Square

Harvard Square is a great place to go if you want to feel young, hip, and smart. Teeming with Harvard professors, students, and wannabes, "the Square" (as it's universally known in the Cambridge-Boston area) can give visitors the sense that they are attending Harvard without the inconvenience of having to take exams.

The center of Harvard Square is a former subway kiosk converted into a Harvard-worthy newsstand. The kiosk is surrounded by steps leading down to what is called "the Pit," a pocket-size park dominated by skateboarders. Restaurants, shops, and what may be the highest density of bookstores in the United States fill the remainder of the square.

Harvard Square wasn't always just a hangout. In 1630 it was the village of Newtowne, the first planned settlement in Anglo North America. Newtowne's street plan remains in use today, as do buildings dating from the early 1700s.

The Square is becoming more homogenized as national chains integrate with local shops. But be sure to stroll over to the Grolier Poetry Book Shop and pick up a volume of Robert Lowell or one of 15,000 poetry titles. Or grab a cup of coffee at a local café and enjoy the ambience of the Square.

An old subway kiosk, now converted to a noteworthy newsstand, stands at the center of Harvard Square.

Freedom Trail

Follow the red brick line along the 2.5-mile Freedom Trail and you'll be able to take in 300 years of American history.

The idea for the Freedom Trail came in 1958 from William Schofield, an editorial writer for the *Boston Herald-Traveler*. He hatched the idea of creating a marked line that would transform Boston's mazelike streets into something that tourists could follow. His campaign succeeded and inspired other "trails," including the Constitutional Walking Tour of Philadelphia and Boston's Black Heritage Trail.

There are 16 stops of historic significance along the Freedom Trail. You can start your tour at any of the stops, but the tour officially begins at Boston Common. The 50-acre common was a British troop encampment during the American Revolution. Today's Bostonians think of the common as the centerpiece of the city's Emerald Necklace chain of parks.

From there, the trail moves to the Massachusetts State House; Park Street Church; and the Granary Burying Ground, where John Hancock, Samuel Adams, and Paul Revere are buried. It continues on to sites including the Old South Meeting House, where Sam Adams signaled the start of the Boston Tea Party; the Paul Revere House; and Bunker Hill Monument, where the ragged colonials held off the British Army.

The Massachusetts State House is the oldest building on Beacon Hill.

The Freedom Trail ends at the USS Constitution, *which became known as "Old Ironsides" during the War of 1812.*

Fenway Park

Fenway Park reigns as a temple of the Great American Game, despite the decades of misfortunes of its principal occupant, the Boston Red Sox baseball club.

Built in 1912, it is not only Major League Baseball's oldest park but its most eccentric. The stadium seats just 33,871 people, and while the team suffered an 86-year dry spell beginning in 1918, Red Sox fans continued to crowd Fenway. Fans were finally rewarded in 2004 when the Red Sox won the World Series.

Fenway Park is among the old ballparks that give their fans the feeling that they are surrounded by the legends—if not the ghosts—of ballplayers past. The right-field foul pole became known as "Pesky's Pole" after weak-hitting shortstop Johnny Pesky hit one of his few home runs just beyond it in the 1940s. Then there's a seat in the right-field bleachers painted red to mark the spot where Ted Williams hit the longest measurable home run (502 feet) at the park in 1946.

One caution: Fenway is also the rare major-league park that sells seats with obstructed views. Still, the atmosphere is magical and not-to-be missed when in Boston.

Fans pack the stands in Fenway Park to cheer on their beloved Boston Red Sox. Painted green in 1947, The Green Monster (inset) is the left-field wall at Fenway. It stands 37 feet high.

Plymouth Rock

People flock to Plymouth, Massachusetts, to watch whales, relax on the beach, kayak, and see the famous ten-ton granite boulder, Plymouth Rock.

Plymouth Rock is hallowed in American history as the place where the Pilgrims set foot in America. They went on to form the first permanent European settlement in New England. While traveling across the Atlantic, they wrote the Mayflower Compact, the New World's first governing agreement, and signed it in Provincetown Harbor.

However, the claim that the Pilgrims landed at Plymouth Rock may be just that, since the first mention of the site came nearly a century after the *Mayflower* landed. No matter—this is the accepted spot where leaders John Carver, William Bradford, and some 100 other Pilgrims landed and started Plymouth Colony. About half of the colonists died the first year.

"Thus, out of small beginnings...as one small candle may light a thousand, so the light here kindled hath shone unto many," Bradford wrote.

Plymouth Rock marks the site where the Pilgrims were thought to have landed in 1620.

Walden Pond

Henry David Thoreau moved to Walden Pond to get a little peace and quiet and to write. He wrote an account of his time in the cabin he built by the pond and called it *Walden; or, Life in the Woods*. His little book, often credited with creating the conservation movement, changed the world.

"I lived alone, in the woods, a mile from any neighbor, in a house which I had built myself, on the shore of Walden Pond, in Concord, Massachusetts, and earned my living by the labor of my hands only," wrote Thoreau. He lived by the pond for two years, two months, and two days, and then moved back in with Ralph Waldo Emerson and Emerson's family.

In Thoreau's day, the land around the pond was one of the few woods left in the area, which was surrounded by farmland. Today, Walden Pond is part of Massachusetts's Walden Pond State Reservation, which includes the 61-acre pond plus another 2,680 acres known as "Walden Woods."

The park preserves Thoreau's temporary homesite; the original chimney was discovered in 1945, and a replica of the house was built there. Travelers can also linger at the statue of Thoreau, the reservation's The Shop at Walden, or Tsongas Gallery. But check in advance: Only 1,000 people are allowed in at a time.

Walden Pond, seen here at sunset, inspired author Henry David Thoreau's most famous work, Walden.

Boston Marathon

The first Boston Marathon was run in 1897. For a sense of perspective, consider that its closest rival, the New York City Marathon, was started in 1970.

The pioneering Boston Athletic Association (BAA) was the primary inspiration for the event. Chartered in 1887, the association provided more than half the U.S. Olympic team for the first modern Olympics in 1896. The next year, it was ready to stage its own BAA Games, the culminating event of which was a

Runners take off from Hopkinton for the Men's Open.

The Boston Marathon is held each year on Patriots' Day.

24.5-mile marathon. The first winner was John J. McDermott, who finished in 2:55:10. The fastest finish in a modern Boston Marathon of 26 miles, 385 yards was Robert K. Cheruiyot, in 2006, with a time of 2:07:14. But the most beloved would have to be Johnny A. Kelley, a winner in 1935 and 1945 who finished a record 58 of the 61 Boston Marathons he ran. Kelley died at age 97 in 2004. The most famous loser was amateur Rosie Ruiz, who in 1980 appeared to be the women's winner. But when the videotape was later examined, it revealed that Ruiz had cheated, slipping into the pack about a half-mile from the finish line.

As a matter of tradition, the Boston Marathon is held annually on Patriots' Day, the third Monday in April. So join the roughly half-million spectators who line the marathon route from Hopkinton to Boston each spring to cheer on the runners—especially the rookies. Supply them with water, snacks, and have a ball!

Boston Harborfest

Independence Day in Boston is celebrated at a mammoth bash called Boston Harborfest, a six-day patriotic extravaganza that crescendos to a dynamic fireworks display on July 4.

Harborfest has been a favorite of Bostonians and visitors for a quarter-century. Celebrants dress the Cradle of the American Revolution with bright trappings of pageantry as Boston revels in its colonial past. There are more than 200 events at the waterfront and downtown areas, including walking tours, lectures, reenactments, and alfresco concerts, plus perennial favorites such as the Chowderfest, Children's Day, tours of the Boston Harbor Islands, and the arrival of the USS *Constitution*, also known as "Old Ironsides," complete with working cannons. About half the events are free.

(Above) *A marching band dressed as British Army Redcoats makes its way down the street during Boston Harborfest.*

At the Harborfest, make your way through crowds of loyalists, royals, and patriots to a favored spot such as the Massachusetts Avenue Bridge to hear the Boston Pops play the 1812 Overture (with traditional cannon fire and church bells). Then watch the fireworks blowout on the Esplanade, the long stretch of parkland along the Charles River.

(Left) *Rebel reenactors ready their reproductions of colonial weapons in a Boston parade.*

Newport Mansions

Newport is a small city on Aquidneck Island, Rhode Island, in Narragansett Bay. It surely must be the home-viewing capital of the world. Each year, 3.5 million visitors come to the city of 30,000.

Many of the millions of tourists who cross Newport Bridge are drawn by the world's most spectacular collection of mansions, most from the 19th-century Gilded Age of the Astors, Belmonts, and Vanderbilts. Among the most famous, Newport boasts Beechwood, the home of Caroline Schermerhorn Astor, inventor of the American social register. Astor renovated the home in 1881 for $2 million, an inconceivable amount at the time. Today, costumed actors conduct tours there. Stunning, too, is The Breakers, Cornelius Vanderbilt II's summer home, with 70 rooms finished in alabaster and rare marble. The Breakers is also open for tours.

Other reasons to visit Newport include the world-famous JVC Newport Jazz Festival each August and the Newport Folk Festival, not to mention lesser-known fests such as the Newport Waterfront Festivals. These include the Great Chowder Cook-Off and the Spring Boat Show. Then there are the exhibits and tournaments at Newport's International Tennis Hall of Fame.

Overlooking the Atlantic Ocean, The Breakers is among the most elaborate of Newport's exquisite mansions. It was named for the waves that crash into the rocks below the estate.

Benefit Street

If you're touring Providence, Rhode Island, and its antique treasures, the best place to start is Benefit Street, also known as the "Mile of History." The best time to visit Benefit Street is during the Providence Preservation Society's annual June Festival of Historic Houses.

Benefit Street was established in 1756 and became home to Providence's well-to-do merchants. During the next two centuries, how-

A three-story 18th-century redbrick home with white trim is representative of the famously restored structures on the "Mile of History."

ever, it crumbled into a tenement slum until the Preservation Society took action to turn the neighborhood into a model for historic restoration worldwide.

Today, almost all of the buildings along the Mile of History have been restored, giving the street the architectural flavor of colonial times. While many of the building interiors are off-limits to the public, visitors can take in the historical ambience of this collection of homes and businesses. One exception is the John Brown House Museum, just around the corner from Benefit Street, which is open for tours.

(Above) *A historic aura permeates Providence's Benefit Street.*

Not to be confused with John Brown the abolitionist, Providence's John Brown was a politician who completed the mansion in 1788. John Quincy Adams proclaimed the house "the most magnificent and elegant private mansion that I have ever seen on this continent."

Benefit Street was also the haunt of authors Edgar Allen Poe and H. P. Lovecraft. Less unsettling denizens have included the patriots at the Old State House on Benefit Street, where Rhode Island declared its independence from the British Crown two months before the nation's founders did so.

Block Island

On one side of Block Island is the Atlantic Ocean; on the other, Block Island Sound. The island lies 12 miles off the coast of Rhode Island and about 18 miles from the tip of Long Island, New York. Visitors can sail or fly a private airplane to get there, but most take the ferry. The new, high-speed ferry has whittled the trip to just half an hour, but why hurry? This retreat offers a kind of time travel, where you can relax and think back to when you had time to skip rocks into the ocean and dig your toes into the sand.

Block Island is a tear-shape isle only three miles wide and seven miles long with about 7,000 acres of rolling hills, sandy cliffs, verdant valleys, timeless beaches, and 365 pocket-size ponds. The signature Victorian homes still set the scene on the inhabited parts of the island.

The island's fierce winters guarantee the permanent population will never rise much above 1,000 residents; in summertime, however, 10,000 or more occupy the island.

Visit the Block Island North Light, built in 1867 on Sandy Point, and Block Island Southeast Light, built in 1873 (Southeast Light is the tallest lighthouse in New England). Both have museums.

Block Island North Light operated from 1867 to 1970. In 1989 the lighthouse was restored and now aids ships in navigating near Sandy Point.

Stonington Borough Lighthouse

The town of Stonington is the oldest borough in Connecticut (Stonington Borough), settled in 1753 and chartered in 1801. Both the lighthouse and the town represent the history and architecture of an archetypal Connecticut town.

The Stonington Borough Lighthouse Museum is in the restored 30-foot granite tower, which looks as much like a fort as a lighthouse. The beacon was first built on Stonington Point in 1823 to guide the many vessels approaching Stonington Harbor from Long Island Sound. While the original lighthouse eroded and was dismantled, materials from it were saved and used to build the current lighthouse, which was completed in 1840. The lantern was visible up to 12 miles at sea thanks to its 10 oil lamps and parabolic reflectors.

The lighthouse museum is a gateway to Connecticut's past. Six rooms of exhibits testify to the rich and varied history of this coastal region, notable for its Stonington stoneware, which is characteristically splashed with cobalt blue and was made between 1780 and 1834 from clay imported from New York and New Jersey.

The museum also features furniture and portraits that give visitors a peek at the lives of the early blacksmiths, potters, farmers, fishers, merchants, and shipbuilders who lived in

In 1927, the Stonington Borough Lighthouse was converted to a museum honoring the maritime history of this quaint coastal village.

Connecticut. One notable portrait is of David Chesebrough, called "King David" in Newport, Rhode Island, for his dominance of the merchant trade. It was painted by John Smibert in Newport in 1732, and hangs over the main room's fireplace mantel. Mystic, Connecticut, with its Mystic Seaport, is about ten minutes away.

Mystic Seaport

The best way to enter Mystic Seaport, logically enough, is from the sea—best of all in a sailboat. Sure, you can come by car or bus, but it's not quite the same. Sailors who approach Mystic Seaport during the day, slightly dazed by the sun and salt spray, secure their boats and step ashore into a replica of an early-19th-century seafaring town, right down to the costumed actors role-playing strollers, printers, bartenders, teachers, bankers, sailors, sailmakers, chandlers, ship carvers, coopers, mast hoop-makers, and clerks at the Geo. H. Stone General Store. Best of all, visitors who sail into Mystic Seaport may enjoy a walk through the 17-acre town at night, when most tourists and impersonators have gone home. During the day, Mystic Seaport seems as if it's a vision of another century. Under the moonlight, you're sure it is.

Mystic Seaport is in Mystic, Connecticut, which is about a three-hour drive from New York City and two hours from Boston. The seaport is where the Mystic River empties into the Long Island Sound. It is one of a string of Connecticut sea-related enterprises ranging from the nearby New London Naval Submarine Base to the more accessible Mystic Aquarium & Institute for Exploration.

The town of Mystic became a shipbuilding center in the 17th century. Historians say ship-

The Charles W. Morgan *is a whaling ship built in 1841 and used until 1921. Mystic Seaport acquired the ship in 1941.*

builders along the Mystic River constructed more than 600 sailing vessels between the late 1700s and the end of World War I. But by then the great wooden sailing ships had been outstripped by steam-powered vessels. Mystic's maritime enterprises, like those in most of New England, began to vanish.

Then three visionary Mystic citizens—a doctor, a lawyer, and an industrialist—devised a plan to turn Mystic Seaport into a living educational institution designed to preserve seagoing culture. Following this model, Mystic Seaport expanded in the 1940s. Historic buildings—including the Buckingham-Hall House, a coastal farmhouse, the Nautical Instruments Shop, the Mystic Press Printing Office, and the Boardman School one-room schoolhouse—were moved from their original locations in New England and put together to form Mystic Seaport, a model New England seagoing village. Mystic Seaport became one of the first living museums.

The project's leaders swiftly assembled one of today's largest collections of maritime history: There are more than two-million maritime artifacts, an impressive selection of maritime photography with more than one-million images and 1.5 million feet of film, and an unparalleled collection of almost 500 wooden sailboats. These collections are available at Mystic Seaport's Collections Research Center storage and preservation facility.

The Joseph Conrad *is both an exhibit and a training ship for the Mystic Mariner Program at Mystic Seaport.*

The Henry B. duPont Preservation Shipyard, launched in the 1970s, gives Mystic the look and feel of a real seaport. In 1998, the shipyard workers re-created the historic schooner *Amistad*, from keel to topmast. Mystic Seaport also is home port to four ships that are National Historic Landmarks, most notably the *Charles W. Morgan*, a three-masted whaling bark built in 1841 in New Bedford, Massachusetts. "She has outlived all others of her kind," the seaport notes, and she alone is more than worth the price of admission.

Chapter Two

Mid-Atlantic

The Cradle of Liberty. Ellis Island. The Liberty Bell.

Independence Hall. The United Nations. The Statue of

Liberty. The Empire State Building. Ground Zero. The

memorials and monuments of Washington, D.C., and the

city's annual Cherry Blossom Festival. These symbols of

the history, ideals, and ambitions of the United States and

its centuries of triumphs and tragedies are represented

in the Mid-Atlantic. However, casual observers may inad-

vertantly neglect the region's natural beauties, such as

Chesapeake Bay and the New Jersey Pine Barrens. The

area offers visitors the best of everything: world-class

cities with diverse cultural offerings within easy reach of

sandy white beaches and pristine wilderness.

Across the East River, the United Nations and Chrysler Building
light up the dazzling New York City skyline.

Statue of Liberty

Standing high over New York Harbor since 1886, the majestic Statue of Liberty has been the focal point of countless photographs—and probably as many tears. She stands for freedom, hope, and possibility. But when you visit, don't let the vivid symbolism prevent you from admiring this matchless work of art.

Study the magnificence of the sculpture, alive with dignity, grace, and movement. It seems she is striding forward, torch in one hand, tablet in the other, with her copper gown flowing around her. The crown is regal, the torch a beacon. Her face is that of everyone.

Consider the scale: Physically, Lady Liberty weighs about 225 tons and stands more than 151 feet high. The sculpture is further elevated by the 65-foot-high foundation and the 89-foot-high granite pedestal. (For years she was the tallest structure in New York City.) The statue is classified as a "neoclassical realistic sculpture," but artistry may not be what comes to mind when you examine her 42-foot arm, her 35-foot waist, and her size 879 sandals. She is not only a work of art—she is a feat of engineering.

The statue is a massive iron pylon with a skeletal structure (engineered by Gustav Eiffel of Eiffel Tower fame) clad with copper skin sculpted by Frederic Auguste Bartholdi. Liberty was first erected in France, then dismantled and shipped to Bedloe's Island in New York Harbor. The transfer required 214 crates, and it took American workers four months to reassemble her.

Pedestal Inscription

"Give me your tired, your poor,
Your huddled masses yearning to breathe free,
The wretched refuse of your teeming shore,
Send these, the homeless, tempest-tossed, to me:
I lift my lamp beside the golden door."

—Emma Lazarus, 1883

"Liberty Enlightening the World" is a tourist attraction, a symbol, an icon, and a monument to Franco–American relations.

(Inset above) From 1892 to 1954, more than 12 million immigrants entered the United States through Ellis Island, which stands in the shadow of the Statue of Liberty.

Initially visitors could climb 354 steps and look out the 25 windows in Lady Liberty's seven-point crown.

You may not know that "Liberty Enlightening the World" (the statue's real name) was originally meant to be a lighthouse. But the night the Statue of Liberty was to be dedicated in 1886, the fog rolled in, the rain poured, and the much anticipated harbor light was at best dim. For years, one electrical system after another was installed in the torch with limited success. Eventually the goal was given up, and the sculpture was declared a national monument and turned over to the Department of the Interior.

Quick Fact
Statue of Liberty Specifications

Height from base to torch	151'1"
Ground to tip of torch	305'1"
Heel to top of head	111'1"
Length of hand	16'5"
Index finger	8'0"
Head from chin to cranium	17'3"
Head thickness from ear to ear	10'0"
Distance across each eye	2'6"
Length of nose	4'6"
Length of right arm	42'0"
Thickness of right arm	12'0"
Thickness of waist	35'0"
Width of mouth	3'0"
Length of tablet	23'7"
Width of tablet	13'7"
Thickness of tablet	2'0"
Ground to top of pedestal	154'0"

On July 30, 1916, during World War I, a cache of dynamite was blown up at a nearby New Jersey wharf. It caused damage to the Bedloe site, popping bolts out of Liberty's right arm. The statue was closed for repairs, but the arm (which, of course, included the torch) never reopened to the public. Gutzon Borglum, better known for creating Mount Rushmore, redesigned the torch that year. He added 600 pieces of yellow cathedral glass to enhance the enigmatic light. Today, through the power of many incandescent and mercury vapor lamps, the torch lights up the harbor, shining many times brighter than the moon.

Many sightseeing opportunities have been curbed since the tragedy of September 11, 2001. But you can still get to the island by ferry, walk the grounds, and visit the multilevel pedestal. It holds museums, memorabilia, tributes to the artisans and engineers who created her, pictures, original pieces replaced in a renovation (including the original flame), murals, and much more. Nevertheless, the star of this show is the armature. It sparks awareness of the brilliance of both the sculptor and the engineer who brought Lady Liberty to life.

The Solomon R. Guggenheim Museum

"I need a fighter, a lover of space, an agitator, a tester, and a wise man...I want a temple of spirit, a monument!" said Hilla Rebay to Frank Lloyd Wright. Rebay was the art advisor to Solomon R. Guggenheim, and the collaboration of these three led to the creation of the fabulous Guggenheim Museum, now known for both its collections and its adventurous architecture.

Guggenheim chose New York City as the site for his new art museum. Wright had reservations about designing the museum for the already overcrowded, overpopulated city, but he reluctantly agreed to the project. The museum opened in 1959.

The Guggenheim Museum remains an iconoclast. Viewed from Fifth Avenue, its exterior is an inverted cone with wide bands rising upward like a child's giant top. Inside, the museum contains an atrium and a spiral ramp where visitors view artwork from a perspective that can be dizzying. Despite its impressive permanent collection of works by Kandinsky, Klee, Calder, Picasso, Rousseau, and many more, visitors sometimes find it a relief to return to the atrium.

Wright's design will forever remain controversial, which might be one reason the museum has been so readily adopted by New Yorkers—despite Wright's feelings that their city lacked merit.

Built to showcase avant-garde paintings and sculptures, the Guggenheim Museum is itself a masterpiece.

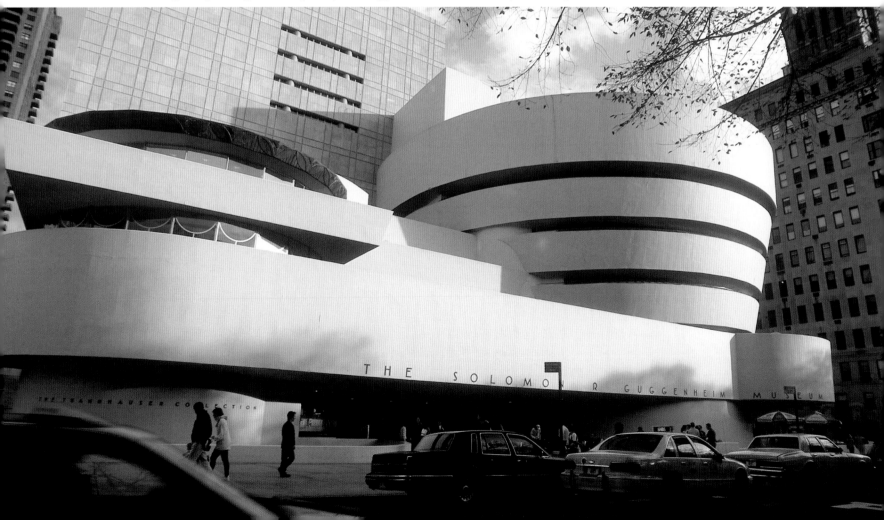

The Metropolitan Museum of Art

Any list of the world's most important art museums includes the Metropolitan Museum of Art, better known as "the Met," which boasts one of the world's greatest collections of—just about everything.

The museum's two-million-square-foot building is a treasure of painting, sculpture, and decorative art collections, including exhibits of American art divided into 24 breathtaking period rooms. The Met also features unsurpassed collections of Dutch Masters, Impressionists, and Post-Impressionists

The American Wing Courtyard at the Met is an interior sculpture garden.

from Monet to Mirot, Modigliani, and Matisse. Its massive antiquities collections include ancient Near Eastern art, Greek and Roman art, Asian art, and the art of Africa, Oceania, and the Americas.

More than five million people visit the Met each year. What makes it so appealing? The Fifth Avenue facade and impressive permanent collections give the Met an aura of excellence.

But the museum also is in a permanent state of flux, attracting visitors with special temporary exhibits of works culled from influential artists or periods.

Plus, it's a great place to take the family. Children and adults alike enjoy the musical instruments exhibitions, the Costume Institute, and the wonderful Arms and Armor collection, which includes armor for men, women, horses, and children. There's also the mysterious and mind-boggling assemblage of 36,000 Egyptian art objects.

Central Park

Central Park is the jogging, bicycling, picnicking, and recreational center of life in Manhattan. The park was designed in 1857 by landscape architect Frederick Law Olmsted and his partner Calvert Vaux to be an island of tranquility in the middle of the roiling city.

Today, Central Park hosts activities from alfresco dining while listening to the Metropolitan Opera to strolling through formal gardens or exploring the zoo. There are also spots to fish, play tennis, ice skate, swim, and rollerblade. The park offers horseback riding

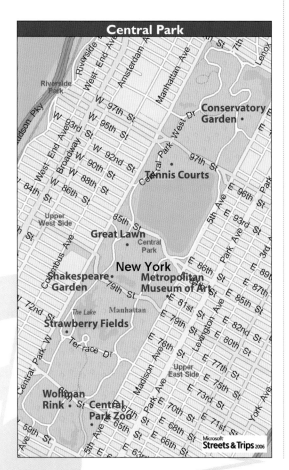

The elegant cast-iron Pine Bank Bridge is located near the southwest entrance of Central Park.

and famous horse-drawn carriages. In the summer, the Public Theater presents a Shakespeare in Central Park series, there are rock concerts in the park, and children can ride the carousel. There are many superb restaurants nearby. On the park's east side you'll find the Obelisk (formerly called Cleopatra's Needle) and the Metropolitan Museum of Art; on the west side are the American Museum of Natural History and Strawberry Fields, the section of the park named after the song "Strawberry Fields Forever" in memory of John Lennon. The west entrance to Strawberry Fields contains a memorial to Lennon—a black-and-white mosaic featuring the word "Imagine."

America's first landscaped public park is big enough for all this and much more; it covers 843 acres and is 2.5 miles long and .5 mile wide. Central Park has a 6.1-mile loop for cars that has parallel paths for riders, joggers, and cyclists during the week, while the park is closed to motorists on weekends. The park earned a reputation for crime decades ago, but those days are long gone. So get out and enjoy!

Tourists leave flowers and memorabilia on the "Imagine" mosaic in memory of John Lennon.

Times Square

New York City's Times Square is a blaring, electrifying, exhilarating, intoxicating, spotlit "crossroads of the world." Don't believe it? Times Square welcomes 26 million visitors annually to its stores, hotels, restaurants, theaters, and attractions.

Times Square has attracted tourists for a century. Its first electric billboard went up in 1917, and ever since the square has been synonymous with glitz. Today there are more high-technology signs, but the famous electronic newswire still lights up the base of One Times Square, and the ball still drops at the top of the building each New Year's Eve, a tradition since 1907. Times Square remains the heart of midtown Manhattan, in part because the area is a gateway to the city's main theater district, known as Broadway, which extends from 41st Street uptown to the Studio 54 Theatre on 54th Street.

Once upon a time, Times Square had a reputation as the worm at the core of the Big Apple, but the sleaziness was cleaned up in the 1990s and replaced with shops, restaurants, and other tourist-friendly attractions. Many large financial and media firms now have their headquarters in the neighborhood. While as crowded and crazy as ever, Times Square today is an amazing place where visitors can feel comfortable bringing the whole family.

Dazzling neon signs and advertisements have made Times Square a New York City icon.

Rockefeller Center

Midtown Manhattan's Rockefeller Center is a complex of 19 commercial buildings a few blocks south of Central Park. The center is a shopping mall, an Art Deco icon, a winter wonderland, the backdrop for a television network's morning program, and the only place on earth where you can nurse a cocktail and watch ice-skaters leap and twirl beneath a big, golden statue of Prometheus.

The center of the complex is 30 Rockefeller Plaza, a 70-story building that towers above the skating rink and the adjacent central plaza. Visitors can enjoy glamorous dancing accompanied by a big band in the Rainbow Room or dine next door at the Rainbow Grill, which provides a glistening view past the Empire State Building through its room-spanning vertical windows.

Rockefeller Center is also home to NBC studios, which includes the legendary Studio 8H. Arturo Toscanini, the NBC Symphony Orchestra, and *Saturday Night Live* have been filmed there. Or take a tour or see a movie or stage show at Radio City Music Hall, the largest indoor theater in the United States, where the sky-high-kicking Rockettes have been knocking out audiences since 1932.

The Plaza at Rockefeller Center is decorated by a golden statue of Prometheus atop a water fountain.

United Nations

"They shall beat their swords into plowshares, and their spears into pruning hooks. Nation shall not lift up sword against nation, neither shall they learn war any more."
—*Inscription on the Isaiah Wall, Ralph Bunche Park, across from the United Nations' world headquarters*

The United Nations (UN) was created during a time when the world's nations aspired to work together to bring about peace. The UN's world headquarters is *in*, but not *of*, New York City: It is an 18-acre international zone belonging to its member nations. Visitors may become startled during a tour of the United Nations when they realize they are in what is tantamount to a separate nation–state with its own fire department and post office.

Offices for the United Nations are located in the Secretariat Building of the United Nations Headquarters.

UN headquarters is often thought of as the striking glass building on the East River—the high-rise visible in movies and on the news. The complex actually combines four major buildings. Three were completed in 1952: the 39-floor Secretariat building, the General Assembly building, and the Conference building. In 1961, the Dag Hammarskjöld Library was added.

The General Assembly Hall, where representatives of the UN's 191 member nations meet, is the headquarters' largest room, seating more than 1,800. A subdued space, it features the UN emblem (a surprising rarity inside the complex) and abstract murals designed by French artist Fernand Leger.

Brooklyn Bridge

"That's the first mistake we've made since that guy sold us the Brooklyn Bridge," Stan Laurel says in the film *Way Out West*.

"Buying that bridge was no mistake," rebuts Oliver Hardy. "That's going to be worth a lot of money to us someday."

The Brooklyn Bridge, designed by architect John Augustus Roebling, towers over New York City's East River.

The Brooklyn Bridge opened on May 24, 1883, linking what would become the boroughs of Brooklyn and Manhattan in New York City. It was an accomplishment of mythic proportions requiring new technologies and new engineering. In its day, the Brooklyn Bridge was the longest suspension bridge in the world with the length of the main span measuring 1,595 feet. Its towers were once the tallest structures in the city.

The design was imaginative: Artists said the Gothic-influenced Brooklyn Bridge demonstrated that aesthetics and technology could coexist. It so inspired the poet Hart Crane that he chose his apartments for their view of the bridge. His masterpiece is the book-length poem "The Bridge."

> "O Sleepless as the river under thee,
> Vaulting the sea, the prairies' dreaming sod,
> Unto us lowliest sometime sweep, descend
> And of the curveship lend a myth to God."
>
> —*Hart Crane, excerpt from the poem*
> *"The Bridge," 1933*

Macy's Parade

Macy's Thanksgiving Day Parade requires the support of 10,000 Macy's employees and volunteers. It draws the attention of 2.5 million spectators along the parade line and close to 50 million television viewers. The Macy's parade—with its marching bands, skyscraping balloon characters (some favorites are Spider-Man and Clifford the Big Red Dog), and aircraft carrier–size floats—has the advantage of being able to roll with the times and with the weather. Technology, too, keeps the parade exciting. A recent addition has been the Macy's parade's first square balloon, which was actually a sphere holding together an external square shape with 610 tie lines.

Macy's employees excitedly helped organize the first parade in 1924. There were marching bands and 25 animals borrowed from the Central Park Zoo. A huge crowd lined the parade route, and the event made history. The first balloon appeared at the parade in 1927—a grinning Felix the Cat.

If you're in the area the afternoon before, watch as workers inflate the balloons around 3 P.M. To see the three-hour parade live the next morning, arrive at Central Park West, Columbus Circle, Broadway, or 34th Street between Broadway and Seventh Avenue at about 6:00 A.M. Bring a large mug of hot cocoa, and get ready to feel like a kid again.

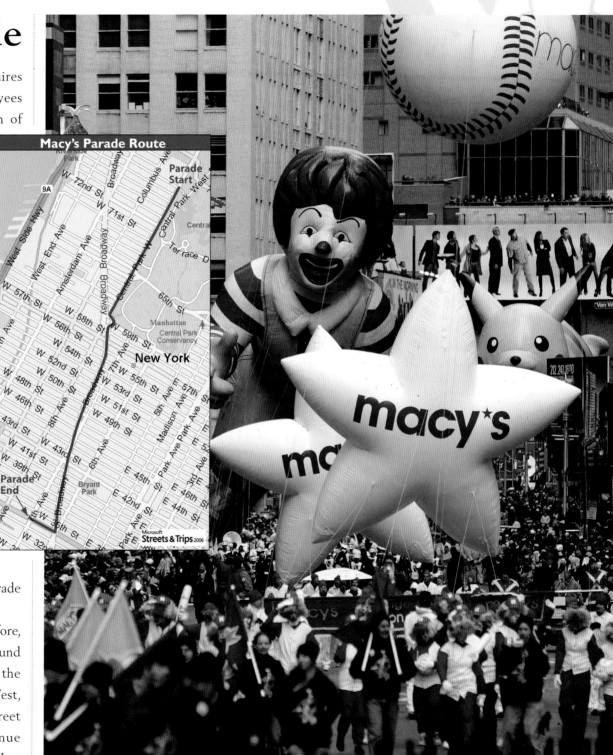

Crowds gather along Broadway to see the Macy's Thanksgiving Day Parade.

Empire State Building

On a clear day, you can see 80 miles from the observation deck of the Empire State Building, all the way to Massachusetts, Connecticut, New Jersey, or Pennsylvania, and, of course, you can see much of New York, the Empire State. Each year almost four million tourists walk through the building's chrome-and-marble lobby and stand in line, sometimes for many hours, to ride an express elevator to the top. And it's worth the wait.

Climb the Himalayas, and you will see more territory. But when it comes to urban views of the world, the Empire State Building is preeminent. This is not only because of the building's height but because of the dazzling views of the New York City skyline. The building overlooks Manhattan and landmarks such as Rockefeller Center, the United Nations, Central Park, the Statue of Liberty, and, seemingly close enough to touch, another Art Deco icon, the Chrysler Building.

The Empire State Building takes up about one-third of the block between 34th Street and 33rd Street and Fifth Avenue and Herald Square. The building measures 1,453 feet, 8.5625 inches (443.2 meters) from its base to the top of its lightning rod. With the World Trade Center towers now gone, it is the tallest building in New York and among the ten tallest buildings in the world. Nowadays, people are permitted to visit the spacious 86th

(Opposite page) *The Empire State Building dominates the New York City skyline.*

floor outdoor observatory, a terrace with a high iron fence. Tourists can also travel to the building's 102nd floor and look out through its 24 tiny windows.

For more than 40 years the Empire State Building was the tallest building in the world.

Stories persist that the Empire State Building was built during the Depression to create jobs. Actually, it was the result of a competition between Walter Chrysler, founder of the Chrysler Corporation, and John Jakob Raskob, founder of General Motors Acceptance Corporation. Both wanted to build the tallest

building. The Raskob team won the contest with the Empire State Building, but the real winners were New York City and the world.

The building's design, while not as spectacular as the chrome-crowned Chrysler Building, has been recognized since its 1931 opening as an architectural success. Viewed from a distance—say, from across the Hudson River in New Jersey—the Empire State Building looks like a shapely bell tower. (Chief architect William Lamb is said to have based his design on the shape of a pencil.) Its exterior was constructed of limestone and granite and trimmed with aluminum and chrome-nickel steel from the sixth floor setback on up, with long, decorative chrome-nickel steel rails along the corners. The 1950 addition of a television tower only added to the building's impressive, graceful immensity, which helps explain the number of tourists who can be seen daily standing on the Fifth Avenue sidewalk, gaping upward at the skyscraper.

Perhaps the most amazing aspect of the building's history was its rapid design and construction. Thanks to Lamb's ingenious plan, the Empire State Building was built in just over 13 months, setting a record for a building that size. Tragic experience has demonstrated that the design stands up to stress: In 1945 an Army Air Force B-25 bomber struck the building between the 78th and 79th floors, and 14 people died. Witnesses said the building shuddered and then stood still again. The fire was extinguished in 40 minutes.

Ground Zero

The site of the former World Trade Center towers, now called Ground Zero, has become one of the United States' most revered memorials. Unlike many other memorials, Ground Zero is not naturally aesthetic, and it has no statues, no music, no fountains, no architectural monuments, and no grand memorial. Perhaps Ground Zero is like Gettysburg before it became a national park, or the site where the USS *Arizona* sunk in Pearl Harbor before a memorial was built there.

Yet each week thousands of people come from all over the world to visit this 16-acre site. Some are confused or disappointed when they arrive because Ground Zero is now a construction site where the World Trade Center Transportation Hub is being built (due to be completed in 2009).

On the tour of Ground Zero, guides explain what is currently at the site, where the buildings used to stand, and what the site might look like in the future. For further context, visitors may want to see some of the other remnants of the attacks on September 11, 2001. One is the Ground Zero Memorial in Union Square. Another is Fritz Koenig's 45,000-pound steel-and-bronze sculpture "Sphere," which had anchored the fountain at the foot of the towers and is now on exhibit in Battery Park.

A "Tribute in Light" memorial was held from March 11 to April 13, 2002, to honor victims of the World Trade Center attacks.

Chrysler Building

Ironically, the best place to see the Chrysler Building is probably from the observation deck of its long-ago archenemy, the Empire State Building. Sadly, the Chrysler Building closed its observation decks long ago, and so gone are its fabled views of midtown Manhattan and close-ups of the building's stainless-steel crown. The Art Deco spikes, triangular windows, and gargoyles of eagles and wings were taken from the Chrysler hood ornament's design, and the building's top was modeled after the Chrysler hubcaps.

Ever since its opening in 1930, the Chrysler Building has struck observers as the perfect architectural expression of the Roaring Twenties, which witnessed a fierce competition to build the tallest skyscraper. The contest was so intense that the Chrysler Building, hailed as the world's tallest building by far in 1930, had to yield first place to the Empire State Building in 1931.

Admire the Chrysler Building from a distance, then see its lobby. Then (if you can resist stopping to shop on Madison Avenue) walk to the restored Grand Central Terminal, the New York Public Library, or Bryant Park on 42nd Street. From there on Fifth Avenue, which was originally designed so that its buildings, all the same height, would form a synthetic canyon, look downtown: You'll feel like you're on top of the world.

The Chrysler Building is a masterpiece of Art Deco architecture symbolizing the spirit of the Roaring Twenties.

St. Patrick's Cathedral

St. Patrick's Cathedral lies in New York City across from Rockefeller Center. Technically, the cathedral was completed in 1879 after 20 years of construction. But the cathedral is the seat of the Archbishop of New York, so an archbishop's house and the rectory were added between 1882 and 1884. In the 1880s, the cathedral's dramatic spires were completed. Later the great rose window and immense bronze doors on the Fifth Avenue side were added.

On the outside, the cathedral is 400 feet long and 274 feet wide, with spires that rise 330 feet above the street. On the inside, it seats 2,200 and has been the site for the wakes of such greats as Polish Prime Minister Ignace Jan Paderewski, New York Governor Alfred E. Smith, and Senator Robert F. Kennedy.

The cathedral admits both the exalted and the humble; about three million visitors come to admire the cathedral each year. Both gawkers and worshipers come to see the St. Michael and St. Louis altar, designed by Tiffany & Company, and the St. Elizabeth altar, designed by Paolo Medici of Rome. There's also the crypt where the former Archbishops of New York are buried under the high altar with their honorary headwear hanging above. St. Patrick's welcomes visitors from 7:00 A.M. to 8:45 P.M. daily, as long as they respect the serenity others seek there.

St. Patrick's is the largest Gothic-revival style cathedral in the United States.

National Baseball Hall of Fame

Visitors to Cooperstown, New York, enjoy the Farmers' Museum, the Fenimore Art Museum, and in summer, the Glimmerglass Opera. The village was named for author James Fenimore Cooper's father, William Cooper, who founded Cooperstown in 1786. He was the first to explore the lake region that was later immortalized as the setting in his son's *Leatherstocking Tales.*

But only one Cooperstown attraction often draws more daily visitors than the population of the village: the National Baseball Hall of Fame on Main Street, known to baseball fans worldwide simply as "Cooperstown."

In 1905, an official commission erroneously ruled that Abner Doubleday invented baseball in the village of Cooperstown in 1839. Almost 100 years later, a village philanthropist conceived of a hall of fame to celebrate Doubleday's centennial, and the idea took off like a Nolan Ryan fastball.

The hall showcases the plaques of the revered first five inductees: Ty Cobb, Babe Ruth, Honus Wagner, Christy Mathewson, and Walter Johnson. Today the Hall of Fame's exhibits and archives celebrate the national pastime in countless ways, living up to the hall's motto: "Preserving History, Honoring Excellence, Connecting Generations."

Outside the Baseball Hall of Fame are bronze statues of Johnny Podres pitching to his Brooklyn teammate Roy Campanella (right) *during a World Series game.*

Atlantic City Boardwalk

Just off the mainland of southeastern New Jersey lies Absecon Island, whose marshes and sandy beaches lay undisturbed until 1854. Then the Camden and Atlantic Railroad Line was built there, and Atlantic City was born. Unfortunately, the hordes of vacationers from New York and Philadelphia dragged volumes of sand through too many marbled lobbies. In 1870, Alexander Boardman, a railroad conductor, proposed constructing a wooden walkway to sift out the sand, and the Atlantic City Boardwalk was born. That first boardwalk measured one mile long. By 1883, almost 100 enterprises had sprung up beside it.

Atlantic City built and rebuilt the Boardwalk until the fifth and final version in 1896. It was more than 4 miles long and 60 feet wide and featured steel pilings and 40 foot steel beams. The Boardwalk helped make Atlantic City an attractive host for innovative events such as the 1921 Miss America Pageant. Later came the legalization of casino gambling in the late 1970s. Today, like Las Vegas, the Boardwalk is open 24 hours a day.

Has the Boardwalk changed all that much from, say, 1885, when the gasoline engine was invented? It is more modern, but visitors still enjoy a range of distractions from saltwater taffy and chocolate fudge stands to the Steel Pier's rides and games.

The Trump Taj Mahal is one of many famous resort-casinos on the Atlantic City Boardwalk.

Cape May

Cape May is a peninsula at the southernmost tip of New Jersey and the nation's oldest seaside resort. It was settled by whalers in the 17th century and is now a magnet for visitors from New Jersey, New York, and eastern Pennsylvania. Because a fire swept the little town in 1878, it was rebuilt in the Victorian style of the day, setting the architectural tone for what remains a charming, old-fashioned resort.

Cape May is the gateway to the 30 miles of sandy Atlantic Ocean beaches along the Jersey Cape that connect the resort towns of Ocean City, Sea Isle City, Avalon, Stone Harbor, and the Wildwoods. You'll find plenty of enticing attractions here. Take a nature walk at the Wetlands Institute in Stone Harbor or Leamin's Run Gardens (25 gardens on 30 acres). Visit Historic Cold Spring Village, an Early American living-history museum on 22 acres, or the Cape May County History Museum in the 1755 John Holmes House. The white Cape May Lighthouse towers 157 feet high and serves as a peaceful sentry over the picturesque peninsula.

The cape offers plenty of amusements that have kept fun-lovers coming back for almost 150 years, such as the boardwalk piers in Ocean City and the Wildwoods. You can also charter fishing boats, rent speedboats, kayak, or parasail. And with 30 miles of pure, white sand, it's possible to find some quiet, too.

Charming Victorian bed-and-breakfast inns are popular with visitors to Cape May.

New Jersey Pine Barrens

People who don't know the New Jersey Pinelands National Reserve, better known as the Pine Barrens, probably don't realize how big the forest really is. The 1.1-million-acre national reserve is about the size of Glacier National Park. More than 700,000 people live in Pinelands' communities, yet much of it remains wild.

The barrens comprise impenetrable bogs and marshes with forests of low pine and oak and sporadic stands of cedar and hardwood swamps. And there are the 12,000 acres of mature dwarf pine and oak commonly called the "pygmy forest." Under the barrens, the Cohansey Aquifer contains more than 17 trillion gallons of water—its acidity seeps into the barrens' bogs and swamps and stains the water a tea color. Aboveground, ribbons of water flow to the Atlantic.

Tourists love hiking, biking, boating, and cranberry picking as well as visiting the historic villages of Batsto and Double Trouble. The Pine Barrens has its share of history and legends, such as the Jersey Devil, said to have the head of a horse, large wings, and claws. For the courageous, the New Jersey Pine Barrens offers Jersey Devil tours.

Pitch pines and blackjack oaks loom over the marshy landscape of the Pine Barrens.

Pittsburgh's Three Rivers

The Duquesne Incline brings tourists atop Mount Washington for a dazzling view of Pittsburgh.

People call Pittsburgh the Steel City: The name dates back to the early 19th century when the steel industry ruled the city. Back then, white-collar workers brought an extra shirt or blouse to work because a black ring would form inside their collars by lunchtime. In the early 20th century, streetlamps burned all day so residents could see through the smoke. Today, the air is clear, and the smoke and mills are mostly gone.

When in Pittsburgh, one of the best ways to see the city is by taking the Duquesne Incline, which, since 1877, has provided public transportation to the top of Mount Washington, a steep hill on the city's south side. Take the incline at night and go to the observation deck overlooking downtown Pittsburgh's Golden Triangle. Fifteen major bridges span the waters of the Allegheny and Monongahela rivers as they flow together to become the Ohio River.

The Renaissance City sparkles like a river of stars. You'll not only be rewarded by the view, but by having landed in the middle of Pittsburgh's Restaurant Row.

Opposite Mount Washington, going north across the rivers, is the Andy Warhol Museum, the Carnegie Science Center, PNC Park, and Heinz Field. While you're on the north side of the rivers, check out the National Aviary. It's a warm refuge on a chilly Pittsburgh day.

Independence National Historic Park and Independence Hall

The United States of America is a relatively young nation, but its history is as illustrious as that of any country, and it should be explored. If you really want to see America, start where the country started: Independence Hall. The area between Fifth and Sixth streets, between Market and Chestnut, in Philadelphia's Center City, is home to the body and spirit of U.S. history.

Independence Hall, which is now part of a 45-acre park (along with 20 or so other buildings), is where America's independence was born. Once called the Pennsylvania State House, this simple building saw the foundations of the Declaration of Independence laid and brought to fruition. It was here that the U.S. Constitution was debated, argued, honed, and signed. (The political debates, the spirit of which continues in today's U.S. legislature, became so heated—and loud—that the windows were always closed, even on hot, humid days in the middle of July.)

Standing in front of Independence Hall, it is difficult to comprehend that this one building, with its subtle charms and small park, is the place where a remarkable gathering of brilliant minds changed the world. It is here that freedom was made possible. Democracy, the keystone of the United States, was established here. It was defined here. And it was celebrated here.

The comely two-story redbrick building now has a steeple with a clock in it. But long ago, that steeple housed a 2,080-pound bell. The bell, of course, is the Liberty Bell. It chimed often (supposedly annoying the neighbors), but most notably, it was rung on July 8, 1776, to announce the first public reading of the Declaration of Independence.

The bell was once moved to a church in Allentown, Pennsylvania, where it was hidden under the floorboards to avoid confiscation by British troops. From the beginning, the bell was adopted as the symbol for many causes (religious freedom and abolition, to name two), so it was displayed around the country. After the Civil War, people hoped that seeing it would help to heal the wounds between North and South, and so it traveled to fairs and exhibitions across the United States.

Now the bell is perhaps best known for its cracks...and its silence. No longer hanging

> **Liberty Bell Inscription**
> "Proclaim liberty throughout all the land unto all the inhabitants there of—Lev. XXV, v.x. By order of the Assembly of the Province of Pensylvania [sic] for the State House in Philada."

The Liberty Bell is now displayed in a glass chamber at the Liberty Bell Center, with Independence Hall in the background.

in the steeple of Independence Hall, it has its own home on the park grounds. The striking history of the bell is available through a video presentation (in several languages) and is sure to get your patriotic heart pumping.

All tours kick off at the Independence National Historic Park Visitor Center (near Market and Arch). The tickets are free, but tours are timed to help manage the crowds. The visitor center will prepare you for an exciting tour (don't expect a square mile of musty musings and memorabilia). The people at the park have gone to great lengths to make history interesting for everyone. There are some artifacts, but there are also high-tech interactive and multimedia exhibits. Some souvenir shops may be of interest. You can even lunch at an outdoor café on the grounds and take in the view that most interests you.

The Independence National Historic Park covers three large city blocks. There are paths (quaint alleys) you can follow to the many historical buildings and fascinating sites, such as Ben Franklin's final resting place in the Christ Church graveyard. The park is tourist-friendly, providing benches, walls, and other seating so you can catch your breath and rest your busy feet. It's hallowed ground you're walking on, so take your time, and try to see as much as you can. It's a visit you'll always remember.

Construction on the Pennsylvania State House, now called Independence Hall, began in 1732 and was completed 21 years later.

Philadelphia's Old City

Philadelphia is made up of many colorful neighborhoods, and Old City is among the most interesting. Laid out by William Penn in 1682, Old City today would surely astonish the great Quaker. It was a lowly waterfront district until artists began buying lofts, restoring dilapidated industrial buildings, and introducing the first theater companies. Soon, architectural firms, art galleries, design firms, restaurants, shops, and bars opened in the neighborhood, all a short stroll from downtown Philly.

The heart of Philadelphia is its Old City neighborhood, where the city began. And the heart of Old City is Elfreth's Alley, the oldest residential street in America. People have lived there since 1702. Three hundred years ago, traders and local merchants lived in the Georgian- and Federal-style buildings on the narrow street, which at just 15 feet wide was sized for horse-drawn carts and pedestrians. Blacksmith Jeremiah Elfreth owned most of the property along the alley and rented his houses to shipbuilders, sea captains, and landlubbers such as pewter smiths.

Today, Old City remains a vibrant neighborhood. Just a short stroll from historic Elfreth's Alley are Christ Church, the Betsy Ross House, and Independence Hall. There's also the Elfreth's Alley Museum, which offers guided tours of the homes built between 1710 and 1825.

Elfreth's Alley in Philadelphia is the oldest residential street in America.

Groundhog Day

Groundhog Day is an American phenomenon. A number of cities boast rodents capable of predicting the advent of spring, but there is only one Punxsutawney Phil.

Punxsutawney Phil is a 20-pound specimen of *Marmota monax* who, on February 2 each year, predicts when spring will arrive. He has also put his western Pennsylvania town on the map while becoming a movie star, especially through roles in films like *Groundhog Day*. Further proof of Phil's status can be found in the form of limited edition Punxsutawney Phil Beanie Babies.

(Above) *If Phil sees his shadow on February 2, it's an omen of six more weeks of winter weather.*

Phil is consulted each year on Gobbler's Knob before a waiting world.

Phil today wears his mantle of stardom lightly, thriving on a special diet of dog food and ice cream in his climate-controlled home at the Punxsutawney Library, where he is cared for by his handler, local funeral director Bill Deeley.

Also remarkable is Phil's longevity. The groundhog event was first recorded in 1841. Official Groundhog Day celebrations began in 1886, and the creature was named "Punxsutawney Phil, Seer of Seers, Sage of Sages, Prognosticator of Prognosticators, and Weather Prophet Extraordinary."

Handler Bill Deeley cares for Phil year-round.

Gettysburg

Gettysburg, Pennsylvania, never asked to be a crossroads of history, but it became one nonetheless. The borough is the seat of Adams County, and it was originally purchased in 1736 by the William Penn family from the Iroquois. The Mason–Dixon Line runs just south of Gettysburg. The settlement was named after its founder, General James Gettys. The community prospered, building roads and bridges. Later these structures were used by troops of the North and South during the Battle of Gettysburg. This fateful, pivotal clash during the first three days of July 1863 led to the defeat of the Confederacy.

Today, Gettysburg National Military Park is in the heart and soul of Pennsylvania Dutch country. It will forever be remembered as the place where General George Gordon Meade's Union forces turned back the Confederate Army of General Robert E. Lee, and as the location where President Abraham Lincoln gave his famous address four months later. Gettysburg offers visitors a surprising array of historic battlegrounds, monuments, and activities such as hiking and biking. Gettysburg includes the national park, the adjacent borough, and the next-door Eisenhower National Historic Site. Located about an hour-and-a-half from downtown Washington, D.C., Gettysburg allows visitors to explore a versatile

Gettysburg National Cemetery is shown here from the Gettysburg National Military Park Tower.

vacationland or take a solemn pilgrimage to the hallowed site where 50,000 soldiers were killed, wounded, captured, or missing in action during the Civil War.

There's also a charming little tourist town next door with attractions such as Gettysburg's American Civil War Museum, the Soldier's National Museum, the Jennie Wade House Museum, the Lincoln Train Museum, and the Gettysburg Battle Theater.

After a visit to the town, continue to the Gettysburg National Military Park Visitor

---

Quick Fact

The Battle of Gettysburg

Fighting at Gettysburg lasted just three days, but it was the largest and bloodiest battle of the American Civil War.

On July 1, 1863, Confederate General Robert E. Lee pushed north with his troops to fight on Union ground and to allow the state of Virginia to rebuild after being devastated during previous battles. Lee scored an early victory at the end of the first day, but it was not decisive. Under the command of General George G. Meade, the Union troops were able to hold off Confederate forces by controlling Little Round Top, East Cemetery Hill, and Culp's Hill during the second day. On July 3, Confederate troops tried desperately to regain ground, most famously through Pickett's Charge: a mass infantry assault of nearly 15,000 soldiers marching across an open field, braving artillery fire, in an attempt to take Cemetery Ridge. Nearly 10,000 of these men were killed in the first hour. The Union succeeded in holding off the Confederacy, and Lee retreated the next day.

Union commander	Confederate commander
General George G. Meade	General Robert E. Lee
Union troops	**Confederate troops**
approximately 95,000	approximately 75,000
Union casualties	**Confederate casualties**
23,040	22,000–25,000

Cannons are positioned on Cemetery Hill as they were during the Civil War.

Center, which features the Electric Map program (a 30-minute orientation program, for a fee), and the renowned Gettysburg Museum of the Civil War (free). Then comes the Gettysburg Cyclorama, a 360-degree painting of Pickett's Charge. The cyclorama was unveiled in 1884 by French artist Paul Philippoteaux, who interviewed survivors of the battle to perfect the details of Cemetery Ridge on the battlefield and the "High Water Mark," the point at which the Confederacy penetrated farthest north. (The Parks Service has embarked on a project to rehabilitate the battlefield; the cyclorama is being restored and will be withdrawn from public view until April 2008.) On the other side of the visitor center is the Gettysburg National Cemetery, site of Lincoln's speech and where many Union soldiers are buried.

But the foundation of Gettysburg is really the 6,000-acre battlefield and its more than 1,400 markers and monuments. It is well worth the trip to see the rolling hills and fields where the tide of the Civil War changed. Here Lincoln dedicated the United States "to the great task remaining before us...that this nation, under God, shall have a new birth of freedom—and that government of the people, by the people, for the people, shall not perish from the earth."

Fallingwater

Frank Lloyd Wright is probably the most famous American architect, and his most renowned building is a house in Mill Run, Pennsylvania, called Fallingwater. Wright designed the house in 1935 for Mr. and Mrs. Edgar J. Kaufmann of Pittsburgh. It was completed in 1939.

The location for the building was inspired by Edgar Kaufmann's love for the waterfall on Bear Run, the stream that runs through these serene woods. Wright also recognized the beauty of the location, and immediately visualized a house with cantilevered balconies on the rock bank over the waterfall.

The Kaufmann family used Fallingwater as a vacation and weekend home from 1939 until the 1950s. In 1963, the son, Edgar Kaufmann, Jr., a curator at New York's Museum of Modern Art, entrusted the family home to the Western Pennsylvania Conservancy.

Fallingwater became the gem of Wright's organic architecture school. A 1991 survey of the American Institute of Architects members judged it the all-time-best work of American architecture.

Today Fallingwater is open to the public and contains the original Wright-designed furnishings and the Kaufmanns' superb modern and Japanese art collections. And, of course, there are the exterior views of the place, which suggest that art and nature are not so very far apart.

The unique balconies of Fallingwater seem to float over the falls.

National Aquarium, Baltimore

The National Aquarium, on the end of Baltimore's Pier 3, anchors Baltimore's Inner Harbor. The aquarium is considered the nation's greatest and is certainly entertaining and thought provoking. It is huge, with more than 10,500 fish and other creatures on display.

You'll rave about the aquarium's exhibitions—not to be missed are its 1,200-seat Marine Mammal Pavilion dolphin show on Pier 4 and the Wings in the Water display, which features small sharks, turtles, and dozens of gliding, pinwheeling stingrays that look as if they're dancing on air.

The aquarium has five levels, with more happening on each than at a three-ring circus. The Atlantic Coral Reef exhibit is a 335,000-gallon tank that surrounds you with hundreds of tropical fish swimming around the world's most accurate fabricated coral reef. Step into the South American Rain Forest exhibit, a recreation of an Amazon River tributary that runs the length of a 57-foot-long acrylic wall with giant river turtles, tropical fish, and dwarf caimans. Or get an up-close look at large sharks in the Open Ocean exhibit, a 225,000 gallon ring-shape tank. Interactive computer stations explain the exhibits.

Anemones and coral populate the Atlantic Coral Reef exhibit.

Baltimore Inner Harbor

Baltimore calls itself "The Greatest City in America," and while some might dispute that, a visit shows why Charm City has every right to burst with pride.

Baltimore's pride and joy is its fantastic Inner Harbor. Not long ago, the city's harbor could have substituted for urban decay's exhibit A. Then, beginning in the early 1960s, a succession of city administrations focused on rehabilitating the old waterfront. They succeeded beyond anyone's wildest dreams, luring many A-list attractions. These range from the Baltimore Orioles' new-yet-classic Camden Yards ballpark to the National Aquarium, the Maryland Science Center, Port Discovery for kids, the Baltimore Maritime Museum, the Baltimore Civil War Museum, the Civil War–era USS *Constellation* (the Navy's last all-sail warship), and much more.

Clearly, the Inner Harbor is designed to satisfy every taste, from the sophisticated to the acquisitive. Shopping centers such as the

The observation level of Baltimore's World Trade Center gives a 360-degree view of the harbor.

groundbreaking Harborplace, which occupies 275,000 square feet in two pavilions, make sure of the latter.

Baltimore Inner Harbor is also home to the Tall Ships, and the best way to see them is the Tall Ship Tour. Another must-see is the Top of the World Observation Level on the 27th floor of Baltimore's World Trade Center.

Assateague Island

Off the coasts of Maryland and Virginia is an island of endless white sand sparkling in the sunshine. Assateague Island is 37 miles long, and its wild horses have galloped along the beach since the 1600s.

The surf is gentle, and stripers, bluefish, weakfish, and kingfish are plentiful. Assateague Island is a barrier island, so it has an ocean side, a bay side, and an interior. The center of the island is a bird-watcher's paradise of ponds and marshes, home to wintering snow geese, green-winged teal, northern pintail, American wigeon, bufflehead, red-breasted merganser, bald eagles, ospreys, red-tailed hawks, kestrels, and merlins.

Three stunning public parks share the island's 39,727 acres (48,000 acres counting

(Above) *The horses on Assateague are descendants of domestic horses that reverted back to the wild. They are only about 12 to 13 hands tall—the size of ponies.*

water boundaries): Maryland's Assateague State Park, Assateague Island National Seashore, and, mainly on the Virginia side, Chincoteague National Wildlife Refuge, which has 14,000 acres of pristine forest, marsh, dunes, and beaches. The refuge also includes three more barrier islands: Assawoman, Metompkin, and Cedar.

The wild horses on the island, made famous by the children's classic novel *Misty of Chincoteague*, are joined not only by deer but by Sikas, Asian elks that have thrived on the island since the 1920s.

Saltwater marshes provide a habitat for marine wildlife and waterfowl.

Chesapeake Bay

Skipjacks were introduced to the Chesapeake in the late 19th century to dredge for oysters. Today some of these versatile old vessels provide tours of the bay.

Chesapeake Bay, the largest estuary in North America, is shared by Maryland, Virginia, and Delaware. The bay stretches almost 200 miles from the Susquehanna River to the Atlantic Ocean and ranges from 4 miles wide to 30 miles wide. The mighty Chesapeake is spanned by the 23-mile Chesapeake Bay Bridge–Tunnel and the shorter and busier Chesapeake Bridge.

The beautiful bay was once the valley of the Susquehanna River, which helps explain why the bay is surprisingly shallow—most of it is less than six feet deep. Nonetheless, the Chesapeake Bay was the site of the American Revolution's critical naval Battle of the Chesapeake in 1781. It was also the site of the standstill battle between the ironclads CSS *Virginia* and USS *Monitor*.

Giant Chesapeake Bay, called "Great Shellfish Bay" by the Algonquin Indians, has benefited from recent conservation and restoration efforts. The devastating pollution of the bay's waters has remained a threat since the 1970s but no longer greatly detracts from its natural beauty. The bay today is a feast of art exhibitions, waterfront festivals, regattas and races, sportfishing contests, and boat shows.

U.S. Capitol

Located on the east end of the National Mall, the U.S. Capitol is an icon of 19th-century neoclassical architecture that houses the country's legislative branches and stands as a symbol of the United States. The building's cornerstone was laid on September 18, 1793, and it's been burnt, rebuilt, expanded, and restored since then.

The original building was designed by William Thornton, a Scottish-trained physician and neophyte architect whose blueprint was selected by President George Washington. When Congress moved from Philadelphia to Washington, D.C., in 1800, only the north wing of the building was complete. Then in 1814 the building was torched by British troops, but a serendipitous downpour spared its complete destruction. The chambers of the Senate and House, as well as those for the Supreme Court, were ready for use by 1819.

By 1850, an expansion was necessary to accommodate the growing legislature: The wings were lengthened, and the rickety wood-and-copper dome was replaced by the the current stately cast-iron dome.

Today the Capitol has a floor area of about 16.5 acres. It houses the legislative chambers as well as a museum of American art and history.

The U.S. Capitol's cast-iron dome was designed by architect Thomas U. Walter and constructed from 1855 to 1866. The Statue of Freedom was placed atop the dome in 1863.

The National Mall

The National Mall in Washington, D.C., is one of the world's great public places. Its 146 acres of renowned monuments, impressive institutions, and grand government offices draw visitors from across the country.

By strict definition, "the Mall" means the greensward and adjacent buildings from the Washington Monument to the U.S. Capitol. When you visit there's no need to stick to this definition; instead, enjoy how the Mall connects the White House to the north; the Potomac River, National World War II Memorial, and Lincoln Memorial to the west; the Jefferson Memorial, Franklin D. Roosevelt

(Below) *The greensward of the Mall extends from the base of the Washington Monument to the steps of the U.S. Capitol and is lined by world-class museums.*

Memorial, and Tidal Basin (with its glorious cherry trees in spring) to the south; and the U.S. Capitol to the east.

Any one of the dozens of the Mall's world-class museums or memorials is worth its own exploration. It might require a day, a week, or a month to do them justice. The Mall includes the National Archives, the U.S. Botanic Garden, the Ulysses S. Grant Memorial, the U.S. Holocaust Museum, the National Gallery of Art, the Korean War Veterans Memorial, the Vietnam Veterans Memorial, Constitution Gardens, West Potomac Park, and the Reflecting Pool. The National Mall is the center of the center, the magnificent green-and-marble heart of the U.S. capital.

The Mall also encompasses the riches of the Smithsonian Institution, which gives visitors a tour of national treasures, from Ray Charles's

(Above) *At 555 feet, the Washington Monument is the city's tallest structure.*

Completed in 2004, the National World War II Memorial honors the 16 million who served in the U.S. armed forces during World War II and the more than 400,000 who died.

sunglasses to the Hope Diamond. The Smithsonian has 15 museums on the National Mall; it's so big that the original "Castle," built in 1855, is now merely its office and visitor information center. Among the Smithsonian museums on the Mall are the National Museum of American History, the Hirshhorn Museum and Sculpture Garden, the National Air and Space Museum, and the National Museum of the American Indian. (Admission is free for all Smithsonian museums in Washington, D.C., but tickets need to be purchased for IMAX shows.)

Surrounded by the greatness of the National Mall, it's hard to remember that it was designed in 1791 by architect Pierre L'En-fant as a "Grand Avenue" of gardens and spacious homes interspersed with, not dominated by, monuments, museums, and government buildings. But Washington, D.C., neglected L'Enfant's plan. In 1901, a committee directed by influential architect Daniel Burnham redesigned the Mall with a focus on restoring it to the uninterrupted greensward envisioned by L'Enfant. Since then, the Mall has grown more urban, federal, and monumental, but the landscaped parks, wide avenues, and open spaces of L'Enfant's vision remain.

The National Mall remains at heart a park that means many things to many people. It can be a springtime stroll under the blossoming cherry trees, a getaway in the middle of a political pressure cooker, or a visit to some of the United States' most hallowed documents and precious works of art. Visitors can take it all in bit by bit, spending hours examining a Vermeer painting at the National Gallery of Art, the Rodin sculpture collection at the Hirshhorn, or Dorothy's ruby slippers at the National Museum of American History. Or they can take in the vista of the two miles between the Washington Monument and the Capitol as one great path under the trees that line the Mall and imagine the nation's capital the way L'Enfant did in the District of Columbia's founding.

The White House

The White House is most amazing for its open-door policy: It is the only residence of a head of state in the world that's open to the public, free of charge. And while visitors can't tour all 132 rooms, they can see some of the more famous ones, including the East, Blue, Green, and Red rooms. (Public tours of the White House are available for groups of ten or more; however, requests must be submitted through your member of Congress six months in advance.)

In 1790, President George Washington laid out his vision for Washington, D.C., to be situated on a plot of land "not exceeding ten miles square . . . on the river Potomac." Washington then worked with city planner Pierre L'Enfant to select the spot for the presidential residence—1600 Pennsylvania Avenue. James Hoban's understated, classical blueprint for the building was selected from a field of nine, and ground was broken in 1792.

Eight years later, John and Abigail Adams became the first residents of the White House—although it wasn't called that until President Theodore Roosevelt gave it that name in 1901. The Adamses made minor changes to the place, as has every president since. In 1949 while Truman was in office, the White House underwent its only major renovation. The original halls, third floor, and roof were retained, but the rest of the interior was stripped and rebuilt on a new concrete foundation. Since then, several presidents have decorated the interior differently, but the architecture has remained intact.

Tours typically convene in President's Park South, the 52-acre park better known as the Ellipse. The Ellipse is home to several monuments and memorials as well as events such as the famed Easter Egg Roll in the spring and the lighting of the National Christmas Tree in December.

The White House, at 1600 Pennsylvania Avenue, has been the president's residence since 1800.

U.S. Holocaust Memorial Museum

The horrors of the Holocaust will never be forgotten. The unspeakable tragedy that took place in Europe in the 1930s and 1940s must be spoken about so that people never forget.

That is the mission of the U.S. Holocaust Memorial Museum in Washington, D.C. The museum is devoted to documenting, studying, and interpreting the history of the Holocaust. It is also a memorial to the Holocaust's six million victims. Beyond educating the public about the tyranny of Nazi Germany against Europe's Jews, gypsies, and members of other minority groups, the museum serves to remind

(Above) *The Tower of Faces contains more than 1,300 photos of Jewish life in the Lithuanian town of Ejszyszki taken between 1890 and 1941.*

A guide discusses the historic photos in the U.S. Holocaust Memorial Museum.

visitors that their responsibilities as citizens of a democracy are never to be taken lightly.

Adjacent to the National Mall, the Holocaust Memorial Museum was chartered by Congress in 1980. Its exhibitions focus on artifacts, art, and other evidence of the Holocaust and the death and destruction it wrought. Every spring, a solemn and reflective ceremony is held on the grounds on Holocaust Remembrance Day.

Supreme Court of the United States

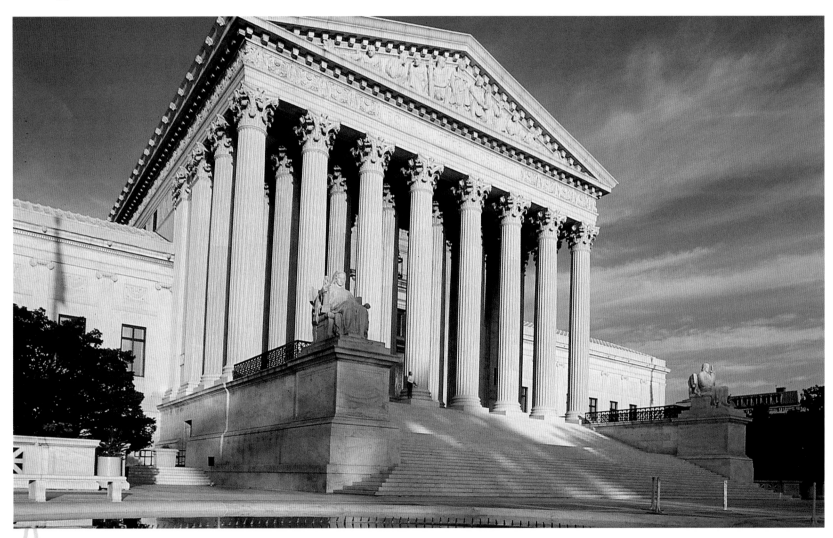

The Supreme Court of the United States is the highest court in the nation. Appointed by the president and confirmed by the Senate, the Supreme Court consists of a chief justice and eight associate justices. The justices serve for life, or at least until retirement, and no justice has ever been impeached.

The Supreme Court was established in 1789 by the U.S. Constitution, but it has only occupied the building across from the U.S. Capitol since 1935. Designed by celebrated architect Cass Gilbert, the building is sheathed in marble that was quarried in the United States. On the front, eight rows of imposing pillars stand under the chiseled motto, "Equal Justice Under Law." Inside the courtroom, however, Gilbert decided domestic marble was not good enough for the highest court in the

The classical Corinthian architectural style of the Supreme Court was chosen to accent its dignity.

land and would settle for nothing less than the finest marble from Italy's lauded quarries. In this setting, the nine justices make decisions that have shaped and will continue to shape the country.

Thomas Jefferson Memorial and Franklin Delano Roosevelt Memorial

Located in East Potomac Park on the eastern shore of the Tidal Basin, the Thomas Jefferson Memorial, with its graceful dome, is a striking site. Known as a writer, philosopher, diplomat, and Renaissance man, the third president of the United States left behind a legacy of political ideas and actions that have passed the test of time with flying colors. A statue of Jefferson stands at the center of the rotunda under the dome, and the surrounding walls are inscribed with words from his most lasting and eloquent writings, including personal letters and the Declaration of Independence.

On the west side of the Tidal Basin, the Franklin Delano Roosevelt Memorial pays respect to the nation's 32nd president. Dedicated by President Bill Clinton in 1997, the memorial consists of four outdoor "rooms," each depicting one of FDR's four terms in office. This memorial is not only about the man, but also the tumultuous times through which he guided the nation.

(Below) *Sculptures at the Franklin Delano Roosevelt Memorial, such as this one of Roosevelt seated in a wheelchair, were based on photographs of the 32nd president.*

(Above) *The Thomas Jefferson Memorial was dedicated in 1943 on the 200th anniversary of Jefferson's birth.*

Lincoln Memorial

At the center of the Lincoln Memorial is a sculpture of Abraham Lincoln, seated with resolve but as if reserving judgment. One hand is clenched, one open. His gaze seems to change with the light but remains focused across the Reflecting Pool to the Washington Monument and the National Mall beyond. He seems to look toward the future and not flinch from it.

The Lincoln Memorial leads visitors to contemplate what Lincoln accomplished and what he stood for. No poet (including Walt Whitman) and no biographer (including Carl Sandburg) has expressed this as well as Lincoln himself in his addresses at his second inauguration and at Gettysburg. Both speeches are carved into the walls of the memorial.

Similar to the Washington Monument, building the Lincoln Memorial was a prolonged process. Congress formed the Lincoln Monument Association in 1867. The original design was for a 12-foot statue of Lincoln surrounded by 6 large equestrian and 31 pedestrian statues. But a lack of funding derailed the initial project, and construction on the current memorial didn't begin until Lincoln's birthday in 1914.

The memorial was made from Indiana limestone and yule marble from Colorado. It was completed in 1922. It is unlike any other structure on the National Mall. The choice of a neoclassical Greek rather than Roman design stirred dismay.

The memorial is majestic in scale and impressive in its ability to share Lincoln's vision. The base covers roughly the same area as a football field. The statue measures 19 feet wide by 19 feet tall—its size was sharply increased when sculptor Daniel Chester French realized it would be overwhelmed by the memorial's size. The building has 36 Doric columns, one for each state during Lincoln's presidency. The memorial has attracted crowds since its creation and has hosted historic gatherings including Marian Anderson's 1939 Easter Sunday concert, an early turning point

Millions of people come to visit the Lincoln Memorial each year. Here they crowd the steps and look up in awe.

"With malice toward none, with charity for all, with firmness in the right as God gives us to see the right, let us strive on to finish the work we are in, to bind up the nation's wounds, to care for him who shall have borne the battle and for his widow and his orphan, to do all which may achieve and cherish a just and lasting peace among ourselves and with all nations."

—*President Abraham Lincoln's Second Inaugural Address*

IN THIS TEMPLE
AS IN THE HEARTS OF THE PEOPLE
FOR WHOM HE SAVED THE UNION
THE MEMORY OF ABRAHAM LINCOLN
IS ENSHRINED FOREVER

The inscription honors the 16th U.S. president.

in the Civil Rights Movement, and Martin Luther King, Jr.'s, "I Have a Dream" speech culminating the historic march on Washington for civil rights in 1963.

The words carved into the marble of the Lincoln Memorial long ago came true: "In this temple, as in the hearts of the people for whom he saved the Union, the memory of Abraham Lincoln is enshrined forever."

The Lincoln Memorial has come to symbolize freedom, democracy, national unity, and social justice.

Arlington National Cemetery

Nearly four million visitors come to Arlington National Cemetery each year. Most come to pay respect to their loved ones, to honor the leaders interred here, or to thank the more than 300,000 people buried here, many of whom were soldiers killed in the line of duty.

The original 200 acres were designated as a military cemetery on June 15, 1864. Soldiers and veterans from every war the United States has fought, from the Revolutionary War to the war in Iraq, are buried here (those who died prior to the Civil War were reinterred in Arlington after 1900).

(Below) *Tomb Guard sentinels, which are volunteers from the elite 3rd U.S. Infantry, guard the Tomb of the Unknowns 24 hours a day, 365 days a year.*

(Above) *Rows of headstones mark the graves of the soldiers and veterans buried in Arlington National Cemetery.*

Three unknown soldiers—from World War I, World War II, and the Korean War—are buried at the never-officially-named Tomb of the Unknowns. (The Vietnam veteran who had been buried here was identified in 1998, and his body was returned to his family in St. Louis.) President John F. Kennedy is buried in Arlington. His grave is marked by the Eternal Flame, designed so that a constant spark of electricity ignites the gas, keeping the flame alive through rain and wind.

Washington National Cathedral

Pierre L'Enfant, Washington, D.C.'s first city planner, conceived of a national church in 1791. In his writings, L'Enfant described his vision of a cathedral "intended for national purposes, such as public prayer, thanksgiving, funeral orations, etc., and assigned to the special use of no particular Sect or denomination, but equally open to all." However, it took some time for L'Enfant's vision to come to pass. The foundation was laid in 1907, but the building was not actually finished for 83 years. Its western towers were completed in 1990.

The National Cathedral has been a focal point for spiritual life in the nation's capital since it opened in 1912. Every president has attended services here while in office. Many people have gathered at the church to mourn the passing of leaders or mark momentous events in world history.

The National Cathedral is a grand structure with intricate architectural details. With towers 676 feet above sea level and a facade adorned with more than 250 angels and more than 100 gargoyles, the church deserves its lofty title.

The National Cathedral is the sixth largest cathedral in the world. Its High Altar (below) is made from stones quarried near Jerusalem.

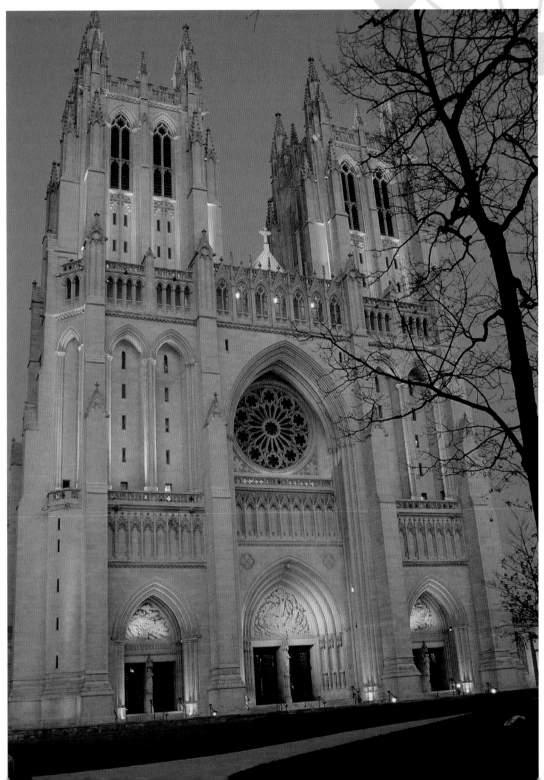

National Cherry Blossom Festival

In 1912, Tokyo Mayor Yukio Ozaki gave Washington, D.C., a gift of 3,000 cherry trees to beautify its streets. Since 1935, the city has commemorated the trees' blooming in late March or early April with one of its biggest festivals. Participants from the United States and Japan kick off the festival with a parade on Constitution Avenue. The festivities continue for two more weeks, with such events as a ten-mile run, concerts, and Sakura Matsuri, a Japanese street festival.

The cycle of giving has continued. In 1965, First Lady Lady Bird Johnson accepted a gift of 3,800 more trees. Then in 1981, Japanese horticulturists came to Washington, D.C., to collect cuttings, which were then planted

Cherry trees bloom each spring along the Tidal Basin in Washington, D.C.

where a flood had wiped out numerous cherry trees in Japan. In 1999, more cherry trees were planted around the Tidal Basin; their common ancestor was a 1,500-year-old tree from the Gifu province in Japan.

Fourth of July Fireworks

Independence Day in the nation's capital is an all-day affair. The morning of July 4 begins with a bustling parade on Constitution Avenue with patriotic floats, military units, marching bands, and important political figures.

While there are all sorts of activities—from art shows to puppet theater—the big event is the evening festivities: one of the country's biggest fireworks displays. This work of incendiary art has an ideal setting above the Reflecting Pool on the National Mall, with the majestic backdrop of some of the country's most beloved monuments and memorials. The multihued fireworks extravaganza is a feast for the ears as well as the eyes: The evening also includes a concert by the National Symphony Orchestra. More than 450,000 people "ooh" and "aah" over the fireworks in person, and millions more take in the spectacle on television. After all, what better place is there to celebrate the birth of the United States than in its capital city?

Each year, on July 4, a dazzling display of fireworks lights up the sky above Washington, D.C.

Chapter Three

The South

Many of the South's enticements are subtle. The region remains the land of warmth and heat, slow talking and long memories, blossoming magnolias and elaborate manners. The South is as hot as Miami's glamorous South Beach and as warm as the front porch of a Louisiana plantation. You don't have to live here to realize the appeal of simple yet refined southern pleasures, such as home-cooked meals with friends. Oddly, the same might be said of the natural wonders, which might or might not be the biggest, highest, or deepest, but whose charms make visitors feel right at home.

Humid air hangs over the sultry swamps and marshes in Florida's Everglades National Park.

Monticello

Monticello, the Virginia home of American founder Thomas Jefferson, is a Roman neoclassical masterpiece. Jefferson moved onto the property in 1770, but the mansion was not completed until 1809, after Jefferson's second term as president.

The domed building features east- and west-facing porticos that bookend an entrance hall and parlor. Jefferson, ever the tinkerer and innovator, made all sorts of improvements to Monticello to maximize space and light. The 43-room mansion has 13 skylights, including one over Jefferson's bed.

On the tour of Monticello, you'll have a chance to see Jefferson's mansion up close. The house was the centerpiece of Jefferson's plan-

The west front of Jefferson's Monticello may seem familiar—it was exclusively featured on the back of the U.S. nickel from 1938 to 2003.

tation, which totaled 5,000 acres at its peak. About 130 slaves worked the land, tended livestock, cooked, and cleaned there during Jefferson's life.

Mount Vernon Estate and Gardens

Mount Vernon was home to George Washington, the first president of the United States. The land was given to George Washington's great-grandfather in 1674, and it remained in the family for seven generations.

Washington spent five years at Mount Vernon as a child and later lived there as an adult with his wife, Martha. The plantation grew to 8,000 acres while Washington served as commander in chief during the Revolutionary War. While Washington was best known as a military and political leader, he also left a strong architectural legacy: He designed and

Washington and his family lived in the "Mansion House Farm" section of Mount Vernon.

built many of the structures at Mount Vernon, including the famed mansion with its distinctive two-story portico.

The estate is now 500 acres, 50 of which are open to the public. In Washington's day, Mount Vernon was essentially a self-sustaining community, and a considerable amount of this heritage is still showcased today.

Colonial Williamsburg

Williamsburg, Jamestown, and Yorktown make up Virginia's Historic Triangle. Known as Colonial Williamsburg, the area is the world's largest, and possibly greatest, living-history museum. Nowhere else is more care taken to create, re-create, and maintain a semblance of pre-Revolutionary life in the United States than here. Actors wear period clothing and interact with each other and the visiting public to simulate life in Williamsburg during the 17th century.

The Yorktown Victory Center gives visitors a look at life on a 1780s Virginia farm.

Quick Fact

Jamestown and Yorktown

These locations were the backdrop for two definitive moments in U.S. history. Jamestown was the first permanent English settlement in the New World. And the decisive battle in the Revolutionary War was fought at Yorktown.

Jamestown was founded in 1607—13 years before the Pilgrims landed at Plymouth Rock. While in Jamestown, visit the living-history area. There are replicas of three ships that sailed across the Atlantic to Virginia, re-creations of the colonists' fort and a Powhatan village, and a "riverfront discovery" area describing the commerce of Jamestown in the early 1600s.

The Yorktown Victory Center commemorates the Siege of Yorktown in 1781. The British surrendered at this battle, ending the six-year Revolutionary War.

Jamestown was the first capital of Virginia, but it lay in a low marsh area that compromised defenses against both hostile native people and malaria-carrying mosquitoes. The Army moved some soldiers to nearby Middle Plantation, five miles away on a high point between the James and York rivers. In 1693, King William III and

Today the Colonial Williamsburg Fifes and Drums are boys and girls ages 10 to 18 who carry on the tradition of military music.

Queen Mary II granted a charter to the College of William and Mary, the colonies' second university (Harvard was the first). In 1699, the settlement was renamed Williamsburg after the king and was declared the new colonial capital. Construction soon began on a new statehouse and governor's house. And so Williamsburg remained for nearly a century, until 1780, when Governor Thomas Jefferson moved the capital to Richmond.

Fast-forward to the 20th century. Williamsburg's neglected center, the old capital, was fast decaying until a local pastor persuaded John D. Rockefeller, Jr., to take an interest. Rockefeller quietly bought property and pri-vately financed a plan for the city's restoration. When the time came, he unveiled the idea to universal applause.

The result is today's 301-acre colonial village, where 88 original buildings were restored or repaired and nearly 500 buildings and out-buildings were reconstructed. Colonial Williamsburg is a living museum, meaning while tourists visit museums, they are also invited to immerse themselves in another century and its homes, handicrafts, clothing, stores, taverns, gardens, and jails, as well as its people.

A great way to arrive at Colonial Williamsburg is to drive the nearby Colonial Parkway, which connects Yorktown to Jamestown via Williamsburg. The parkway's 23 miles of picturesque scenery through the Colonial National Historic Park have been protected from roadside development. Even traffic signs are minimized.

For an authentic 17th-century thrill, visitors can stay in period accommodations in Colonial Williamsburg. The Colonial Houses program offers accommodations inside the old city at 28 guesthouses, which are authentically furnished and range in size from one room in a tavern to a 16-room home. The adjacent Williamsburg Lodge, built by John D. Rockefeller, Jr., and listed on the National Register of Historic Places, is equally as exciting.

Virginia Beach

Virginia Beach is a modern magnet for outdoors buffs—namely surfers, anglers, golfers, and boaters. Today the city is a favorite getaway with attractions ranging from amusement parks and miniature golf courses to historic sites and vibrant art. The beach is a wide, sandy strip on the central Atlantic coast, fronted by a three-mile boardwalk and oceanfront resorts with all the trimmings.

The big event here is the Neptune Festival, which has been held annually in late September since 1974. It's now one of the biggest festivals on the entire East Coast, drawing hordes to surfing contests, concerts, "Boardwalk Weekend," and the ever-popular North American Sandsculpting Championship.

Thanks to its location at the mouth of Chesapeake Bay, Virginia Beach also has made history. Just north on Route 60 is Fort Story, home to the Cape Henry Lighthouses. The original lighthouse, built in 1792, was the first lighthouse structure authorized, completed, and lighted by the federal government. While the old lighthouse still stands, a new lighthouse was added in 1878.

The first Europeans—a party that included Captain John Smith—landed at Cape Henry on April 26, 1607. In 1621, they settled what is now Virginia Beach. The Cape Henry Memorial Cross at Fort Story commemorates where these colonists made landfall.

The new Cape Henry Lighthouse stands an impressive 164 feet tall.

Mabry Mill

The historic fixture of Mabry Mill lies alongside Virginia's sublime stretch of the Blue Ridge Parkway. It's located on Rocky Knob, a beautiful mountain known for its crystalline quartz formations and apple orchards.

The mill's namesake, Ed Mabry, began construction on the complex in 1905. The mill was an active gristmill and sawmill in the early part of the 20th century. The complex also included a blacksmith's shop, a whiskey still, and a wheelwright's shop.

In modern days, Mabry Mill has emerged as a living-history center with regular demonstrations of old-fashioned smithing, spinning, and weaving techniques. A short hike on the Mountain Industry Trail reveals what life was

The wonderfully preserved Mabry Mill is one of the most popular attractions on the Blue Ridge Parkway.

like in rural Virginia a century ago. Hikers may also glimpse turtles, ducks, and other wildlife. Better yet, on Sunday afternoons there are festive events with traditional music and dancing.

Shenandoah Valley

For years, the Blue Ridge Mountains seemed an insurmountable obstacle blocking the westward expansion of the United States. Many pioneers stopped cold in their tracks, but a spectacular sight greeted those who made it to the top of the ridge—the lovely Shenandoah Valley. This green paradise of endless forests and meadows cut by winding rivers and streams was so inviting that the valley seemed to hold all the promise of the West.

Shenandoah is in large part protected as a national park. It's also a place where people

The lush Shenandoah Valley stretches from Harpers Ferry, West Virginia, to Roanoke and Salem, Virginia.

have lived for many generations. When the park was established in 1935, much of the area consisted of eroded hillsides, worn farmland, and thin second- or third-growth forests. Today, the forests are mounting a comeback, sheathing the scars of grazing, farming, and logging. Native wildlife is returning as well; black bears, raccoons, and opossums (Amer-

ica's only marsupial), roam here, just as they did in pioneer days.

Skyline Drive runs along the crest of the Blue Ridge, providing 75 overlooks and magnificent vistas of forests, mountains, and the valley. For a real treat, visit the valley in the spring or fall to see the fabulous blossoming flowers or autumn leaf displays. More than 500 miles of trails wind through the valley, including part of the Appalachian Trail. There are also numerous waterfalls—a dozen in the park drop more than 40 feet.

Monongahela National Forest

The Monongahela National Forest in West Virginia is one of the largest tracts of protected Eastern woodlands. This naturally makes it a mecca for outdoorspeople of all stripes—fishers, hikers, mountain bikers, and paddlers. When

The Monongahela National Forest covers 919,000 rugged acres.

visiting, make good use of the forest's extensive network of backcountry trails. The landscape is dotted with highland bogs and dense thickets of blueberries. The forest is made up of five different federally designated wilderness areas at elevations ranging from 900 feet above sea level to 4,861 feet atop Spruce Knob, the loftiest peak in the entire state.

The size and scope of Monongahela is impressive by any standard, and so is the breadth of life in the forest. Black bears, foxes, beavers, woodchucks, opossums, and mink are among the mammals found there. There are also dozens of types of fish in the streams, more than 200 feathered species in the skies and the treetops, and 75 types of trees rooted there.

Kentucky Derby

It's called "the most exciting two minutes in sports" and features 20 world-class athletes culled from a field of more than 30,000. Perfectly chiseled, they line up. A bell sounds. And they're off!

The athletes in question are three-year-old thoroughbred horses. The winner covers the 1.25-mile track at Churchill Downs in Louisville, Kentucky, in just about two minutes at a gallop averaging almost 40 miles per hour.

The first "jewel" of the three races collectively known as the Triple Crown (along with the Preakness Stakes and the Belmont Stakes), the Kentucky Derby is no ordinary sporting event. It's a raucous party, a longstanding tradition, and a vibrant pageant. The race caps the three-week Kentucky Derby Festival, which includes steamboat and balloon races, spectacular fireworks, marathons, and the lively Pegasus Parade.

Run every May since 1875, the Derby is steeped in tradition. In many ways, these time-honored traditions and their year-to-year evolutions are just as amazing as the actual race.

The most visible tradition at the "Run for the Roses" might be the derby hat. Spectators have worn formal attire to the race since its 19th-century founding, and the icing on the cake has always been the women's headgear, wide-brimmed and adorned with flowers or other ornaments. It's said that you don't

choose your hat to match your outfit on Derby Day, but your outfit to match your hat! While more modest styles prevailed in the 1870s, today's derby hats are emblems of excess: the bigger, more colorful, and gaudier, the better

---

Mint Julep

Don your fancy hat and enjoy a refreshing mint julep on Derby day!

2 cups water
2 cups sugar
sprigs of fresh mint
crushed ice
Kentucky bourbon

Boil sugar in water until dissolved, about five minutes. Combine with six to eight sprigs of fresh mint and refrigerate, covered, overnight, to create a mint syrup. Fill each glass with crushed ice, one tablespoon of the mint syrup, and two ounces of bourbon. Stir, and garnish with an extra sprig of fresh mint.

The mint julep is traditionally served in a chilled silver cup, but any festive glass is acceptable. Chill cups in the freezer for 30 minutes beforehand to attain the preferred frosty effect.

Even men get in on the act nowadays with wilder hats every year.

More than 150,000 people attend the Derby each year. "Millionaire's Row," frequented by Very Important People of every stripe, is one place from which spectators can view the action. Another spot is the infield; this area is much rowdier and muddier and can hold up to 80,000 people. A flash of silk and a cloud of dust are about all you can expect to see from here, though.

A prevailing tradition at the Derby is the mint julep. This Southern cocktail—consisting of mint, crushed ice, sugar, and bourbon—has long been the refreshment of choice for the spectators at Churchill Downs.

Mint juleps are perfect for washing down a bowl of savory burgoo, the Derby's traditional Kentuckian stew. Served from vast iron kettles that sometimes measure ten-feet across, burgoo is a time-tested stew that has no established recipe but usually includes lamb, okra, lima beans, and plenty of spices. It's said that a spoon should stand straight up in a bowl of good burgoo.

The traditional silks worn by the jockeys have their origins in early 18th-century England, where riders' colors would denote the duke, earl, or king for whom they raced. Now the silks are a symbol of the horse's owner.

It's also traditional for a long shot to pay off at Churchill Downs. Only two favorites have won in the last 26 years. In 2005, a 50-to-1 long shot won the race.

Legends of races past seem to gallop alongside the contenders. Secretariat is often mentioned as the greatest athlete in Kentucky Derby history. In 1973, the legendary thoroughbred ran the race in a record time of 1 minute, 59 and ⅖ seconds.

(Opposite page) *Enthusiastic spectators cheer on their favorite horses at Churchill Downs.*

Beale Street

The neighborhood surrounding Beale Street might be quiet, with the trolley that runs along Main Street creating the only significant sound. But when you arrive at the southern doorstep of downtown Memphis, the quiet gives way to the raucous neon-and-brick music clubs that line Beale Street.

Beale Street is not just a spectacle for the eyes, it's also an experience for the taste buds. Pots of gumbo and red beans and rice simmer at every corner. However, the smells and tastes of Beale Street are just side dishes: The main course is the music. Blues, soul, and rock 'n' roll claim the perfectly imperfect city of Mem-

Memphis is home to Sun Studio, the label that signed Elvis Presley to his first recording contract in 1954.

(Above) *Memphis touts itself as the "Birthplace of Rock 'n' Roll," and it's got a strong case for the title. In the mid-1950s, Memphis's blues legacy fused with country music, creating a new sound that found fans across the country. Beale Street has remained the heart and soul of music in Memphis.*

phis as their birthplace. And all three get people dancing on Beale Street every night.

Beale Street has long been a feast for the senses. In the early 20th century, it was one of the busiest markets in the South, with European immigrants selling goods of all kinds to a largely African-American clientele. In the 1980s, Beale Street was redeveloped into an open-air, pedestrian-only center for music, nightlife, and more music. And it's caught on—now the old marketplace hosts musicians, dancers, and sellers every night of the week.

As the neon on the Rum Boogie Cafe advises: "Eat. Drink. Boogie. Repeat."

Grand Ole Opry

The Grand Ole Opry is a cultural phenomenon. At its heart, it's a radio program that showcases American country music. In fact, it's the longest-running live radio program in the United States. But country music is just the starting point. The Opry is the centerpiece of Opryland, a comprehensive resort and convention center that covers everything from golf to shopping to, of course, country music.

It all began back in 1925 when a brand-new Nashville radio station, WSM, hired a former

Shows at the Grand Ole Opry are magical to the performers and audience alike.

Memphis newspaper reporter named George Hay to host a weekly program called the "WSM Barn Dance." In 1927, the show was renamed the "Grand Ole Opry," and its popularity snowballed. By 1932, WSM's new 50,000-watt transmitter blasted the program across the country and even to parts of Canada. Over the years, the Grand Ole Opry

has become home to the "Who's Who" of American country music.

The six-foot circle of dark oak wood at the Opry House Stage is magical for the performers and audience. The section was cut from the Opry's former home, Ryman Auditorium, and today's performers feel a connection with the country legends who first sang there. From April through December, the Opry hosts Tuesday Night Opry shows—a perfect way to take in the heart and soul of country music.

Graceland

In his youthful heyday, Elvis Presley was the personification of American cool. He bought Graceland mansion in Memphis's Whitehaven neighborhood in 1957 when he was just 22 years old. He paid $102,500 for the property, an 18-room mansion on nearly 14 acres of country estate surrounded by towering oak trees.

Presley never thought he would see much money in his life. He was born in a sharecropper's shack in Tupelo, Mississippi. But after becoming an international superstar, Presley was rich enough to buy Graceland. Depending on whom you ask, the estate was named for the original owner's wife's aunt, Grace Toof. Presley bought the estate as much for his parents—especially his mother Gladys—as for himself. But Gladys died in 1958 and never got to enjoy the house to the extent Elvis had hoped. The King of Rock 'n' Roll lived in the mansion for most of the second half of his life.

Graceland is strikingly modest, especially by modern standards. Built in 1939, it's a manageable mansion, smaller than most celebrity homes. The house is not unlike a traditional luxury home in the suburbs—except for the King's famously extravagant touches, of course.

Corinthian columns and a limestone facade mark the exterior of the instantly recognizable home. The interior has been preserved as it

Visitors to Graceland pay their respects to Elvis Presley at his grave in the Meditation Garden.

was at the time of Elvis's death in 1977. Like a bug in amber, Graceland captures the 1970s era in all of its possibilities. Elvis's legendary taste included his so-called "Jungle Room," replete with an in-wall waterfall and green shag carpeting on the floor and ceiling; his eclectic billiards parlor, plastered in yards of ornately patterned fabric; and his TV room, with a yellow, white, and blue color scheme and three television sets Presley watched simultaneously. Outside are the pool, his father Vernon's office (next to Elvis's firing range), and a building with a racquetball court, which now houses the King's gold records and other awards.

When visiting Graceland, take the audio tour to learn about the history of Elvis. Then you can pay your respects to Presley, who is buried alongside his parents and his grandmother behind the mansion in the serene Meditation Garden. Beyond the mansion and estate, take a peek at the automobile museum housing the King's cars (Elvis's 1955 pink Cadillac and 1956 purple Cadillac convertible are on display), a pair of his private planes, and restaurants and gift shops that sell Elvis souvenirs of every imaginable variety.

Graceland is now on the National Register of Historic Places, and it's become a magnet for Elvis fans everywhere. Fan clubs from as far away as Asia and Europe regularly send flowers and tributes to his grave. The enduring appeal of Elvis and his music is perhaps the most amazing thing about Graceland. His house attracts upward of 750,000 fans a year more than 30 years after his death—a testament to Elvis's lasting popularity.

The music gates were added after Elvis bought the mansion in 1957.

Quick Fact

Top Ten Sites at Graceland

1. **Music gates**—these were not part of the property when Elvis purchased it in 1957, but they were added later that year.

2. **Hall of Gold**—located in the Trophy Room just behind Graceland mansion, the Hall of Gold contains gold records and honors that Elvis received as a performing artist.

3. **Firearms collection**—on display in the Trophy Room are Elvis's 37 firearms, including pistols, machine guns, and a sawed-off shotgun.

4. **Badge collection**—also on display in the Trophy Room are the badges Elvis collected from law enforcement and security agencies across the country.

5. **Elvis's record collection**—this exhibit, called Sincerely Elvis, is across the street from Graceland and features Elvis's diverse taste in music.

6. **RCA display**—With 111 titles certified as gold, platinum, or multiplatinum, Elvis's collection is the largest presentation of gold and platinum records in history.

7. **Meditation Garden**—this small garden at Graceland is now the final resting place for Elvis and his immediate family.

8. **Elvis's jet, the *Lisa Marie***—purchased by Elvis in 1975, the jet named after his daughter is now on display at Graceland.

9. **The pink Cadillac Elvis bought for his mother**—this 1955 Cadillac, along with some of Elvis's other trademark cars, is on display at the Auto Museum.

10. **Wedding dress and suit**—Elvis's black paisley brocade jacket, matching vest, and plain black trousers and Priscilla's white silk organza dress are on display in the Sincerely Elvis exhibit.

Great Smoky Mountains National Park

Shrouded in thick deciduous forest, the Great Smoky Mountains are the United States' highest range east of South Dakota's Black Hills. They are also one of the oldest mountain ranges on the planet. The park's highest point is the 6,643-foot peak of Clingman's Dome, which is just across the North Carolina state line in Tennessee. On clear days, you can see as far as 100 miles from the peak. A cool, damp, coniferous rain forest covers much of the mountain.

The mountains are made of primeval rock and are considerably older than their rough, craggy counterparts out West. Today, the Great Smoky Mountains are protected as a national park but perhaps loved too much—more than nine million visitors take their toll each year.

The Smokies' vast forest is also one of the oldest on the continent. The park often feels like a vestige of an ancient era when trees ruled the planet. Today, over 100 species of trees and 1,300 varieties of flowering plants grow in the park. The respiration of this plant life produces the gauzy haze that gives the mountains their 'smoky' moniker.

The ridges of the Great Smoky Mountains trail off into the humid air.

Biltmore Estate

The largest home in the United States is the centerpiece of an immaculate 8,000-acre estate that includes lush gardens, active vineyards, and a luxury inn. Originally the country retreat of the Vanderbilt family, Biltmore has evolved into a swanky tourist attraction with a fascinating historical pedigree.

Biltmore mansion is the estate's distinguishing feature. It was the vision of George W. Vanderbilt. In the late 1880s, he purchased 125,000 acres in the Blue Ridge Mountains near Asheville, North Carolina, for the estate. He commissioned his friend, architect Richard Morris Hunt, to design the mansion.

Construction began in 1889 and lasted six years, requiring the labors of more than 1,000 workers. The fruit of their labor was this 250-room French Renaissance château. It was one of the most technologically advanced buildings of its time. Biltmore had indoor plumbing, electricity, elevators, and some of the first lightbulbs and telephones. There are 65 fireplaces, an indoor pool, a bowling alley, and numerous antiques. The gardens, designed by landscape architect Frederick Law Olmsted, are similarly superlative.

The Walled Garden on the Biltmore Estate blooms with a progression of color from spring through summer.

Cape Hatteras

Cape Hatteras is a largely untamed string of barrier islands about 70 miles long. This natural wonder has a distinct culture and fascinating history. The dunes, marshes, and woodlands that mark the thin strand of land between North Carolina's coastal sounds and the Atlantic Ocean are a diverse ecosystem defined by the wind and the sea. Nearly 400 species of birds have been sighted in the Cape Hatteras area. Hawks, shorebirds, and songbirds are common in spring and fall; terns and herons populate Cape Hatteras in the summer; and ducks and geese make the area home in winter.

Countless shipwrecks have earned Cape Hatteras a treacherous reputation and the nickname "The Graveyard of the Atlantic." The navigational dangers led to the construction of several lighthouses, including Cape Hatteras Lighthouse and Ocracoke Lighthouse (built in 1823, it's the oldest operating lighthouse in North Carolina).

While crowds are few and far between, Cape Hatteras is a popular recreational destination. Try the waters on either side of the island—they are considered some of the best on the entire East Coast for surfing. The cape is also excellent for surf, sound, and pier fishing.

The 208-foot-tall Cape Hatteras Lighthouse is the tallest in the United States. Visitors may climb the 268 steps to its top for a commanding view of the shoreline.

Roanoke Island

In 1587, Sir Walter Raleigh of England sent an expedition to the New World to Roanoke Island, a 27-acre isle in Croatan Sound off what is now the North Carolina coast. About 116 settlers, mostly families, sailed across the Atlantic Ocean and established a village there. But they arrived too late in the year to plant crops, and their leader, John White, returned to England for supplies.

Because of tensions between England and Spain, White couldn't return to Roanoke Island until 1590. When he arrived, the village

(Below) Elizabeth II, *docked at Manteo Harbor, is a composite design modeled after the original* Elizabeth, *one of the ships that sailed to the New World in 1585.*

(Above) *Today Roanoke Island is a fishing community and home to shopkeepers and artists.*

was deserted. Roanoke became known as the "Lost Colony." The mystery remains unsolved to this day.

Modern Roanoke Island is home to a historic park that tells this story and others through living-history demonstrations, a replica of a 16th-century sailing ship, and an interactive museum. A walk along the boardwalks and nature trails reveals native wildflowers and protected maritime forest. There's also an outdoor pavilion that hosts a performing arts series.

Blue Ridge Parkway

The Blue Ridge Parkway glides along the ridgetops of the southern Appalachian mountainside. The peaks are more than 6,000 feet above sea level, offering remarkable views of the verdant fields and country towns far below.

Construction crews began building the parkway in the 1930s to link Shenandoah National Park in Virginia to the Great Smoky Mountains National Park in North Carolina and Tennessee. Construction was paused during World War II.

By 1968, all that remained unfinished was a rugged stretch around North Carolina's Grandfather Mountain. But connecting the dots took nearly 20 more years and required building the Linn Cove Viaduct, a 1,200-foot suspended section of roadway. Considered an engineering marvel, it remains one of the most successful unions of road and landscape on the continent.

The Blue Ridge Parkway was officially dedicated in 1987, a full 52 years after construction began. It now offers a portal into the history, culture, and natural wonder of southern Appalachia.

"America's Favorite Drive" winds 469 miles from Shenandoah National Park to Great Smoky Mountains National Park.

Myrtle Beach

South Carolina's Grand Strand, Myrtle Beach, has been a favorite sun-and-sand destination for more than a century. The beach is named for the numerous wax myrtle trees growing

Sand and surf are prime attractions at Myrtle Beach. Apache Pier, (left), is the longest pier on the East Coast.

along the shore. The Seaside Inn, which opened in 1901, became the first of many increasingly sophisticated resorts that have made this one of the top tourist areas on the East Coast.

Myrtle Beach shares its name with the adjacent city. The beach itself bustles with all sorts of activity. Parasailers fly above the ocean, surfers hang ten on the tide, and divers explore the depths below. Pushcarts stocked with frozen lemonade and shops overflowing with T-shirts and bright beachwear are always close at hand, as are plenty of children. Myrtle Beach is known for its great family atmosphere, thanks to a lively boardwalk and numerous waterfront tourist attractions, including an amusement park.

Hilton Head Island

Hilton Head Island is one of the premier beach getaway destinations in the Southeast. It was named for William Hilton, an English sea captain who explored the island in the 17th century. The foot-shape barrier island is only 42 square miles. But the semitropical

(Below) *The Harbour Town Yacht Basin is a favorite attraction on Hilton Head Island.*

paradise of white-sand beaches, salt marshes, lagoons, and lush forests of mossy oaks, palmettos, magnolia, and pine is irresistible.

The island's pristine natural environment is balanced with the graceful aesthetics of some of the finest resorts and golf courses. The combination is a magnet for visitors: Though the year-round population is just 31,000 people, Hilton Head Island sees more than 2.5 million

(Above) *Hilton Head Island is known for its world-class golf courses, some of which are ranked among the top 100 in the nation.*

tourists each year. They come not only for the lush scenery, posh resorts, and great golf, but also for many deep breaths of fresh coastal air, abundant peace and quiet, and those beautiful sunsets that play out over the mainland on the western horizon.

Fort Sumter National Monument

At 4:30 A.M. on April 12, 1861, a 10-inch mortar tore through the air at Fort Sumter, located off the South Carolina coast near Charleston. The fort—then controlled by Union troops—was besieged when the Confederate Army launched a naval offensive. The event was the fuse that lit the Civil War.

South Carolina delegates had voted to secede from the United States the previous year in protest of the election of President Abraham Lincoln. Tensions had been running high leading up to the siege of Fort Sumter, and its bombardment marked the official beginning of the Civil War.

After 34 hours of bombardment, the Union soldiers defending Fort Sumter surrendered to the Confederacy on April 13, 1861, and the fort was controlled by the South until the end of the war in 1865. Reconstruction of Fort Sumter began in the 1870s.

Today, the perfectly preserved fort is a national monument and a symbol of Southern pride. Visitors can see the original cannons and brickwork at the fort. The inside of the battery has been converted to a Civil War museum. And from the upper level of the fort, take in the panoramic view of Charleston and its harbor.

Fort Sumter was restored after being severely damaged during the Civil War. It became a U.S. National Monument in 1948.

Martin Luther King, Jr., National Historic Site

Martin Luther King, Jr., was born in a modest, comfortable, Queen Anne–style home in the heart of Atlanta's "Sweet Auburn" district (the city's prosperous African-American downtown in segregated days). Visitors to the Martin Luther King, Jr., National Historic Site in Atlanta, Georgia, are reminded that the great civil rights leader could have lived a cozy, middle-class life as a respected man—and never risked his life for his beliefs. Instead King spent the 11 years from 1957 to 1968 traveling over six million miles and speaking more than 2,500 times in support of civil rights for all Americans. He took part in protests, most notably the peaceful march on Washington, D.C., where he delivered his moving "I Have a Dream" speech.

The historic site evokes the memory of King's dreams. The visitor center has a helpful video and exhibits aimed at young visitors.

The King Center, established by King's widow, Coretta Scott King, in 1968, features exhibits on King; Coretta Scott King; and Mahatma Gandhi. The center is the site of King and his wife's graves. He is entombed beside an eternal flame, but King's real eternal fire lives on in those who hear his message.

The King Center is a memorial to and final resting place of Martin Luther King, Jr.

Cumberland Island National Seashore

You may have to make an effort to visit beautiful, mysterious Cumberland Island National Seashore. This is due to a policy that permits a maximum of 300 visitors per day and has only one developed campsite, Sea Camp (reservations can be made up to six months in advance). But a trip to the remote island is worth the hurdles.

The lucky few who make it have Cumberland Island seemingly to themselves. The island is three miles wide ringed by a beach almost

Cumberland Island is covered by white-sand beaches, dunes, and saltwater marshes.

18 miles long. It's covered by acres of marsh, tidal creeks, sand dunes, blinding white sand, and historic ruins and museums that compel admiration and amazement. And this doesn't even take into account the island wildlife. Georgia's southernmost barrier island is a sanctuary for gigantic loggerhead sea turtles. Herds of wild horses roam here, too. It's said

they were left behind by Spanish explorers in the 16th century. Cumberland Island's maritime forest of oaks and palmettos, draped with Spanish moss, envelop the island's trails. Summer tanagers, yellow-throated warblers, and pileated woodpeckers as well as armadillos and bull alligators thrive here.

Cumberland Island is dotted with picturesque, haunting ruins. To help make sense of them, the Ice House Museum covers island history dating back to its first inhabitants.

Chippewa Square, Savannah

Savannah, Georgia, is America's first planned city. General James Edward Oglethorpe (who had previously founded the colony of Georgia) founded Savannah in 1733. He designed his new capital as a series of neighborhoods centered around 24 squares. His layout remains intact today: Twenty-one squares still exist in Savannah. Each has a distinctive architecture, history, and folklore.

Johnson Square, laid out in 1733, was the first Savannah square. Oglethorpe Square, which was called "Upper New Square," was laid out in 1742 by General Oglethorpe. And Orleans Square was built in 1815 in memory of the heroes of the War of 1812.

Chippewa Square is at the center of the downtown historic district between Hull Street and Perry Street. At the square's heart, a statue of Oglethorpe commemorates the founding of Georgia. Excerpts from the original Georgia charter are inscribed on the pedestal, designed by Henry Bacon.

Built in 1815, the square gets its name from the Battle of Chippewa in the War of 1812. By the 1820s, Chippewa Square became Savannah's nightlife center, in part because the Savannah Theatre is just one block north. The showbiz tradition continues to this day: The square served as the backdrop for the famed park-bench scene in *Forrest Gump*.

A statue of General James Edward Oglethorpe stands at the center of Chippewa Square in Savannah, Georgia.

Tybee Island

Eighteen miles east of Savannah, Georgia, Tybee Island is an exclusive beach getaway with plenty of opportunities to relax and sightsee. This barrier island's three-mile beach is backed by mesmerizing sand dunes. Tybee means "salt" to some Native Americans, but visitors to the island enjoy far more than just the ocean.

Tybee is a laid-back resort town where you can choose to stay at luxury hotels, deluxe condominiums, quaint cottages, or bed-and-breakfasts. More than 30 restaurants on the island serve up fabulous food: Some have dishes with a Caribbean kick, and some feature chef specialties of seafood dishes such as crab, oysters, shrimp, or fish.

Enjoy boat cruises, fishing trips, or kayaking. Venture into the salt marshes to go bird-watching. Or check out local marine life on display at the Tybee Island Marine Science Center—exhibits feature species from the marsh, shoreline, and reef. There are also biking and hiking trails across the island.

If you have a passion for history, visit Tybee's historic sites. Fort Screven was a former coastal artillery fort, and Fort Pulaski played a vital part in the Civil War. And at 154 feet, the Tybee Island Lighthouse is the oldest and tallest lighthouse in Georgia.

Since 1736, the Tybee Island Lighthouse has guided mariners. Over the years, it has been rebuilt and repainted with various striped patterns.

Stone Mountain

Stone Mountain, Georgia, is the world's largest exposed piece of granite—7.5 billion cubic feet of rock. This immense, bulging monolith is just a half-hour drive from Atlanta.

But it's not just the size of the mountain that drives people to visit. Stone Mountain's outstanding feature is the Confederate Memorial Carving. Three southern heroes from the Civil War have been carved into the rock: Confederate President Jefferson Davis, General Robert E. Lee, and General Thomas J. "Stonewall" Jackson. The relief is massive, spanning 90 by 190 feet, and is surrounded by a carved surface that covers three acres. While planning for the sculpture began in 1915, it was not completed until 1972.

Stone Mountain can be visited by taking a cable-car ride up the north face. Intrepid visitors can hike along various trails to get closer to the amazing mountain. A visit to the top reveals rock pools and views of a downtown Atlanta that seems close enough to touch.

The massive Confederate Memorial Carving honors Confederate Civil War heroes Jefferson Davis, Robert E. Lee, and "Stonewall" Jackson.

Located just outside the park's west gate is Historic Stone Mountain Village. The village was established in 1839 and offers more than 50 specialty shops and restaurants. Visitors can browse through quaint antique stores as well as shop for art and jewelry created by local artisans.

Jekyll Island

Jekyll Island is one of Georgia's Golden Isles. It is Georgia's smallest barrier island and lies off the coast midway between Savannah, Georgia, and Jacksonville, Florida. But this small island has a fascinating history and an assortment of relaxing activities for modern-day visitors.

In 1886, a group of famous entrepreneurs including William Rockefeller, Joseph Pulitzer, and J. P. Morgan founded the Jekyll Island Club. The island became a winter retreat for some of America's most elite families. In addition to soaking up some sun during the winter months, the men also met for discussions and dinners. "Secret" meetings at the club are rumored to have led to the creation of the Federal Reserve System and helped William McKinley be reelected to his second term as president. But the blows of the Great Depression and World War II brought about an end to the club. In 1947, the state of Georgia bought the island and turned it into a state park.

The Jekyll Island Club Hotel is both a historic landmark and elegant resort on Jekyll Island.

Today tourists can visit the many mansions built by club members (they referred to the homes as merely "cottages"). You can feel like a billionaire for a day at least when you take a carriage ride through the historic district.

The island also has three 18-hole golf courses. For outdoors types, there are ten miles of pristine beach waiting to be explored. Year-round guided nature walks explain Georgia's coastal life. The saltwater marsh, freshwater rivers, and ocean are all great for fishing. And if you feel adventurous, try sailing, sea kayaking, or canoeing.

Amicalola Falls

A hiker's paradise unfolds at Amicalola Falls State Park. Twelve miles of trails weave through the picturesque Appalachian Mountains. Daring adventurers can brave the eight-mile approach from the park to Springer Mountain. This path is an access point for the 2,150-mile Appalachian Trail that winds all the way up to Maine. It passes through the Amicalola Watershed to Amicalola Falls.

At 729 feet, this is the tallest waterfall east of the Mississippi River. Its name means "Tumbling Waters" in Cherokee. Amicalola Falls is one of Georgia's Seven Natural Wonders (the others being Okefenokee Swamp, Stone Mountain, Providence Canyon, Tallulah Gorge, Warm Springs, and Radium Springs).

Visitors can stay at the modern lodge near the falls, which has 57 rooms. The visitor center has scales where hikers can weigh their packs before departing. Travelers can also stay at the remote Len Foote Hike Inn, accessible by a five-mile hike along the Hike Inn Trail. The secluded inn's 20 rooms are arranged around a two-story lobby. The rustic inn provides many gorgeous panoramas of oak and hickory forests with mountain laurel and rhododendron. It also is an access point for winding mountainside trails where you can catch a glimpse of warblers, vireos, white-tailed deer, rabbits, raccoons, and bears.

Amicalola Falls, seen here from the crossover bridge, is the tallest cascading waterfall east of the Mississippi River.

World of Coca-Cola

Coca-Cola was invented in Atlanta in 1886, and it quickly became a favorite beverage across the world. The Coca-Cola Company's showcase museum, the World of Coca-Cola in Atlanta, Georgia, is a tribute to the brand. As one scholar wrote, "If Coca-Cola is a superstar, then the World of Coca-Cola is Coke's Graceland: the institutionalization of that superstardom. Or, to use another metaphor, it is the Vatican of Coca-Cola." So if you've ever enjoyed a cold Coke on a hot day—whether in

The World of Coca-Cola in Atlanta, Georgia, houses the world's largest collection of Coca-Cola memorabilia.

Cleveland or Cairo, Atlanta or Athens, Virginia City or the Vatican—the World of Coca-Cola might be just the tonic for you. If you are one of countless hard-core Coke collectors, the place is a must-see.

The three-story museum traces Coke from its early days, when it was rumored to be a

mix of kola nuts and cocaine, to the drink's triumph as a beverage of global reach. The exhibition begins with "Creating a Classic," a collection of memorabilia from 1886 to 1926 with interactive video stations. The second gallery, "The Pause That Refreshes," comprises a replica 1930s soda fountain with a real "soda jerk." The museum goes on from there until visitors reach the real objective for many of them: Club Coca-Cola, where they may sample all the soft drinks they wish.

Everglades National Park

It's a bright day, and you're walking on a boardwalk a few feet above water. The heavy woods thin out into sawgrass, and the water below deepens and clears. You hear a cuckoo and see an anhinga bird with dark, furry-looking feathers and a hooked bill. A cormorant plunges into the water and eats a fish, then settles on the rail just ahead of you. You look down into the water and see a large, primitive-looking garfish and what appears to be a bass. An alligator surfaces; first its broad

back appears, then its head and tail. In the distance, past a shimmering purple gallinule bird, a coral snake uncoils around a branch. The cormorant flaps its wings and flies away.

These exotic species and more inhabit Everglades National Park at the southern tip of Florida. Scarcely more than a 90-minute drive from Miami, the park is home to gorgeous fish, turtles, otters, lizards, and birds including great blue herons, ibis, wood storks, and red-cockaded woodpeckers. There are plenty of alligators and crocodiles lurking in the freshwater and saltwater swamps. And if you are *very* lucky, you might even spot a rare Florida panther.

The Everglades are a diverse ecosystem of swamps and marshes where freshwater and saltwater meet. This unique environment is home to animals including the American alligator (inset).

The cypress groves in Everglades National Park are home to many species of waterfowl. More than 350 species of birds have been sighted in the park.

Just four miles from the park entrance near Homestead, the Anhinga Trail at the Royal Palm Visitor Center is one of the world's most amazing boardwalks. The walkway is built above Taylor Slough, one of the park's many ecosystems. The freshwater slough is something like a stream in the middle of a marsh, where the water moves about 100 feet per day. Other Everglades trails take you through freshwater marl prairie, pinelands, hardwood hammocks, cypress groves, mangrove forests, marine estuaries, and more. Near the Anhinga Trail, the Gumbo-Limbo Trail (which is a quarter-mile long and wheelchair accessible) takes you through a dense hammock of royal palms and gumbo-limbo trees.

The Everglades is a limestone shelf spilling toward the ocean. In the northwestern Everglades and Big Cypress National Pre-serve, freshwater from as far away as Orlando flows over the Tamiami Formation (limestone formed eons ago by the sand, silt, and calcium of an ancient sea) and mixes with saltwater as it flows into the ocean. The result is a splendid but fragile environment.

Everglades National Park, which covers 1.5 million acres and is the third-largest national park in the continental United States, has five entrances. Most adventurers start at the Ernest F. Coe Visitor Center by the main entrance on the eastern edge of the park. The Royal Palm Center is about four miles west. The Flamingo Visitor Center, 38 miles southwest from the main entrance, takes travelers deep into the park for hiking and canoeing; some areas are bike- and wheelchair-accessible, too. The territory near the center of the park is the preferred place for croc-watching, and Eco Pond, one mile past the Flamingo Visitor Center, is prime gator habitat. (The Everglades is the only place on Earth naturally occupied by both crocodiles and alligators.) In the park's northwest corner, The Gulf Coast Visitor Center lies across the water from the 10,000 Islands, a haven for fishing in the scenic backwaters. And the Shark Valley Visitor Center, on the Tamiami Trail (Highway 41) on the park's northern border, is an outpost on Florida's "River of Grass."

Novelist Marjory Stoneman Douglas founded Friends of the Everglades in 1969. "There are no other Everglades in the world," she wrote. "They are, they have always been, one of the unique regions of the earth; remote, never wholly known. Nothing anywhere else is like them"—not that visitors to this precious preserve need to be reminded.

Ringling Estate, Sarasota Bay

In its time, the Ringling Bros. and Barnum & Bailey Circus was the greatest show on earth. It became the world's most successful and enduring circus, formed in 1919 when the Ringling Bros. (led by John Ringling) and Barnum & Bailey circuses merged.

John Ringling had a passion for art, collecting works while touring Europe. In 1924, he and his wife, Mable, began building their Italian Renaissance–style mansion on Sarasota Bay. The building was called Cà d'Zan, meaning "House of John" in Venetian dialect. The mansion is a work of art. The building is capped by a 60-foot tower that was illuminated when the Ringlings were home. Its living room (called the Court)

is two-and-a-half stories high. An impressive 8,000-square-foot marble terrace offers awe-inspiring views of Sarasota Bay.

In 1927, the Ringlings began building the John and Mable Ringling Museum of Art (now also known as the State Art Museum of Florida). The Ringlings wanted to share their love of and collection of art with the people of Florida. Their art treasures include more than 10,000 paintings, sculptures, drawings, prints, photographs, and decorative arts. The museum holds the largest private collection of paintings and drawings by Peter Paul Rubens as well as masterworks by Lucas Cranach the Elder, Nicolas Poussin, Frans Hals, and Anthony Van

Dyck. All in all, there are 21 galleries of European paintings (including more then 700 Old Masters), antiques, Asian art, American paintings, and contemporary art.

A new addition to the estate in 1948 was the Circus Museum. Visitors can relive the magic of the circus through exhibits of costumes, wagons, performance equipment, and other memorabilia that convey its history. Among the attractions is a scale model of the Ringling Bros. and Barnum & Bailey Circus as it was from 1919 to 1938.

The elegant Cà d'Zan is 200 feet long, with 32 rooms and 15 baths.

Miami's South Beach

Buildings in the Art Deco District of South Beach have a distinct whimsical flare.

South Beach, a section of Miami Beach, is an arts, entertainment, and recreation center of global scope. South Beach is the southernmost 23 blocks of Miami Beach. This district has exquisite restaurants, hip nightclubs, and luxurious oceanfront hotels. Topless sunbathing is common on some beaches.

It is also home to the historic Art Deco District. Most of the hotels and apartment buildings here were built in the 1930s and have the rounded corners and geometric highlights of Art Deco architecture.

The district has spawned smaller, hipper neighborhoods. One such is SoFi, short for South of Fifth Street, a laid-back neighborhood with sizzling spots such as Opium Garden and Nikki Beach. SoFi is also home to the Bass Museum of Art which houses a collection ranging from Botticelli and Rubens to Miami Beach architectural photographs.

South Beach was recognized when its first bar, Mac's Club Deuce, opened in 1906. Today, some diehards consider Club Deuce the last real bar in South Beach. It's now surrounded by a kaleidoscope of glitzy, trendy nightclubs that regularly change names or owners in search of the latest craze. All of this razzle-dazzle begs the question: Has South Beach replaced Los Angeles and the Big Apple as America's hottest nightspot? You decide.

Cape Canaveral

Cape Canaveral is a barrier island off the east coast of Florida that's spacious enough to include the 58,000-acre Canaveral National Seashore, John F. Kennedy Space Center, and Cape Canaveral Air Force Station. Its 220 square miles are covered by marshes and many miles of shimmering beach.

Visitors are welcome at the Kennedy Space Center, whose tours give an in-depth behind-the-scenes look at NASA, including visits to launch pads and rockets. Outer space may be the island's main attraction, but Cape Canaveral proves that Earth has its share of beauty and mystery, too. The space center borders the Merritt Island National Wildlife Refuge. There, manatees graze underwater in the shadow of a launch pad, and endangered sea turtles swim to shore to lay their eggs in the silence of the night.

The cape is home to many exotic wildlife species. Canaveral National Seashore records indicate there are 1,045 plant species and 310 bird species in the park, including endangered creatures such as the peregrine falcon, the West Indian manatee, the southern bald eagle, and the eastern indigo snake. The park's 24 miles of undeveloped beach comprise the longest stretch on the east coast of Florida.

The Rocket Garden at the John F. Kennedy Space Center gives visitors an up-close look at the rockets and capsules that first launched NASA astronauts into space.

Key West

Key West, Florida, has long been famous as one of America's top destinations for fun-and-sun vacations. Key West has retained its charm, remoteness, intriguing history, natural beauty, and idyllic weather (once the hurricane season subsides) since the 1920s. About the same number of people live there now as then. Its small town feeling exudes all the characteristics necessary to lure visitors back every year.

Located at the southernmost tip of the Florida Keys, Key West's average temperature

Tropical Key West is home to the southernmost point in the continental United States.

is a temperate 77.8 degrees. Storms aside, Key West has few highs or lows—just steady sunshine, perfect for relaxing on the beach to soak up some sun. A daily treat, Key West's Mallory Square hosts the Sunset Celebration each evening, with food vendors, fire-eaters, tightrope walkers, and arts and crafts exhibits.

Key West, which has also been called "Margaritaville" or the "Conch Republic," didn't always have a reputation for laid-back sun and fun. The name "Key West" is in fact a corruption of *Cayo Hueso*, meaning "Island of Bones." This haunting name was bestowed by early

The Key West Lighthouse, built in 1847, offers spectacular views.

Spanish explorers impressed by the human remains left on the beach.

Key West has become known for its most famous visitors, including artists Winslow Homer and John James Audubon, actor Cary Grant, President Harry Truman, and novelist Ernest Hemingway. Hemingway wrote many of his best works while on the island, and today Hemingway House is Key West's top tourist attraction.

Castillo de San Marcos, St. Augustine

Castillo de San Marcos and its 25 acres of old parade grounds are a St. Augustine must-see. The fortress, built by Spaniards between 1672 and 1695, is a marvel of a relic constructed to defend the conquistadores' treasure routes against British attacks from the north. The fort is star-shape to provide a maximum view of, but minimum exposure to, an approaching enemy. It includes a 40-foot moat and double drawbridge. The walls are made from coquina, a limestone formed from compacted shells and coral, which is quite durable and could shrug off cannon fire. The fort's upper level, with its watchtowers and cannon, gives visitors a long view out to sea.

St. Augustine's Old City and Castillo de San Marcos reflect Florida's successive historic developments like tree rings. In 1513, after sailing with Columbus on his second voyage to the New World, Juan Ponce de León (he of the Fountain of Youth) was the first explorer to set foot in Florida. He landed just south of St. Augustine.

King Philip II of Spain established St. Augustine in 1565 as the sword and shield for the American outpost of his great empire. He commissioned Admiral Pedro Menéndez

Castillo de San Marcos has served a number of nations in its history, but it was never taken by military force—control was passed by treaty.

Watchtowers on the fort's bastions gave its occupiers time to prepare for incoming attacks.

de Avilés to remove the French from Florida. Avilés defeated a French fleet of five ships in Matanzas Bay and founded St. Augustine. The settlement joined the Spanish Empire (said to be the *first* empire upon which the sun never set), which stretched from Manila to Mexico City and back to Madrid.

Yet, the sun did set on the Spanish Empire, and the king's fort in St. Augustine passed to the British, then back to Spain. Later it belonged to the United States, then the Con-

federate States, then the United States again. All this back-and-forth resulted in an unclassifiable Old City that is southern with Spanish and Moroccan accents, definite Britishisms, reminders of 18th- and 19th-century America, and echoes of the ages before that.

In 1738, Fort Mose, just north of the city, became the first settlement created for free African-Americans. This makes St. Augustine the oldest continuously occupied European and African-American settlement in

the United States (excluding Puerto Rico). In that spirit, visit St. Augustine's Lincolnville Historic District. Founded in 1866 by freed slaves, and a bastion of the Civil Rights Movement of the 1950s and 1960s, the district is now noted for its Victorian architecture and Gothic churches. Its Yallaha Plantation House, built in 1800, is one of the oldest in Florida. (The oldest home of all is the Old City's Gonzalez–Alvarez House, which was built shortly after the British siege in 1702.)

Little Havana

The heart of Cuban life in Florida is the vibrant commercial strip in Little Havana called Calle Ocho, or Eighth Street. This bustling neighborhood is southwest of downtown Miami between 12th and 17th avenues.

Calle Ocho is the epicenter of an ethnic explosion that includes immigrant commu-

Residents of Little Havana gather in Maximo Gomez Park to challenge each other to games of dominoes.

nities from around the world. One of the many highlights is the authentic Cuban cuisine—restaurants serve up seafood paella, succulent marinated pork, and hearty beans and rice. Visitors can also sample the cuisines of Peru, Nicaragua, the Dominican Republic, and myriad other Latin lands. Tourists and locals

Each year more than one million people gather for the Calle Ocho Festival, which has been called the "world's largest block party."

alike dote on the neighborhood's trademark hand-rolled cigars, merengue and salsa music, and chess and dominoes games.

Then there are the celebrations! The last Friday of each month is known as *Viernes Culturales*, or Cultural Friday. This Latin street party showcases Cuban music, dancing, street performers, food, and local artists. In March, the Calle Ocho Festival is one of the world's largest free festivals, drawing more than one million people.

Vulcan Statue

The 56-foot statue of Vulcan in Birmingham, Alabama, is the largest cast-iron statue in the world. The creation of the glorious sculpture is tied closely to the roots of the city.

Birmingham began as a mining town for coal, limestone, and iron ore, which were forged to make steel. By the 20th century, it was a formidable industrial power, and the city's business leaders sought to promote Birmingham. Their audacious answer was to have Italian sculptor Giuseppe Moretti create a cast-iron sculpture of Vulcan, the Roman god of fire, volcanoes, and the forge. The sculpture was unveiled at the 1904 St. Louis World's Fair, where it was a hit and won the mining and metallurgy exhibition grand prize.

Unfortunately when the statue was moved back to Birmingham, its arms were reassembled improperly. The statue was neglected and became a three-dimensional billboard, cradling giant-size Heinz pickle jars and even sporting painted-on jeans. In 1939, Vulcan was finally moved to his proper place on Birmingham's Red Mountain. Restoration of the statue was completed in 2004, and Vulcan Park reopened for the statue's centennial. Today the statue and its panoramic view come closest to fulfilling Moretti's original vision of a brawny, ambitious Birmingham.

The cast-iron Vulcan Statue in Birmingham has been restored to symbolize the town's steel history.

Natchez Trace

Natchez Trace, which runs from Mississippi to Tennessee, began as a series of tribal trading routes worn into the earth.

Natchez Trace originated thousands of years ago. Big animals such as deer and bison were the first to tramp along what became the Old Natchez Trace. Then the Choctaw and Chickasaw connected the paths, and the trail became the region's premiere trade route. Arriving Europeans grasped its potential, and by the late 1700s the Natchez Trace bustled with boaters. They would sell their cargo and flatboats or keelboats for lumber in Natchez or New Orleans and then travel back north to Nashville and beyond. The boaters carried their money in gold and silver coins, and the Natchez Trace became legendary for its cut-throat gangs. In 1801, the United States signed a treaty with the Choctaw allowing roads to be built along the route.

Today, Natchez Trace has many meanings. It is the 444-mile Natchez Trace Parkway, which follows the road from Natchez, Missis-sippi, to just outside Nashville, Tennessee. The parkway's one visitor center is located near Tupelo, Mississippi, birthplace of Elvis Presley. Four sections of trails along the parkway make up the Natchez Trace National Scenic Trail. Crimson clover, butterweed, Japanese honey-suckle, ground ivy, and many other species of wildflowers dot the scenery along the parkway. Adventurers can enjoy numerous hiking trails, picnic sites, and campgrounds, too.

Gulf Islands National Seashore

From above, the Gulf Islands National Seashore looks like a sandy string of pearls off the coasts of Florida and Mississippi. Along the water are miles of snow-white beaches, bayous, saltwater marshes, maritime forests, barrier islands, and nature trails. Of the more than 135,000 acres of national seashore, 80 percent of the park is underwater.

The environment is diverse, but visitors to the seashore usually focus on the beach. Miles and miles of white powdery sand extend through the sparkling water. Especially intriguing are the barrier islands, notably the Horn Island and Petit Bois Island wilderness areas, each about ten miles out from the Mississippi coast. Camping is permitted anywhere on the islands.

A sub-specialty of Gulf Islands National Seashore is the 19th-century forts. Four of them are on the Florida panhandle side of the park. They were built after the War of 1812 to defend Pensacola Bay. The largest, Fort Pickens, was completed in 1834. Today the fort doubles as one of the park's most popular beach areas. Along with Perdido Key, Okaloosa, and Davis Bayou (on the Mississippi side), it ranks among the most popular beaches in the area.

But the barrier islands are still a buffer to protect the mainland—the park has been bruised by storms such as Hurricane Ivan in 2004. Check for closures before you go.

The white sand of Gulf Islands National Seashore is believed to have eroded from rocky areas to the north.

Delta Blues Festival

Performers entertain the crowd at Greenville's big annual event.

The Mississippi Delta Blues Festival is the king of blues festivals. Founded in 1978, the Greenville-based blues festival is the second oldest continuously operating festival of its kind in the country.

The festival is Mississippi's largest single-day event. Perhaps it has earned its regal status because of the way it was born—from the heart and passion of the state's civil rights and antipoverty movements. The blues were born out of a folk culture context drawing elements from work songs, love songs, slow drags, rags, and spirituals. The Mississippi Delta Blues Festival is the flagship of the Delta Arts Project, founded by the Mississippi Action for Community Education Incorporated (MACE). Its mission is to confront the human rights issues that gave birth to the blues and empower African-Americans.

The festival began as a community gathering where locals played traditional blues on acoustic instruments. While it's still seen as a community event, the festival has drawn top-notch blues artists such as B. B. King, Bobby Rush, Albert King, Bobby Blue Bland, John Lee Hooker, Johnny Winter, Muddy Waters, Furry Lewis, and Big Joe Williams.

Blanchard Springs Caverns

Blanchard Springs Caverns is the jewel of the Ozarks. This three-level cave system has almost every kind of cave formation: from soda straws to bacon formations to rimstone cave pools. The most famous formation in these haunting caverns is the 70-foot-high joined stalagmite-stalactite called the Giant Column.

Anthropologists have found evidence of human visitors in the caverns as early as 900 A.D. But it was the pioneering spelunkers and environmental activists in the mid-1950s and 1960s that led to further exploration. Early expeditions took adventurers about 1.4 miles into the cave. With careful planning, the caverns have remained a healthy, "living" cave system.

Visitors can choose from three scenic trails through Blanchard Springs Caverns. The Drip-

The cavern's namesake river, Blanchard Springs, leaves the cave as a waterfall.

stone Trail is a one-hour trail around the upper level that is stroller- and wheelchair-accessible. The Discovery Trail is a longer section that winds through the middle level. If you're look-

The shimmering Ghost Room is a highlight of the Discovery Trail.

ing for a challenge, the four-hour Wild Cave Tour is an introduction to spelunking requiring athleticism, endurance, and equipment available only by reservation.

But even the claustrophobic can enjoy the wide-open serenity of the Ozark National Forest. There are campsites and opportunities for fishing, hiking, and watching wildlife. While in the area, tour the Ozark Mountain Folk Center. And if you're craving more caving, there are tours of other caves in the area including Bull Shoals Caverns, Hurricane River Cave, Mystic Caverns, and Cosmic Cavern (the site of the Ozark's largest underground lake).

Hot Springs National Park

Hot Springs National Park is the smallest and oldest national park in the United States. It is also one of the most unusual. For one thing, much of Hot Springs National Park is a National Historic Landmark District located in downtown Hot Springs, Arkansas. Most important, it contains what some veteran visitors call the world's best hot springs water. About 850,000 gallons of water per day percolate from the side of Hot Springs Mountain at 143 degrees Fahrenheit in 47 hot springs.

The popularity of the park has been bubbling, too, rising to about 1.5 million annual visitors.

The importance of preserving these waters was evident to early Americans, and the main mission of the National Parks Service today is to maintain the springs. The Bathhouse Row historic district shows visitors how their predecessors enjoyed the park. The many matchless examples of Gilded Age architecture show how the resort early on earned the title "The American Spa."

The architectural style and interior details of the Fordyce Bathhouse pay tribute to the "life-giving" waters of the hot springs.

Yet there's much more to Hot Springs National Park than a relaxing soak. Favorite recreations include hiking, crystal prospecting, camping in Gulpha Gorge Campground, and driving or hiking up Hot Springs Mountain to enjoy the 40-mile view from Hot Springs Tower.

Ouachita National Forest

Ouachita National Forest spans 1.8 million acres in a broad swath north of Hot Springs, Arkansas, that reaches all the way to eastern Oklahoma. The forest is renowned for its glistening streams and pristine lakes. It is the oldest national forest in the South: President Theodore Roosevelt created Ouachita National Forest in 1907.

The Ouachita Mountains first gained praise in 1541 from Hernando DeSoto, and later from French explorers, who named the mountains for the native word for "good hunting ground." The modern motto might be "good fishing": Today the forest contains about 700 acres of fishing ponds and lakes. You can use nonmotorized boats to reach favorite fishing spots. Or if you're water-weary, choose from the extensive trails for hiking, mountain biking, and horseback riding that provide optimum scenic views.

The Ouachita Mountains might be best known around the world, however, as heaven for geology enthusiasts and rock collectors. The mountains were built by orogeny, the folding of the earth's crust. The exposed surface then eroded over time. It has taken millions of years, but the results include astounding finds of diamonds, what many say are the world's finest quartz crystals (especially near Hot Springs and Mount Ida), and ridges made of novaculite flint, a dense, hard rock used for whetstones.

Autumn foliage heightens the beauty of the riverbanks in Ouachita National Forest.

Mardi Gras

Now the biggest annual party in North America, New Orleans's Carnival (also known as "the greatest free show on Earth") is an over-the-top street party that typically attracts more than a million people from all over the world. Carnival culminates with Mardi Gras, or Fat Tuesday, the wild event that turns New Orleans into a center of celebration.

Mardi Gras gives way at midnight to Ash Wednesday, the first day of Lent. While the party has roots in pagan rituals that predate Christianity, it was recognized as a day of celebration by Pope Gregory XIII in 1582 when he placed it on his Gregorian calendar. The Catholic Church in Europe co-opted Mardi Gras as a season of excess before the self-discipline of Lent.

French explorers were the first to celebrate Mardi Gras in the New World, though it's a point of contention whether the first Mardi Gras in America was hosted in Louisiana or Alabama. Some say the first Mardi Gras was celebrated in 1699 on Mardi Gras Island just downstream from present-day New Orleans on the Mississippi River. Others claim the first was in Mobile, Alabama, in 1704.

For the last century or so, however, nobody has thrown a bigger party than the city of New Orleans. Carnival begins with the Feast of Epiphany, on January 6, the twelfth day of Christmas. But because Fat Tuesday falls between February 3 and March 9 every year, most people don't get serious about Carnival until the two-week window before Mardi Gras.

Visitors crowd Bourbon Street for the annual Mardi Gras parades and celebration.

The last five days of Carnival—starting with the Friday before Mardi Gras—are the most intense of the celebration. New Orleans's famous French Quarter—in particular, Bourbon Street—becomes a wild party with famous people, frozen cocktails, competition for beads, and tons of fun.

The parades are the flamboyant soul of Carnival. Each parade is organized by a krewe, or group with hereditary membership. There are about 60 krewes in New Orleans. Each krewe selects a king and queen to reign over the parade. The parades put on by the Comus, Rex, and Zulu krewes are among the longest standing and most loved in New Orleans. Elaborate multicolor floats carry krewe members in ornate costumes. They toss trinkets, beads, doubloons, small toys, and candy into the crowds, sometimes in exchange for a wink, a hug, or a flash of flesh.

The parades snake through New Orleans until they reach their destination—a big, bawdy ball. Many of these balls are masquerades where traditional king cake is served to revelers. The king cake is made from roll-like dough brushed with icing. A trinket, usually a bean or tiny plastic baby representing the Christ child, is baked inside. Whoever gets the piece with the trinket is bestowed special status for the remainder of the party.

When the clock strikes midnight on Mardi Gras, the party is officially over. New Orleans

Quick Fact

The French Quarter

After Hurricane Katrina damaged structures in the French Quarter in 2005, some television personalities questioned whether its unique atmosphere would change. Didn't these experts understand that the French Quarter is eternal?

Here they say, *"Laissez les bons temps rouler"* ("Let the good times roll"), and clearly the good times will return to this famous district. It took months to restore telephone service to New Orleans, but the decision to go ahead with the next Mardi Gras took only weeks. "We've got to have this party," said Blaine Kern, also known as "Mr. Mardi Gras." The French Quarter and Mardi Gras are the heart of New Orleans. Locals and tourists flock to the French Quarter for the crazy party each year, with its parades raining beads, costumes a dozen feet wide, jazz in the streets, and dancing.

While Mardi Gras comes only once a year, the French Quarter has plenty of entertainment to keep visitors delighted year-round. Restaurants serve up some of North America's finest cuisine, with specialties such as po-boys, jambalaya, crawfish etoufée, and shrimp Creole. The French Quarter is also known for its incomparable coffee and Sazerac cocktails.

Stay for a sample of the music that was born in New Orleans. The beats of blues and jazz, stride and boogie-woogie, Dixieland, big band, and rock 'n' roll can be heard in clubs throughout the district.

police officers on horseback clear upper Bourbon Street and send the partiers home. Beginning on Ash Wednesday, many of the city's citizens give up a few pleasures for Lent.

And Mardi Gras will go on, despite—or perhaps to spite—Hurricane Katrina in 2005. This is one party that's impossible to stop.

The St. Louis Cathedral towers over Jackson Square in the French Quarter.

Chapter Four

The Midwest

At the heart of the United States is the Midwest. The "nation's breadbasket" has its roots in agriculture, but the Midwestern spirit has come to encompass more than traditional farmland and rural communities. Treasures abound throughout these plains, stretching from the foothills of the Appalachians through the Great Lakes region to the Rockies. Among the wonders in this chapter are Michigan's landmark Grand Hotel and isolated Isle Royale, Chicago's earthy blues clubs and chic Magnificent Mile, and Ohio's enigmatic Serpent Mound and lush Cuyahoga National Park.

Illuminated at sunrise, the faces of Washington, Jefferson, Roosevelt, and Lincoln grace Mount Rushmore in South Dakota's Black Hills.

Rock and Roll Hall of Fame and Museum

Rock 'n' roll lives on today, more than a half-century after its beginning. One reason is Cleveland's Rock and Roll Hall of Fame and Museum. Designed by architect I. M. Pei, the building expresses the raw power of rock music. The geometric and cantilevered forms are often compared to a turntable or pyramid. The striking building and its 162-foot tower anchor Cleveland's North Coast Harbor.

The hall began operation in 1986 with the ceremonial induction of its first class of rock stars: Chuck Berry, Elvis Presley, Little Richard, Sam Cooke, the Everly Brothers, and Buddy Holly, among others. Inside it holds a collection of rock memorabilia and features groundbreaking exhibitions. Broadcasts from the Alan Freed Studio are a fan favorite, as are the exhibitions of Janis Joplin's Porsche, Jim Morrison's Cub Scout shirt, and Ringo Starr's Sergeant Pepper uniform. The permanent collection contains rock rarities from pioneer Louis Jordan to present-day stars. Celebrity sightings are frequent, so put on your blue suede shoes and rock, rock, rock!

The Rock and Roll Hall of Fame is the world's first museum honoring rock music.

Professional Football Hall of Fame

In 1920, Canton, Ohio, was home to the Canton Bulldogs, which were then part of the American Professional Football Association. While the team lasted just a few years, its legacy is a permanent part of the Professional Football Hall of Fame. A seven-foot statue of Jim Thorpe, once a star athlete for the Bulldogs, stands at the Hall of Fame's portal.

Built in 1963, the building has since been expanded three times. Today it measures 83,000 square feet. The Hall of Fame Enshrine-ment Gallery is the most revered attraction: Each Hall of Famer is commemorated with a bronze bust. The gallery was updated in 2003 to add space and high-tech interactive features. The most innovative attraction is the GameDay Stadium, which shows recordings of professional NFL games in a turntable the-ater featuring a unique 20- by 42-foot Cin-emascope screen.

Once visitors pass the Thorpe statue, they ascend into a rotunda showcasing the 100-

Each year, the Professional Football Hall of Fame inducts three to six players, coaches, or sports-casters, who must be retired.

year history of the sport, followed by the Pro Football Today display, a history of the NFL's 32 teams. Even if you're just a casual fan, try a game of Hall of Fame Teletrivia or QB-1-Call-the-Play-Theater using the interactive displays. And, of course, no trip would be complete without a stop at the Tailgating Snack Bar.

The Cincinnati Museum Center

The Cincinnati Museum Center at Union Terminal is an Art Deco masterwork that attracts viewers from around the world enticed by its headquarters and gallery building. Like so many other great American buildings, Union Terminal opened during the depths of the Great Depression, in 1933. The building was an architectural icon from the beginning. When it was built, the ten-story Art Deco limestone half-dome was the only building of its kind on the continent. After train travel

Originally the Union Terminal train station, the building reopened as the Cincinnati Museum Center in 1990.

dwindled, the terminal was declared a National Historic Landmark in 1977 and stood empty for more than a decade.

Today the beautiful terminal is home to five major Cincy cultural organizations: the Cincinnati History Museum, the Cinergy Children's Museum, the Museum of Natural

History & Science, the Robert D. Lindner Family OMNIMAX Theater, and the Cincinnati Historical Society Library. The Cincinnati History Museum features re-creations of the Cincinnati Public Landing wharf of the mid-1800s, including a 94-foot side-wheel steamboat. The Museum of Natural History & Science invites visitors to enter the Ohio Valley ice age of 19,000 years ago in a re-created limestone cave featuring underground waterfalls, streams, and a live bat colony.

Serpent Mound

Serpent Mound, a winding mound of earth one-quarter mile long and three feet high, remains a mystery despite all the science that has been thrown at it.

There are many Native American mounds in North America, but Serpent Mound State Memorial, near Peebles, Ohio, is the largest prehistoric animal effigy, or image, in the world. Snakes were important in the art and religion of the Maya of Mexico, the Navajo, the Hopi, and other Native American tribes. But what, if anything, that has to do with the mystical Serpent Mound is unknown.

Serpent Mound uncoils in seven curved stages along a bluff over Rush Creek in Ohio and is completed by an oval that appears to represent the head and mouth of the serpent. Some believe that the serpent's head points toward the summer solstice. Park archaeologists say that the builders carefully planned the serpent's form, outlined it with stones, and then covered it with baskets of earth. There are neither signs of burial nor aboriginal civilization. The mystery continues: Serpent Mound was created on a rare raise called a "cryptoexplosion structure"—in other words, a bluff created by a big bang that remains, naturally, a mystery.

The enigmatic Serpent Mound winds over one-quarter mile.

Cuyahoga Valley National Park

Cuyahoga Valley National Park lies between Akron and Cleveland in Ohio. It may be the park service's most urban-friendly environment. The park preserves 33,000 acres along the Cuyahoga River, called "crooked river" by the Mohawk Indians. The forests, plains, streams, and ravines of Cuyahoga Valley National Park contain an astonishing array of fauna, flora, and recreational opportunities.

The park's wetland habitats and woods provide a home to 54 butterfly species, almost 200 bird species (including threatened non-breeding bald eagles), and 32 mammal species (including the endangered Indiana bat, first discovered in the park in 2002).

A 22-mile stretch of the Cuyahoga River dominates the park, and almost 200 miles of streams course through it. Cuyahoga Valley National Park abounds in marshes and waterfalls, the highest being 65-foot-high Brandywine Falls. Amazing geological features such as the skyscraping Ritchie Ledges are not to be missed. The Beaver Marsh, a beaver dam built along the defunct Ohio & Erie Canal, is a favorite short hike and critical wetlands biosphere.

The park has almost no roads, but you can explore plenty of bike and hiking paths. A perennial favorite is the 20-mile Towpath Trail. Don't miss the cultural exhibits and events such as historic displays and outdoor concerts.

Cuyahoga Valley National Park is a serene, natural haven amid the urban areas of Ohio.

Pictured Rocks National Lakeshore

Pictured Rocks National Lakeshore spans 42 miles of Lake Superior shoreline, covering more than 73,000 acres of Michigan's Upper Peninsula. It is a preserve of spectacular scenery and cascading sand dunes. The most photographed location is the five miles of "perched" dunes and sparse jack pine forests of the Grand Sable Dunes. Of the signature sculpted sandstone cliffs, such as Indian Head, Miners Castle, Grand Portal, and Lovers Leap,

Miners Castle is the highlight of a 2.5-mile cruise around Pictured Rocks. Tourists can enjoy a close-up view by hiking to the formation.

all but Miners Castle can be viewed only by water. Cruises are a spectacular way to take in these views.

Despite the remote location, almost 400,000 visitors each year seek out Pictured Rocks for hunting, fishing, hiking, and boating

in spring and summer. In fall and winter, snowshoeing, snowmobiling, ice fishing, and cross-country skiing are popular.

You can hike to astonishing waterfalls, including Spray Falls, Alger Falls, Wagner Falls, Chapel Falls, and Laughing Whitefish Falls, with its dramatic 100-foot drop. The 1874 Au Sable Light Station, thought to be the Great Lakes' finest masonry lighthouse, also draws crowds.

Isle Royale National Park

Isle Royale, which was carved and compressed by glaciers, is the largest island on Lake Superior: It's 45 miles long and nine miles wide at the widest point. It exists in splendid isolation—you can only get to the island by boat, seaplane, or ferry. Together with numerous smaller islands it makes up Isle Royale National Park, located off of Michigan's Upper Peninsula. (The park is closer to Canada than it is to Michigan.) Only about 20,000 people visit this remote, tranquil setting each year. Those who do often spend at least three days absorbing the peaceful wilderness.

About 85 percent of the park's 850 square miles is water. The island is home to 20 species of mammals, though the mainland has more than 40. Scientists speculate that the moose on the island were brought from the mainland.

There are no roads on the island, but you can choose routes from among the 165 miles

The Rock Harbor Lighthouse at the northeast end of Isle Royale was built in 1855.

of hiking trails. The most striking hike is Greenstone Ridge, a trail more than 40 miles long along a basalt flow that was formed by lava and tinted green by copper. Diving for shipwrecks is another favorite activity—there are more than ten major wrecks below the serene water.

Mackinac Bridge

The mighty Mackinac Bridge straddles the Straits of Mackinac between Lakes Michigan and Huron to connect Michigan's upper and lower peninsulas. Pronounced *MA keh nah*, Mackinac is short for Michilimackinac, which was an Indian territory on what is now Mackinac Island. Measured the conventional way, between towers, Mackinac Bridge is the world's ninth longest suspension bridge. Mea-

sured by impact, it ranks right up there with the Golden Gate Bridge. No wonder Michiganders call it "Mighty Mac."

Ceremonies to celebrate the official beginning of construction were held in 1954; it opened in 1957. The Mackinac Bridge has had

a lasting impact on travel in Michigan—on the day it opened, the ferry service to the Upper Peninsula ended. Crossing the seemingly endless bridge can be its own reward, with the added bonus of entering another world: Michigan's incomparable Upper Peninsula.

The nearly five-mile-long Mackinac Bridge, including approaches, links the upper and lower Michigan peninsulas.

Quick Fact	
Mighty Measurements	
Total length of bridge	26,372 feet
Length of suspension bridge	8,614 feet
Length of main span between main towers	3,800 feet
Height of main tower above water	552 feet
Total length of wire in main cables	42,000 miles
Total concrete in bridge	466,300 cubic yards
Total weight of bridge	1,024,500 tons
Total weight of concrete	931,000 tons
Total number of workers at bridge site	3,500
Total number of engineers	350
Total number of blueprints	85,000
Architect	David B. Steinman

Grand Hotel

Cars are banned on Michigan's Mackinac Island, preserving the "all natural" theme of a park where time seems frozen. Here you can take in the serenity and enjoy horse-and-buggy rides, bicycling, or walking.

Many hotels call themselves "Grand," but the island's astonishing entry earns the title. The hotel is grand, great, glorious, and grandiose. As you travel to the island by ferry, the hotel becomes visible over the waters of Lake Michigan. From a distance, it looks like a great Queen Anne–style ship. The hotel's highlight is its 660-foot porch.

Opened in 1887, the Grand Hotel is the world's largest summer hotel. It's open only from May through October each year. The hotel's 385 rooms are each unique, and a daily full breakfast and five-course dinner (evening dress is required) are included in the room charge. The hotel boasts of many famous luminaries having visited over the years, with four first ladies and five presidents among them.

More than 125,000 annual flowers create the Grand Hotel's gardens, and 2,500 geraniums in 260 planting boxes line the front porch.

Stellar attractions are just beyond the porch of the Grand Hotel. Mackinac Island State Park covers 80 percent of the island; Fort Mackinac was built by British soldiers during the American Revolution; and Old Mackinac Point Lighthouse aided ships through the Straits of Mackinac from 1892 to 1957.

Tulip Time Festival

The roots of the Tulip Time Festival in Holland, Michigan, reach back to 1846 when 60 Calvinist separatists departed Holland for the New World. Fast-forward to 1927, when Holland High School biology teacher Lida Rogers brought up the idea of celebrating the town's hardy forebearers with a festival. The city council purchased 100,000 tulip bulbs and sold them to Hollanders for a penny apiece. In 1929, the tulips bloomed, and the annual Tulip Time Festival began. Today Tulip Time attracts one million visitors annually to a town of barely more than 35,000.

Year-round touchstones of Holland include the restored Victorian downtown and cobblestoned Dutch Village. Also worth a visit are Holland's Veldheer Tulip Gardens, the De Zwaan Windmill (a 12-story, 240-year-old import from the Netherlands), Holland State Park, and "Big Red," the Holland Harbor Lighthouse.

Tulip Time begins each May with a town crier walking through the city, hollering, "The streets are dirty, and they must be scrubbed!" whereupon cadres of costumed scrubbers begin to wash the streets to traditional Dutch standards. Then there's the Dutch Market, fireworks, Dutch and pop concerts, Klompen dancing—and for a historically accurate clean-up, more street scrubbing.

Children don costumes reflecting their Dutch heritage and march in the Kinderparade during the festival.

(Above) *The De Zwaan Windmill, whose name means "the swan," overlooks fields of blooming tulips on Windmill Island.*

Indianapolis 500

Start with four straight sections of asphalt, two long and two short, connected by four turns, each exactly a quarter-mile in length and banked at an angle of 9 degrees and 12 minutes. Mix in 33 of the best cars money can buy and upward of 300,000 fans. Add Memorial Day weekend and nearly a century of tradition, and serve. That's the recipe for the legendary Indianapolis 500.

The race's home is the Indianapolis Motor Speedway, also known as the Brickyard. The speedway first opened in 1909, but numerous poorly attended seasonal races led the owners to focus on one big annual event. That big

The Indianapolis Motor Speedway, also called the Brickyard, is the famed home of the Indianapolis 500.

event was the Indianapolis 500 Mile Race, first held in 1911 on May 30—Memorial Day. It was a breakthrough success for the fledgling track, attracting 80,000 fans who cheered when driver Ray Harroun crossed the finish line first.

Named for the number of miles covered by circling the 2.5-mile track 200 times, the Indianapolis 500 became an instant rite of spring for the country's racing community. The race has been held every Memorial Day since 1911 with the exception of six years during World War I and World War II. Nicknamed "The Greatest Spectacle in Racing," it is one of the longest-standing and richest motorsports events in the world.

The speedway's founders would be hard-pressed to believe how their race and

racetrack have evolved since 1911. While Harroun averaged 75 miles per hour in his six-and-a-half-hour triumph, modern winners sometimes finish the race in less than three hours. The race now has the largest single-day attendance of any sporting event on the planet.

Many 500-goers are more interested in partying than watching the race. On race day, the track's infield hosts a tailgate party of

Quick Fact

About the Indy Racing League (IRL) Cars

- Engines are limited to a 3.0L normally aspirated engine to curb top speeds.
- The engines can produce about 650hp, nearly four times that of an average street car.
- These racing cars get only about two miles per gallon of fuel.
- They can accelerate from 0 to 100 miles per hour in less than three seconds.

Indy Racing League cars zoom around the 2.5-mile track at top speeds near 220 miles per hour.

mythic proportions. Speedway regulations allow those who park their cars in the infield to fire up barbeques and tap kegs of beer. Deep in the infield, the race is an afterthought evidenced only by the roar of cars speeding down the track's straightaways. The track infield also holds a museum, part of an 18-hole golf course, concert stages, corporate "tent parties," and just about everything else one could shoehorn into a couple hundred acres of former farmland.

Like the logistics inherent in organizing the event, the physics of the race are nothing short of astounding. The cars hit top speeds near 220 miles per hour, meaning the drivers are rocketing through space, covering the length of a football field every second. They're also subjected to g-forces that are four times the earth's normal gravitational pull—in other words, about the same force experienced by the space shuttle's passengers when blasting off from Cape Canaveral.

As for drivers, A. J. Foyt is an all-time legend of the Indianapolis 500. He competed in a record 35 consecutive races. Foyt won four times, the first of only three racers to do so (the others were Rick Mears and Al Unser), after which he enjoyed the traditional winner's refreshment: a jug of ice-cold milk.

The Indianapolis 500 is an undeniable testament to America's love affair with cars, speed, and tailgating.

The College Football Hall of Fame

South Bend, Indiana, with a population just over 107,000, probably would have remained an ordinary college town were it not for Notre Dame's Fighting Irish football team and the countless legends it has engendered. Thus, it seemed logical when the College Football Hall of Fame moved from Ohio to the downtown district of South Bend in 1995.

The Hall of Fame today is highlighted by an unusual architecture of ramps, spirals, and tunnels. The main museum hall is underground. Visitors wind around a giant circular staircase to visit the Hall of Honor. They then branch out to exhibits such as the Great Moments Kiosk and the Pantheon, which showcases recipients of especially prestigious awards, equipment displays, a strategy clinic, and a practice field where visitors can pass, block, and kick. The Pantheon's centerpiece is the Stadium Theater, a re-creation of a live football game that makes visitors feel as if they are on a stadium field among the players, cheerleaders, and 106,000 screaming college football fans.

The first Hall of Fame inductees were selected in 1951. Among the original 54 legends inducted were Walter Camp, Jim Thorpe, and Red Grange. Today more than 900 college football players and coaches are enshrined.

Some exhibits at the College Football Hall of Fame in South Bend contain sports equipment and artifacts from behind-the-scenes of the game.

The Magnificent Mile

Chicago's Magnificent Mile stretches along North Michigan Avenue between Oak Street and the Chicago River. The 100-story John Hancock Center may be the most prominent building on this stretch, but don't overlook the other architectural gems. The Tribune Tower, with its decorative buttresses and gothic design, was once called "the most beautiful and eye-catching building in the world." Park Tower, a 67-story skyscraper, preserves the facade of the landmark 1917 Perkins, Fellows & Hamilton studio. There's also the distinctive Old Water Tower. Built in 1869, the tower was one of the few buildings to survive the Great Chicago Fire; it has become a symbol of Chicago. Today the tower stands near Water Tower Place, a mall with more than 100 specialty shops.

Which brings us to the truly magnificent part of the Magnificent Mile: Bloomingdale's, Louis Vuitton, Chanel, Gucci, Lalique, Ralph Lauren, Neiman Marcus, Giorgio Armani, Hugo Boss, and Hammacher Schlemmer.

Chicago's Magnificent Mile—bring your credit card.

The Old Water Tower was one of the only buildings to survive the Chicago fire of 1871. (Inset) The Magnificent Mile in the heart of downtown Chicago has become a hub for high-end fashion retailers.

Chicago Blues

During the 20th century's "Great Migration" of blacks from the American South, many Mississippi Delta blues musicians moved north to the frigid Windy City and found themselves playing in smoky, noisy nightclubs. In the 1930s, blues musicians added electric guitars, electric bass, and drums, and their sound cut through any nightclub's din. By the 1940s, Chi-town blues icons such as Muddy Waters and Howlin' Wolf had created what is now called the Chicago Blues.

One way to sample the Windy City grooves is the Chicago Blues Festival, which features a half-dozen stages and scores of blues acts. The festival takes over Grant Park for four days each June. Or you might prefer to sample the music at the dozens of clubs south of downtown and on the city's south side. Well-known clubs such as Buddy Guy's Legends, Lee's Unleaded Blues, Kingston Mines, Frankie's, House of Blues, Checkerboard Lounge, and Rosa's Lounge can be touristy but fun. Don't miss the smaller clubs dotting the Windy City, too—they yield rich musical rewards.

Crowds are captivated by the soulful melodies and beats at the Chicago Blues Festival.

Wrigley Field

Chicago Cubs fans are among the most devoted fans of any sports team. Nowadays, most people worship winners. But the Cubs, a baseball team that has not won a World Series championship since 1908, are the most lovable losers of America's pastime.

Both the Cubs and their fans prize their quaint home ballpark, Wrigley Field. Wrigley was built in 1914 for $250,000 and featured baseball's first permanent concession stand. It's the second oldest major league park, next to Fenway Park in Boston. And in 1988, it

became the last MLB field to host night games when lights were finally added to the park.

The "Friendly Confines" of Wrigley are known for eccentricities. Fickle winds can change the outcome of the game: Watch for home runs when the breeze blows toward Lake Michigan. And hard-hit balls have been getting stuck in the ivy-covered outfield walls since they were erected in 1937.

Wrigley's capacity is relatively small—a mere 41,160 (with new seats added in 2006), plus the apartment rooftops across Sheffield

Fans flock to Wrigley to cheer on the Cubs— some even crowd the rooftops of buildings on Sheffield Avenue beyond right field.

and Waveland avenues. However, any seat will yield a great view of the playing field (the park is well-known for this attribute). Most games are sellouts, but it's worth it to grab a ticket, hot dog, and beer and sit among the famous Bleacher Bums. Afterward, join the untiring Cubs fans at neighborhood bars and restaurants just steps from Wrigley.

The Art Institute of Chicago

The Art Institute of Chicago boasts more than 300,000 works, including treasured paintings such as Edward Hopper's "Nighthawks," Grant Wood's "American Gothic," and Georges Seurat's "A Sunday on La Grand Jatte." It is one of the most astounding art museums in the world, with an impressive permanent collec-

This stately lion is one of two that guard the entrance to the Art Institute. "The Bean" (inset right) has also become a symbol of Chicago.

tion and featured exhibits throughout the year. The striking Italian-Renaissance architecture gives the building a distinctive look among the skyscrapers of downtown Chicago.

The Art Institute's collections of early Italian, Dutch, Flemish, and Spanish works include paintings by El Greco, Hals, Rembrandt, and Goya. The comprehensive Impressionist collection features one of the largest collections of Monet's works. The museum is also renowned for its arms and armor, Chinese art, prints and drawings, and decorative arts such as porcelains, textiles, and glass. Then there are the period-furnished rooms and the Thorne Miniature Rooms, tiny reproductions of furnished historic interiors.

If you crave a breath of fresh air, step outside and enjoy the 24.5-acre

Quick Fact

Fraternal Twins

Take a second look—the two magnificent bronze lions that guard the Art Institute's entrance are not identical. The south lion stands in an attitude of defiance, while the north lion is on the prowl.

During the holidays, these proud kitties are adorned with evergreen garlands around their necks.

Millennium Park just across Monroe Street. The park, which opened in 2004, has become a global center for music, art, and architecture. Among its most famous attractions are the Jay Pritzker Pavilion, a sophisticated outdoor concert venue designed by Frank Gehry; Ourie Garden; and the popular "Cloud Gate" sculpture, more commonly referred to as "The Bean."

Abraham Lincoln Presidential Library and Museum

Abraham Lincoln's wisdom, compassion, and leadership were unmatched in his time. The Abraham Lincoln Presidential Library and Museum in Springfield, Illinois, combines scholarship and showmanship to sweep visitors along from Lincoln's humble beginnings in a log cabin to his presidency during the Civil War. The library opened in 2004, the presidential museum in 2005. Only six months after it opened, the museum welcomed its 400,000th visitor—a record for presidential libraries.

People stream to the Lincoln Library to see books, papers, and artifacts from the life of the Great Emancipator and from the Civil War. Replicas of Lincoln's boyhood home, the Lincoln White House, and his box at Ford's Theatre give an aura of realism to the exhibits.

The Abraham Lincoln Presidential Library and Museum devotes 200,000 square feet to telling Lincoln's tale. The 46,000-square-foot space devoted to permanent exhibits is twice the size of the next largest presidential library.

Since its opening in 2004, the Lincoln Library has become one of the most popular presidential libraries in history.

Lambeau Field

"The Lambeau Field experience" is common knowledge to the citizens of the football-delirious city of Green Bay, Wisconsin. Lambeau Field is one of those magical stadiums where the game experience evokes a rich past. The history of the stadium begins with Vince Lombardi, head coach of the Packers from 1958 to 1967. He was the first to coach the team in the new stadium and was known for sayings like, "If winning isn't everything, why do they keep score?" and "Show me a good loser, and I'll show you a loser."

Lambeau Field was built in 1957 for less than one million dollars and was named in 1965 for the Packers' great first coach, Earl L. "Curly" Lambeau after his death. The stadium was renovated in 2003, but that hasn't diluted the Lambeau Field magic. It seats more than 72,000 people. It has been continuously occupied longer than any other stadium in the National Football League, and it seems to give the Packers a huge home-field advantage. Insiders say Lambeau Field also has the NFL's nicest fans. Stop by and see if they're right—and don't forget to wear the traditional gear: a large cheese-shape hat!

Despite Wisconsin's often frigid weather, Packers fans cheer on their beloved football team with unmatched zeal.

Captain Frederick Pabst Mansion

The front of the Pabst Mansion in Milwaukee is a looming gate reminiscent of a Renaissance fort. The heavy, square architecture was patterned after the 16th-century palaces and fortresses in Flanders, Belgium. Today, Pabst Mansion is called "the Finest Flemish Renaissance Revival Mansion in America."

The magnificent mansion was the 1892 creation of the prolific Frederick Pabst, whose

In 1889, Milwaukee architect George Bowman Ferry was commissioned to design the Pabst Mansion.

many titles during his lifetime included sea captain, beer baron, real estate mogul, philanthropist, and patron of the arts. Not only does the architecture harken back to the Renaissance, the custom furniture and art do, too.

In 2005, 11 paintings that had been part of Pabst's original collection were repurchased and returned to the property.

With 37 rooms, 12 baths, and 14 fireplaces, the mansion lives up to its name. In its time, the house was a hi-tech marvel featuring electricity, plumbing for 9 bathrooms, and 16 thermostats. The foyer and massive wood-carved Grand Stair Hall are breathtaking.

Taliesin

Taliesin is regarded as a prime example of Frank Lloyd Wright's organic architecture. The house is located in Spring Green, Wisconsin, an hour's drive from Madison.

Construction began in 1911, but the project was soon wracked by nightmarish conflicts. In 1914, while Wright was away, a servant murdered seven people, including Wright's mistress, with an ax and set fire to Taliesin. Much of the building was destroyed. Wright fought through his agony and rebuilt the residential wing of the home, naming it Taliesin II. But this wing was again consumed by fire in 1925. The home visitors enjoy today is Taliesin III, which Wright tinkered with until his death in 1959.

The spacious interior of Taliesin incorporates local limestone, an aspect of Wright's organic architecture.

Taliesin was the start of many experimental ideas that characterized Frank Lloyd Wright's designs.

Wright built the house in the valley settled by his Welsh ancestors and named it after the Welsh bard Taliesin. The house was originally constructed with local limestone, plaster made from sand gathered along the Wisconsin River, cedar, and glass. Wright's technique of building the house from native limestone made it look organic, as though the house was part of the hill on which it was built. In 1976, Taliesin was recognized as a National Historic Landmark.

Today, tours of Taliesin begin at the Frank Lloyd Wright Visitor Center, the only Wright-designed freestanding restaurant. On the tour, you'll see many structures Wright built on the 600-acre estate: the Romeo and Juliet Windmill Tower, Hillside Home School, Tan-y-deri, and Midway Barns.

Apostle Islands National Lakeshore

The 21 islands of Apostle Islands National Lakeshore dot the coast of northern Wisconsin just off Bayfield Peninsula. The popular Madeline Island is the largest of the group and the only one that permits commercial growth. Nesting bald eagles at Bay State Park are this island's main attraction.

Winter brings cross-country skiers and ice fishers to the islands. During warmer weather, visitors enjoy hiking, picnicking, scuba diving,

The cool blue waters of Lake Superior lap at the sandstone rocks along the shores of the Apostle Islands.

swimming, sportfishing, hunting, excursion cruises, kayaking, camping, and sailing.

Once past Madeline Island, take in the beauty of the sandscapes, sea caves, and waterfalls of the lakeshore. There are woods of hemlock, white pine, and northern hardwood and

pristine old-growth forests on Devils, Raspberry, Outer, and Sand islands. Deer and beavers are common on the islands, as are black bears, mink, muskrat, otters, red foxes, and snowshoe hares. Fishing has become a favorite pastime, too, with the successful restoration of lake trout. Lake sturgeon, brook trout, lake whitefish, northern pike, smallmouth bass, and many other types of fish are found in these serene waters.

Milwaukee Art Museum

When you think of Milwaukee, beer, brat-wurst, and Milwaukee Brewers baseball come to mind. But while some weren't looking, Milwaukee turned into a sophisticated city with an amazing, world-class art museum.

In 1957, the Milwaukee Art Center opened its Eero Saarinen Building, named after the architect who designed it (he is also the acclaimed architect of the St. Louis Gateway Arch). The building itself is a work of art. It has a floating cruciform shape with four large wings that cantilever in space. The striking building has set the stage for the growth of the museum. It hosts a masterful collection

(Right) *The Quadracci Pavilion was the first building designed by Santiago Calatrava to be completed in the United States.*

(Above) *The Milwaukee Art Museum in downtown Milwaukee overlooks Lake Michigan.*

of more than 20,000 works from ancient artifacts to modern masterpieces. Works by Degas, Homer, Monet, O'Keeffe, Picasso, Rodin, Toulouse-Latrec, and Warhol are just some of the treasures.

In 2001, the Quadracci Pavilion, designed by Santiago Calatrava, was added to the building. The prominent pavilion has attracted attention worldwide, and no wonder: It has a light, lacy facade that curves like a sail, despite being built from 20,000 cubic yards of concrete. The addition features a 90-foot-high reception hall enclosed by the Burke Brise Soleil, a sunscreen that can be raised or lowered, making it a moving sculpture. The pavilion expanded gallery space by almost a third.

Sculpture Garden and Walker Art Center

It's hard to believe, but the epicenter of contemporary art in the United States is a garden in downtown Minneapolis. The Minneapolis Sculpture Garden, along with the Walker Art Center, contains fine examples of modern art.

Especially in warm weather, a lunch hour in the garden can mean eating egg salad on rye beside "Spoonbridge and Cherry," which is a sculpture-bridge of a humongous spoon holding a gigantic cherry. Then take a leisurely stroll over to James Turrell's "Sky Pesher." The installation is approached through an under-

Inspired by a novelty item, "Spoonbridge and Cherry" has become a beloved icon. It was designed by Claes Oldenburg and Coosje van Bruggen.

ground tunnel that leads visitors to a room with a 16-square-foot opening at the top of its curved white ceiling. "Sky Pesher" uses lighting to create an illusion that's said to "bring the sky down."

Minneapolis's stellar art institutions have kept pace with the competition. Expansions

at the Walker Art Center in 2005 doubled its exhibition space. Later that year, the Sculpture Garden, which was already the largest in the United States, was expanded to 15 acres. The Minneapolis Sculpture Garden now features more than 40 sculptures as well as the all-glass Cowles Conservatory and its displays of orchids, palms, and other native and exotic plants. All of it is framed by the Irene Hixon Whitney Bridge, a stunning pedestrian bridge that spans 16 lanes of highway to link the garden to Loring Park in central Minneapolis.

Voyageurs National Park

At Voyageurs National Park, it helps to know your way around canoes and other watercraft. Voyageurs is the only national park in the United States that has no roads; if you want to visit, be ready for a voyage—the park is accessible only by waterway. Voyageurs National Park covers nearly 220,000 acres and hosts a quarter-million visitors each year.

The park extends along the southern edge of the great Canadian Shield, also called Laurentian Plateau, an enormous stretch of North America that includes most of Canada and parts of Minnesota, Wisconsin, Michigan, and northern New York. Voyageurs lies in Minnesota close to International Falls. Fifty-five miles of the park run along the U.S.–Canadian border.

The northern parts of the park are tundra; farther south are immense forests of pine, hardwoods, swamps, bogs, lakes, and beaver dams. Four lakes together make up almost 40 percent of Voyageurs: Kebetogama, Namakan, Rainy, and Sand Point.

Rock formations rise in Voyageurs near the edge of the Canadian Shield. These ancient formations of exposed Precambrian rock were scoured by glaciers, which scraped the rocks into rugged shapes. Some areas, including the park's North Woods, are now covered by a thin layer of topsoil sufficient for tree growth. The park's most treasured wooded site is the 75,000-acre Kabetogama Peninsula, a vast forest interspersed with hills, swamps, and small lakes.

Ten millennia ago, the glaciers covering what is now Voyageurs National Park vanished, and hunters and gatherers began to arrive. The park currently hosts more than 220 archeological sites.

When the Europeans came, the region became a paradise for trappers. Fur companies

Vibrant sunsets over the tranquil lakes and bays of Voyageurs are stunning.

hired "voyageurs" to transport goods between remote spots. These iron men often worked 14 or more hours per day, paddled at a rate of almost a stroke per second when necessary, and portaged 26-foot canoes carrying at least 180 pounds of goods.

Today you can travel to Kabetogama Peninsula and other areas of the park by watercraft in warm weather or by skis, snowshoes, or snowmobiles in winter. How cold are the winters in Voyageurs? They're cold enough that nearby International Falls has been called the "Icebox of the Nation." Automobile makers and other manufacturers test their products against the brutal cold there.

You don't have to be able to portage a canoe to enjoy Voyageurs. Unlike the Boundary Waters Canoe Area Wilderness next door, this national park permits motorized watercraft. Boat tours on *The Sight-Sea-Er*, the craft that cruises Lake Kabetogama, are perfect for viewing the park's cormorants, great kingfishers, loons, blue herons, ospreys, eagles, wolves, and coyotes. You also can cruise to the historic Kettle Falls Hotel, a spot on the National Register of Historic Places that can be reached only by boat or seaplane.

Carved by glaciation, the rugged landscape of Voyageurs includes ponds, lakes, and islands.

Song of the Voyageurs

To us the river and clear water
To us, who are no longer lost in their secrets
With us the woods and mysteries
Are where the forests rise
My canoe of fine bark
Rides over the white swells...
My oar is of honest wood.

When the snow masses in the woods
I march through it up to my knees
I take my snowshoe and I drive out
The moose and the caribou
But when the shade of the evening arrives
I have a good bed of fir tree
Sleeping near the jumping flames
I sleep, I dream until the morning.

Boundary Waters Canoe Area Wilderness

The Boundary Waters Canoe Area Wilderness is the busiest wilderness area in the United States. This may seem like a contradiction, but it isn't: More than 200,000 people visit Boundary Waters each year.

The vast size (over one million acres) of the preserve and its picturesque terrain are a draw for tourists. Some say there are more than 2,000 lakes, but motorized vehicles are only allowed on a handful of these.

The Boundary Waters lie southeast of Voyageurs National Park and stretches along almost 150 miles of the Canadian border. Canada's Quetico Provincial Park lies on the other side of the border. The region is a mass of marshes, lakes, and bogs on terrain once raked by glaciers at the edge of the Canadian Shield. Waterfalls plunge off cliffs, and you can catch a glimpse of native wildlife such as otters, deer, moose, beavers, ducks, loons, osprey, and bald eagles.

(Above) *Canoe routes weave through the preserved wilderness of the Boundary Waters.*

For recreation, try canoeing, fishing, and camping. Choose from 1,200 miles of canoe routes. Fish for catfish, crappie, sunfish, smallmouth bass, largemouth bass, muskie, walleye, lake trout, panfish, or northern pike that grow to close to 50 pounds. Camping is available by permit on thousands of sites, where you can immerse yourself in this beautiful wilderness.

Motorized vehicles are allowed on only a handful of lakes in the Boundary Waters, but canoes can be used throughout the park.

St. Paul Winter Carnival

St. Paul has celebrated the Winter Carnival since 1886, and the freeze-fest has evolved over the decades into the cold-weather equivalent of New Orleans' Mardi Gras. The Winter Carnival hosts about 80 events and, in some

> On a tall hill outlined in vivid glaring green against the wintry sky stood the Ice Palace. It was three stories in the air, with battlements and embrasures and narrow icicle windows, and the innumerable electric lights inside made a gorgeous transparency of the great central hall.... "It's beautiful!" he cried excitedly. "My golly, it's beautiful, isn't it! They haven't had one here since eighty-five!"
>
> —*from* The Ice Palace *by St. Paul native F. Scott Fitzgerald*

years, features a glorious ice palace. Celebratory events include ice carving (of course!), parades, art shows, fire-truck rides, skating, softball, winter golf, and searching for a medallion in the snow, a tradition that goes back more than half a century.

Like Mardi Gras, the St. Paul Winter Carnival has a creation myth. In this case, it is of King Boreas, "King of the Winds," and his conflict with the Fire King, Vulcanus Rex. When Vulcanus triumphs, the carnival concludes.

Historically speaking, the St. Paul Winter Carnival began when a high-handed New York reporter said St. Paul was "another Siberia, unfit for human habitation." Local residents were determined to prove him wrong—and they did.

Artists carve intricate ice sculptures each year for the Winter Carnival.

Amana Colonies

America has always had a strong utopian streak, whose sweetest fruit is on display in eastern Iowa's gently rolling hills where you can find the seven communities that make up the Amana Colonies.

The Amana Colonies made up a historic utopian society in Iowa's River Valley. Established shortly before the Civil War by German immigrants of the Community of True Inspiration sect, the colonies today are on the National Park Service National Register of Historic Places.

The Amana communities encompass 20,000 acres and 31 historic places. They were one of the world's longest active communal societies, lasting from 1855 to 1932. Hundreds of buildings were once part of the communities; almost 500 have survived, including the Ox Yoke Inn, the Colony Inn Restaurant, the Amana Woolen Mill, Roger's Anvil/Industrial Machine Shop Museum, the Amana Furniture Shop, and the striking Millstream Brewing Company.

Probably the best place for visitors to start, however, is the Museum of Amana History, which helps explain what the communities' religionists called "the Great Change" away from shared life. The Amana Church remains pivotal in the communities: Residents still attend services and live their lives infused by their faith.

Many of the Amana Colonies' original buildings have been preserved.

(Above) *Blankets and fabric were produced at the Amana Woolen Mill. Most of its wool came from sheep raised in nearby East Amana.*

Bridges of Madison County

Madison County, Iowa, used to be a typical Midwestern farm area. Less than an hour's drive south of Des Moines, the county was notable as the birthplace of John Wayne, for the home of the 18-acre Madison County Historical Society building, and for its rustic covered bridges. Then Robert James Waller wrote *The Bridges of Madison County*, a best-selling novel. Today, Madison County's covered bridges have become such a tourist draw that the county now is building reproductions of lost covered bridges.

Madison County at one time tallied 19 picturesque covered bridges; today just five of the original ones survive. These are the Cutler-Donahoe Bridge, Hogback Bridge, Holliwell Bridge, Imes Bridge, and Roseman Bridge, all listed on the National Register of Historic Places. A suspected arson fire destroyed Cedar Bridge in 2002. County officials have offered a reward for information leading to the arrest and conviction of the perpetrator. A replica Cedar Bridge was dedicated in 2004.

While Waller's book tells a romantic tale, the bridges' origins were quite practical: The Madison County Board of Supervisors ordered they be covered to preserve their large flooring timbers, which were more expensive than the lumber used to cover the bridges' sides and roofs.

The Holliwell Bridge is one of the five original bridges still standing in Madison County.

Iowa State Fair

As the preeminent state fair in the country, the Iowa State Fair has been a Midwestern tradition since 1854. The inaugural fair was held in Fairfield on a budget of $323 and attracted upward of 10,000 people. After the fair traveled through eight other towns over the next 23 years, its organizers bought land for permanent fairgrounds in Des Moines.

In 1879, the gates at the Iowa State Fair and Exposition Ground in Des Moines swung open to the public for the first time. More than a century later, the nearly 400-acre site made its way onto the National Register of Historic

(Right) *The Stock Pavilion is part of the permanent fairgrounds in Des Moines.*

(Left) *Visitors sample tasty treats at the largest state fair in the country.*

Places. At the fair's sesquicentennial in 2004, attendance topped a million for the third year in a row.

At its heart, the Iowa State Fair salutes the state's strong agriculture industry. Competitions involve farming and ranching skills, livestock, fruits, vegetables, tractors, and just about everything else. The event also features concerts, an art show, and a midway with thrill rides and carnival games.

The competitions are the soul of the state fair. In a given year, over 10,000 human entrants test their mettle against their peers in hog calling, auctioneering, fiddling, tractor

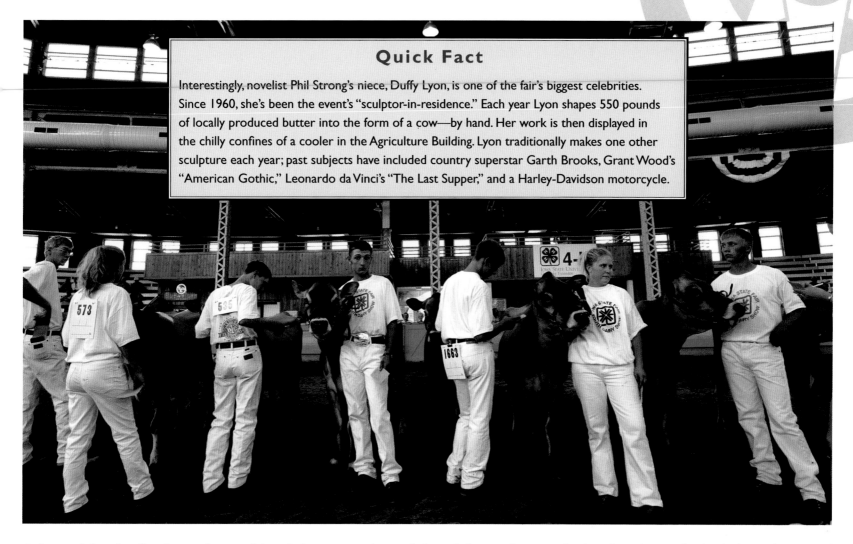

Quick Fact

Interestingly, novelist Phil Strong's niece, Duffy Lyon, is one of the fair's biggest celebrities. Since 1960, she's been the event's "sculptor-in-residence." Each year Lyon shapes 550 pounds of locally produced butter into the form of a cow—by hand. Her work is then displayed in the chilly confines of a cooler in the Agriculture Building. Lyon traditionally makes one other sculpture each year; past subjects have included country superstar Garth Brooks, Grant Wood's "American Gothic," Leonardo da Vinci's "The Last Supper," and a Harley-Davidson motorcycle.

Calves and their handlers line up for one of the livestock competitions.

pulling, horseshoe pitching, and backgammon. Animal categories run the gamut from cats and dogs to horses and cows to llamas and pigeons; plants include pumpkins, tomatoes, and soybeans as well as dahlias and bonsai trees.

Then there are the cooking competitions. Bakers face off with their pies and cakes. Marmalades and preserves go head-to-head. Chili,

hot wings, Asian dishes, fudge, and pretty much every imaginable edible is sampled and judged. Big food corporations even get in on the act: Spam, Crisco, Vlasic, and other companies have sponsored past contests in which their products are required ingredients.

In addition to the goods entered in the fair's competitions, there are plenty more that are sampled and sold to visitors. Organizers tout the availability of more than 20 different kinds of food "on-a-stick," including pork chops, dill pickles, cheese, cotton candy, veggie corn dogs,

chocolate cheesecake, hot bologna, honey, and deep-fried Twinkies. If stick-served food isn't your idea of a meal, there's also plenty of fare delivered on plates.

The Iowa State Fair has been an inspiration for authors and artists, namely Phil Strong's 1932 best-selling novel *State Fair*, a morality tale about the tightly knit Frake family. It in turn inspired the 1945 Broadway musical *State Fair* by Richard Rodgers and Oscar Hammerstein as well as a number of Hollywood movies, both musicals and nonmusicals.

St. Louis Gateway Arch

Sunlight reflects brilliantly off the stainless-steel-faced St. Louis Gateway Arch.

The St. Louis Gateway Arch soars 630 feet high and spans 630 feet. This Gateway to the West has been the tallest memorial in the United States since its 1965 unveiling. The arch is actually part of the Jefferson National Expansion Memorial, dedicated to the western pioneering movement.

Architect Eero Saarinen's bold concept of an almost imperceptibly elongated catenary arch with a thinner top was the basis for the design. From afar, the arch seems to be a sculpture of thin light; up close, it's a majestic building. Even at a massive 43,000 tons, the Gateway Arch, miraculously, seems to soar.

A tram to the top of the arch yields glorious panoramas of St. Louis, the Mississippi River, and southern Illinois. At the arch's bottom, the Museum of Westward Expansion commemorates American Indians and 19th-century pioneers, including the Lewis and Clark expedition that departed from that area.

Branson Strip

Today, most Americans know this once-small town in the Ozarks as the "Branson Strip": The little city improbably became one of the entertainment capitals of the world.

Branson, Missouri, was a quiet, humble town until the Presley family (no relation to Elvis) began performing at Branson's Underground Theatre (now called Presley's Jubilee Theatre) in 1963. Soon other music acts (country and otherwise) crowded the venues along Highway 76. A building boom followed, and the Branson Strip was born.

The town has a population of just 7,500, but it greets seven million visitors each year. Branson today packs a bundle of top-drawer attractions. Built on a country music foundation, the strip offers acts from country favorites Mel Tillis and the Gatlin Brothers to the Acrobats of China and Russian comic Yakov Smirnov; in all, there are 46 music theaters and more seats than there are on Broadway.

Developing the Branson Strip brought bright lights and theaters to this once-small town.

Dodge City

Wyatt Earp, Bat Masterson, Boot Hill, and Dodge City—to anyone who has ever read Western lore or watched cowboy movies, these are legendary names.

The lawless, gun-slinging reputation of this Kansas frontier town was well deserved. Beginning in the 1860s, Dodge City drew all sorts of people who traveled along the Santa Fe Trail (and later the Atchison, Topeka, and Santa Fe Railroad). Gambling and prostitution ran rampant, and the term "red light district" was coined here after the train masters who would take their red caboose lanterns out with them. With no law in town, disagreements often led to sudden death—and the need for a town cemetery. Boot Hill was born, so-named for the number of men who died in shootings with their footwear still on.

Today Dodge City celebrates its past. Re-creations of Front Street, the Long Branch Saloon, and Boot Hill Cemetery are a reminder of the Old West and its colorful history (the buildings represent Dodge City in 1876). There are also tours of Fort Dodge and the Mueller-Schmidt House Museum (built in 1881, the oldest house in Dodge City on the original site).

Actors reenact famous gunfights along Front Street in downtown Dodge City.

Carhenge

In the small town of Alliance, Nebraska, is the unusual sculpture known as Carhenge. Carhenge is a replica of Stonehenge in terms of size and orientation, but the story of its origin is a bit different.

As creator Jim Reinders explained, it was just "something to do at our family reunion." Reinders wasn't kidding: Carhenge was built

Jim Reinders and his family arranged old cars, painted gray, to match the configuration of Stonehenge.

during a reunion at the family farm in 1987. Reinders and 35 of his relatives grabbed their backhoes, found a forklift, and worked seven 8-hour days to position the 38 cars. Among

them, classic Cadillacs, an AMC Gremlin, and a Willys pickup, were stacked in formation and painted battleship gray in accordance with Stonehenge's appearance.

People were immediately drawn to Carhenge. Despite its rather remote location (the closest freeway is 90 miles away), an estimated 40,000 to 80,000 folks visit each year.

Chimney Rock and Scotts Bluff National Monument

Chimney Rock rises to a spire almost 325 feet above the North Platte River Valley in Nebraska. It can be seen from miles away, so it was the ideal landmark for pioneers traveling the Mormon, California, and Oregon trails. Today, Chimney Rock is a National Historic Site that still marks the place where the plains give way to the Rocky Mountains.

Modern-day visitors often travel the Oregon Trail, today known as US Highway 26, about 45 minutes from Chimney Rock to see Scotts Bluff National Monument, another important three-trail landmark. Especially after a long trip across the prairie, whether by covered wagon or station wagon, the monument is striking for its key features—Scotts Bluff and South Bluff and their dramatic cliffs.

Most of the park is native mixed-grass prairie, which has the virtue of looking as pristine and undisturbed as in the days of the pioneers. Gazing out over the landscape, you can feel a kinship with these brave travelers. The monument also boasts barren badlands between Scotts Bluff and the North Platte River, amounting to an amazing variety of landscape packed into 3,000 acres. A museum on the national monument grounds houses exhibits on the area's history.

Chimney Rock (top) *and Scotts Bluff* (bottom) *are two distinct formations that can still be seen along the historic Oregon Trail.*

Badlands National Park

Badlands National Park in southwestern South Dakota is 244,000 acres of buttes, pinnacles, and spires. It is the largest mixed grass prairie in the United States and resembles miles and miles of ethereal moonscape.

Strange shapes carved into soft sedimentary rock and volcanic ash dot the landscape of Badlands National Park. Because the land is so dry, wind and water cause rapid erosion (an average of one inch per year) of the sprawling rock formations. The result is a rugged terrain unlike any other in the United States.

Despite the area's forbidding name, American Indians hunted there for 11,000 years and camped in secluded valleys that had fresh water and game. More than a century ago, seven tribes of the Great Sioux Nation roamed the area. Today, visitors are likely to encounter fossil hunters—the Badlands have been a trove for paleontologists since the 1840s.

The park is about 80 miles east of Rapid City, South Dakota, and is divided into two separate sections of four units. The most visited unit is the Cedar Pass Area, near Interior, South Dakota. Try to visit the Badlands Wilderness Area Sage Creek Unit, a primitive camping area, as well.

Rapid erosion of the plateaus of soft sediment and volcanic ash etched the Dakota Badlands.

Mount Rushmore

Four faces, each 60 feet high—the visages of United States Presidents George Washington, Thomas Jefferson, Theodore Roosevelt, and Abraham Lincoln—look out over South Dakota.

From Grand View Terrace, you can pose for photos and gape at the formidable scope of these massive granite busts. Chosen for their accomplishments and leadership, the four men immortalized on Mount Rushmore are Washington, the Revolutionary War hero and stoic first president; Jefferson, who penned the Declaration of Independence and negotiated the Louisiana Purchase; Roosevelt, the conservationist who set the wheels in motion for the country's national park system and ensured construction of the Panama Canal; and Lincoln, who led the country through the bloody Civil War and the abolition of slavery.

Mount Rushmore's immense scale is integral to the artist's message—sculptor Gutzon Borglum insisted that the dimensions of the monument reflect the importance of the events it commemorated.

Besides the available space, Borglum had several reasons for choosing this mountain in the Black Hills of South Dakota. He liked the granite because it was smooth, homogenous, and durable, eroding just an inch every 10,000 years. He liked the mountain because it dominated the surrounding landscape. He also liked that Mount Rushmore faced southeast, so sunlight would illuminate his masterpiece as much as possible.

Building Mount Rushmore has been one of the most monumental public art projects in U.S. history. From 1927 to 1941, Borglum led a team of 400 men and women, who would climb a 700-step staircase every workday just to get to the punch clock. Then they would spend the day jackhammering granite, setting off dynamite (the tool that shaped 90 percent of the mountain), or chiseling while strapped into a chair on the mountain's face, held aloft by a rope. The work was hard, but it was the Great Depression, and jobs were scarce.

Gutzon Borglum masterminded the operation until he died unexpectedly in March 1941. Under the direction of his son, Lincoln, the team labored for seven more months until funding ran dry. Lincoln lobbied Congress for more money to complete his father's vision—

Gutzon Borglum originally had envisioned a grand "Hall of Records" carved in the canyon behind Lincoln's face—but with World War II on the horizon, federal funds were scarce.

In some ways, Mount Rushmore has remained a work-in-progress since October 1941, and, strangely enough, it wasn't officially dedicated until 1991. However, Gutzon's vision came to a fruition of sorts in 1998 when the National Park Service installed a titanium time capsule, a variation on the Hall of Records, in the canyon behind Lincoln.

There have been suggestions to add a fifth president on Mount Rushmore. A few recent calls were for Ronald Reagan's visage to be immortalized. Others have campaigned for Franklin D. Roosevelt, Dwight Eisenhower, and John F. Kennedy.

But it's extremely unlikely that a fifth face will ever grace the mountain: It would not only require an act of Congress and the president's signature, but it would also require different geology. With Gutzon Borglum's design for four presidents, there simply isn't enough fault-free granite left on the mountain for another 60-foot bust.

(Opposite page) *George Washington, Thomas Jefferson, Theodore Roosevelt, and Abraham Lincoln gaze over South Dakota.* (Left) *The Avenue of Flags displays the 56 flags of the states and territories of the United States.*

Crazy Horse Memorial

Crazy Horse was a fierce chief who fought to preserve the Lakota Indians' way of life. His magic has lasted to the present day. For proof, go see the magnificent Crazy Horse Memorial near Rapid City, South Dakota.

Both the Crazy Horse Memorial's story and its sheer size are amazing. The memorial's completed face of Crazy Horse—87 feet, 6 inches high—is taller than the entire Mount Rushmore. When the statue is completed, it will be larger than the Sphinx in Egypt and taller than the Washington Monument. Its outstretched arm will be longer than three football fields.

The memorial's story began in 1939. A group of Lakota Sioux chiefs, insulted by Mount Rushmore, asked sculptor Koczak Ziolkowski to create Crazy Horse. The artist studied Crazy Horse for years and began the mammoth project in 1946, first sculpting a marble Crazy Horse, scaled 1-to-300 to the final product.

Only the face of the colossal memorial to Crazy Horse (background), *modeled after Ziolkowski's sculpture* (foreground), *has been completed.*

Ziolkowski died in 1982, but his family has carried on his vision, finishing Crazy Horse's face in 1998. The sculpture has been privately financed and will be completed... someday.

Because Crazy Horse Memorial is incomplete, some visitors don't grasp its full impact, but most are properly awed.

Sturgis

For 51 weeks of the year, Sturgis, South Dakota, is a sleepy town of about 6,000. But for one week in August, it hosts one of the biggest and best parties on the North American continent.

The Sturgis motorcycle legacy began in 1936 when local merchant J. Clarence "Pappy" Hoel purchased a franchise from the Indian Motorcycle Company. His shop

Motorcyclists from across the country gather for the Sturgis Rally each August.

(Above) *Bikers line up their motorcycles in downtown Sturgis.*

became the leading Indian dealership (per capita) in the nation. The first rally was launched in 1938. The event has always involved touring cycling shows, races and competitions, and a couple of beers afterward. The rally attracts enthusiasts from hard-core bikers to doctors, lawyers, soldiers, police officers, and philanthropists, all dedicated to having a good time. The rally customarily begins with an enormous pancake breakfast and goes on to motorcycle demos, cycle exhibits, vendors selling motorcycle-theme art, parades, concerts, mobile malls, light shows, and a lot of happy local Sturgis merchants.

Hog Heaven
"A sea of humanity and chrome-laden hogs greeted us at the Mecca of Motorcycling—the Sturgis Motorcycle Rally—in the Black Hills of South Dakota. Nowhere in America can you find such a collection of seasoned riders, rank amateurs, and wonderful women…"

—attendee, 2005 Sturgis Motorcycle Rally

Fort Abraham Lincoln and Fort Mandan

Fort Abraham Lincoln's Web site proclaims: "Welcome to 1875, enjoy your visit." And a trip to this picturesque frontier fort and national historic park on the upper Missouri River will indeed take you back to another century, to the time when this fort was the largest and most important on the Northern Plains.

Visitors are invited into the home of General George A. Custer, appointed exactly as it was in 1875 before he rode off to meet his destiny at Little Bighorn, and into the barracks of the 7th Cavalry (decorated with the biographies of the men of Company I).

The fort also contains the remains of the Mandan Indian settlement On-a-Slant Village, discovered by explorers Lewis and Clark in 1804. The settlement was abandoned and collapsing by the time Lewis and Clark found it, so they canoed north to find shelter for the winter. They encountered a Mandan trading town. Today, that location is Fort Mandan National Historic Park—it's a 70-minute drive from Fort Lincoln. When visiting Fort Mandan, see the fascinating Lewis and Clark Interpretive Center. And don't forget Knife River Indian Villages National Historic Site and Fort Union Trading Post National Historic Site; both are located nearby.

The Fort McKeen Blockhouse once protected the infantry at Fort Abraham Lincoln (top). *Visitors can learn about Lewis and Clark's expeditions at the replica of Fort Mandan* (bottom).

Theodore Roosevelt National Park

This rugged landscape inspired Theodore Roosevelt's conservationist drive.

Part of the expansive North Dakota badlands, Theodore Roosevelt National Park commemorates the conservation policies of the 26th U.S. president. The park covers more than 70,000 acres, of which 30,000 are wilderness.

The park is divided into three units: The South Unit (the most-visited area), Elkhorn Ranch (Theodore Roosevelt's ranch), and the North Unit (70 miles north of the South Unit near the headwaters of the Little Missouri River). Roosevelt first visited the badlands in 1883 to hunt buffalo and returned there over the next few years. While there, he grew alarmed at the overhunting of the buffalo and destruction of their habitat due to farming and ranching. This fueled his desire to enter politics, and he became known as a conservationist. While in office, he established 150 national forests, 51 wildlife refuges, 18 national monuments, and 5 national parks.

If you hike or ride horseback through the park today, you can spend days out of sight of civilization. Take a leisurely drive and stop at the overlooks to view the ragged landscape or tour the nearby restored cowtown of Medora. Or, hike the half-mile Wind Canyon Trail to see a remarkable view of the strangely beautiful badlands and the Little Missouri River.

North Dakota State Capitol

The North Dakota State Capitol, a 19-story building known as "The Skyscraper on the Prairie," towers over Bismark. In this city of 50,000, the skyscraper is startling, especially in spring when the front lawn of the building is decorated with some 5,000 petunias that spell out "North Dakota." While the capitol stands only 241 feet, 8 inches tall, in winter, its upper stories often disappear in low-hanging clouds.

Like the Empire State and Chrysler Buildings, North Dakota's capitol is an Art Deco gem with an interesting story. And like the two Manhattan skyscrapers, it was completed in 1934 during the Great Depression. But to save money, the builders simplified the building's exterior, canceling plans to etch stylized decorations on the steel panels and cornice stones. The result was exemplary of the Art Deco International Style—a stripped-down offshoot of the Bauhaus School.

The capitol's grounds have become the site for many memorials and museums in the years since it was built. Enjoy the North Dakota State Heritage Center Museum and Fountain Garden, the capitol's Judicial Wing, the Pioneer Family Statue, the Statue of Sakajawea, and the North Dakota Hall of Fame. Guided tours of the building, including a visit to the 18th-floor observation deck, are also available. If weather permits, take a stroll along the capitol complex's lovely 132 acres.

This Art Deco skyscraper replaced the original state capitol, which burned down in 1930.

International Peace Garden

Spanning the invisible line where North Dakota becomes Manitoba is the 2,339-acre International Peace Garden. Its crux is the long-standing goodwill between the United States and Canada. Officials from both countries dedicated the garden in 1932 after selecting an idyllic spot, cradled in the gentle green wrinkles of the Turtle Mountains between a sea of wheat to the south and woodland to the north. The garden consists of more than 150,000 flowers, planted annually and shaped into a dramatically beautiful landscape among trees and fountains. Most displays change from year to year, but the traditional arrangements in the shape of the Canadian and United States flags are a permanent feature.

The monuments to peace include girders from the World Trade Center and seven "Peace Poles"—gifts from Japan inscribed with "May Peace Prevail" in 28 languages. At the garden's center, there are two 120-foot towers—one on each side of the border—rising above a chapel whose limestone walls are engraved with words of peace.

Two towers rise above the lush landscape, marking the international border.　　*Blossoming flowers and fountains bring the garden to life each spring.*

Chapter Five

The Southwest

It can be hard to separate legend from reality in the Southwest: Tales dating back to ancient civilizations have been passed on from one generation to the next. The region has become a cultural mosaic with a colorful history. One trait that binds the Southwest is the shared culture between the United States and Mexico. The borderlands are a region with a unique identity rich in language, cuisine, religion, and tradition.

The amazing places in Texas, Oklahoma, Arizona, New Mexico, and Nevada are strikingly diverse. Pueblos in New Mexico look much like they did hundreds of years ago. Innovations such as the Hoover Dam have supplied cities with water and power in the arid desert. And the lure of the vast Grand Canyon is unmatched on the continent.

The sun's setting rays cast shadows over the chasms of Arizona's Grand Canyon: This breathtaking view is from Bright Angel Viewpoint on the North Rim.

San Antonio: The Alamo and Riverwalk

Texas's most visited site, the Alamo, is more modest than its reputation might suggest. But the architecture of this historic mission church now surrounded by modern downtown San Antonio is hard to forget. Violent events nearly two centuries ago made the site legendary. Now, about three million visitors come annually to pay their respects to those who died here.

Spanish missionaries established the Mission San Antonio de Valero in the vicinity of the Alamo in 1718 and worked to convert the local people to Catholicism. They began building the Alamo in 1724 after a hurricane destroyed the original site. The Spanish secularized the mission in 1793. However, it was abandoned before the legendary battle of 1836 broke out.

Today, the missionaries' one-time living quarters, the Long Barrack, have been turned into a museum that recounts Texas's turbulent past, emphasizing the memorable two-week Battle of the Alamo. Visitors can watch a film on the Alamo here. The famed church displays artifacts from the battle as well. Also onsite are the serene Alamo Gardens, which provide a good spot to rest and reflect.

The church and the Long Barrack are the only two structures from 1836 that are still standing. But people hungry for more Alamo history need only look beyond today's modern urban backdrop: Much of the fighting took place in Alamo Plaza, which still approximates the boundaries once marked by the old fort's walls. Visitors can also see the original foundation stones of the Low Barrack, which was the fort entrance before serving as Jim Bowie's living quarters, near the stairway leading down to the Riverwalk to the west.

The popular Riverwalk, also known as Paseo del Rio, makes a vibrant circle around downtown San Antonio. Named by Spanish missionaries in the late 17th century, the San Antonio River has a long, rich history. After the HemisFair exposition in San Antonio in 1968, commercial development along the Riverwalk boomed, and hotels, galleries, restaurants, cafés, and boutiques now crowd the river's banks. The river bustles with activity; there are holiday boat parades on its waters, and river taxis are available every day of the week. Visitors can also take narrated tours along the river, which last about 35 to 40 minutes and are available daily. Nearby theme parks, museums, theaters, and nightlife and entertainment options are a few of the other gems San Antonio has to offer.

(Opposite page) *Rivercenter Mall is a hub for shops and restaurants on the Riverwalk.*

Quick Fact

"Remember the Alamo!"

The Alamo is an American and Texan icon, an emblem of a series of events that's often misinterpreted, and the subject of numerous books and movies. In March 1836, General Antonio López de Santa Anna's Mexican troops crushed the resistance led by Jim Bowie, Davy Crockett, and William Travis, killing all 189 Texas troops and volunteers who had fought to defend the Alamo. About 600 Mexican soldiers were killed or wounded in the battle.

"Remember the Alamo!" became an instant rallying cry for all of Texas. Six weeks later, General Sam Houston's army defeated Santa Anna at the Battle of San Jacinto, ending the Mexican rule in what is now the Lone Star State. The Republic of Texas was born, beginning another chapter in Texas's stormy history. This era of sovereignty, however, proved short-lived. It ended less than a decade later: In 1845, Texas became the 28th state, though its disputed southern border led in part to the Mexican War one year later.

The Alamo remains an icon and reminder of Texas's struggle for independence.

Big Bend National Park

Nicknamed "the last American frontier," Big Bend National Park is in the middle of nowhere—and that's a good thing.

The park is named for the turn of the Rio Grande along the park's southern boundary. Surrounded by beautiful, gnarled desert, the

The chasms chiseled by the Rio Grande draw adventurous rafters to explore Big Bend National Park.

heart of Big Bend is the Chisos Mountain Range. Some peaks in the Chisos soar to nearly 8,000 feet in elevation. Cloaked in green forest, the lush mountains are a sharp contrast to the arid surroundings.

While the Chisos are the prime destination for Big Bend's visitors, they're just the tip of the iceberg, so to speak. The Rio Grande has carved three of the continent's most striking canyons—Boquillas, Mariscal, and Santa

Elena—with elevations as low as 1,800 feet along the river. Rafters are drawn to travel the river, and hikers climb trails winding through the mountains, with the desert acting as a gateway to the north.

Despite the harsh topography, there is an abundance of wildlife in Big Bend. Snakes, scorpions, birds, bats, tarantulas, deer, and javelinas, the wild pigs of the Southwest, all thrive here.

Presidio County Courthouse

The Presidio County Courthouse regained its original splendor after a 2001 restoration. The gray dome is topped with a statue of Lady Justice.

Texas is home to some of the United States' most majestic courthouses, and the Presidio County Courthouse in the small west Texas town of Marfa is the state's crown jewel. The 1887 Victorian courthouse, clad in pink stucco and capped with an ornate gray dome, dominates the horizon for miles and is a work of art inside and out. The observation deck on the fifth floor is open to the public and offers a sublime view of Marfa, which is known for its cattle, minimalist art, and starring role as the setting for the classic film *Giant*.

Legend has it that in the 1890s a convicted outlaw managed to shake free of his captors and fire off a shot at Lady Justice, perched atop the courthouse's dome. His bullet took out the scales that were in the statue's hands as he cried, "There is no justice in this country!"

The Presidio County Courthouse was thoroughly restored in 2001. The price tag for the job: $2.5 million, or about 40 times the original budget of $60,000 to build it. The only thing that wasn't refurbished was Lady Justice's still-missing set of scales.

Austin

Austin stands out from most Texan metropolises. With more than 650,000 people, this is no small town (though it's certainly much smaller than Dallas and Houston). Austin has a Bohemian aura, due in part to the University of Texas campus. And politics prevail here: Austin is Texas's capital city, and its capitol is the largest in the country.

The Congress Avenue Bridge spans the Colorado River in downtown Austin.

The aroma of barbecue and Tex-Mex cuisine hangs in the air, and the nightclub-lined Sixth Street is one of the best spots for live music in the entire world. Then there are the 1.5 million Mexican free-tailed bats that hang

from the downtown Congress Avenue Bridge, which spans the Colorado River. Crowds gather from March through November to watch them emerge en masse at sunset.

It's hard to capture the city's laid-back vibe in words. Maybe the city's unofficial slogan, seen on T-shirts and Volkswagen bumpers all over town, says it best: "Keep Austin Weird."

Texas Gulf Coast

The Texas Gulf Coast is in many ways the United States' forgotten coast, lacking the hype of the East and West coasts. However, its numerous assets run the gamut from remote islands to charming Victorian ports.

Galveston Island was once the state's commercial center, but after it was devastated by a massive hurricane in 1900, many businesses moved to Houston. While the population boomed inland, Galveston recovered and evolved into a resort area. The Strand National Historic Landmark District lies at the cultural

(Above) *The USS* Lexington, *a World War II Essex Class aircraft carrier, was decommissioned in 1991 and converted to a naval aviation museum in Corpus Christi.*

(Above left) *Warm water from the Gulf of Mexico laps at the shores of South Padre Island.*

center of Galveston. Once known as the "Wall Street of the Southwest," it is now chock-full of antique stores, restaurants, and art galleries, and its buildings feature abundantly delightful architecture.

To the south, Corpus Christi hosts beautiful beaches and the Texas State Aquarium. About 43 miles to the southeast, North Padre Island, designated a national seashore in 1962, is said to be the longest remaining stretch of undeveloped barrier island on the planet. Subtropical South Padre Island is more developed and has been called the "Tip of Texas." It is host to many resorts, a thriving sport-fishing industry, and idyllic beaches.

(Below left) *Sunsets on the harbors of the Texas Gulf Coast streak the sky with violet.*

Guadalupe Mountains National Park

At the tip of the Trans-Pecos region (the far west Texas panhandle bordered to the north by New Mexico, the south by the Rio Grande, and the east by the Pecos River) and just southwest of New Mexico's Carlsbad Caverns, the Guadalupe Mountains loom over the surroundings like mighty centurians. The rocky cliffs that define the park developed long ago when today's desert was an ancient ocean. The now lofty mountains were once a reef. As the water receded, it left fossil records of Cambrian sea life on today's craggy peaks.

The modern park contains both Guadalupe Peak, which at 8,749 feet above sea level is the highest point in Texas, and McKittrick Canyon, believed by many to be the prettiest spot in the state. The former is a backpacker's dream: The summit offers sublime views of the surrounding desert. The latter is a vestige of the last ice age that explodes with color in the fall.

At first glance, the desert surrounding the Guadalupe Mountains appears dry and barren. However, the park supports several different ecosystems—from the harsh Chihuahuan desert to streamside woodlands, rock canyons, and mountaintop pine forests. Coyotes, rattlesnakes, mule deer, black bears, and elk can all be spotted within the park's limits.

It's easy to get away from it all here—Guadalupe Mountains is one of the least-visited national parks.

Rising to 8,085 feet above sea level, the impressive El Capitán soars over the rugged landscape of Guadalupe Mountains National Park.

Big Thicket National Preserve

East Texas's Big Thicket National Preserve is 97,000 acres of biological crossroads. This is where the sultry swamps of the South, the verdant forests of the East, and the seemingly endless savannah of the Great Plains meet and mingle. Meadows are scarce, as flora thrives in the rich soil and wet climate.

The unique environment translates into a habitat for all sorts of wildlife. In Big Thicket's diverse biosphere, desert roadrunners live alongside swamp critters such as alligators and frogs, not to mention deer, mountain lions, and 300 species of nesting and migratory birds. This is the only place on the planet where many of these species live side by side. The presence of all these animals in the same lowland forest have earned Big Thicket the nickname "the American Ark."

Big Thicket provides a unique habitat of rich wetlands and thick forests that harbors diverse plant life.

The range of plant life in Big Thicket is even broader: Cacti grow alongside hickory, cypress, and pine trees. And the swampland allows 20 types of orchids and four species of insect-eating plants to thrive as well.

Space Center Houston

As the official visitor center for NASA's Johnson Space Center, Space Center Houston gives visitors an in-depth look at the United States' space program. The visitor center is a museum of space science and NASA history, with exhibits including the Kids Space Place and the Astronaut and Starship galleries. The giant-screen theater shows films on space exploration, and interactive simulators allow lay people to get a feel for space travel.

The fascinating behind-the-scenes tram tour is the best way to observe the nuts and bolts of NASA. The tram makes stops at hangars throughout the operational Johnson Space Center, historic Johnson Mission Control, and the International Space Station Assembly Building. The tram tour has been known to stop at the facilities where astronauts train—allowing visitors to peek at how they prepare for a space flight.

(Right) *Pete Conrad's spacesuit from the Apollo 12 mission to the moon is part of the Astronaut Gallery at Space Center Houston.* (Inset above) *Visitors can explore the outdoor Rocket Park, a collection of rockets from NASA's early days.*

Houston Livestock Show and Rodeo

First held in 1932, the Houston Livestock Show and Rodeo takes over most of the city each year in February and March—it's the largest livestock show and rodeo in the world.

It's also home of the World Championship Bar-B-Que Contest, where more than 300 chefs test their mettle—and brisket—against one another. The cooking competition is held three days before the rodeo.

Beyond the rodeo, the show, and the savory barbecue, music concerts take center stage after nightfall. Elvis Presley performed there in 1970 and 1974, and Alicia Keys sang to a record crowd in 2005.

This event keeps getting bigger and better. In 2006, with attendance nudging two million, it was the most-profitable show of its kind in history. Competitions for 4-H and FFA expanded; attendees could witness calves being born at the Barnyard Babies Birthing Center; and the "old-fashion" Ferris wheel and mechanical bulls still got hearts pumping.

The rodeo showcases seven events: bareback bronc riding (inset above), barrel racing, bull riding (right), saddle bronc riding, steer wrestling, team roping, and tie-down roping.

Lake Amistad

Lake Amistad is an oasis in the Texas badlands. This confluence of the Rio Grande, Devils, and Pecos rivers on the United States–Mexico border has been alive with human activity for thousands of years. The limestone canyons of the Lower Pecos region have been trafficked by people for more than 10,000 years. In their travels, these people left behind one of the world's most spectacular collections of rock art. The artifacts are scattered throughout nearly 250 known sites that include some of North America's largest multihued rock paintings.

In 1969, the rivers were dammed here, creating Lake Amistad. The 67,000-acre reservoir extends up the Rio Grande for 74 miles, Devils River for 24 miles, and Pecos for 14 miles.

(Right) *The Pecos Bridge spans the Pecos River near where it feeds into Lake Amistad.*

The shoreline wraps around 850 miles, and many people are enticed by the striking blue water, which is extraordinarily clear due to the lack of loose soil. Visitors can traverse the lake on watercraft of all kinds. Many people enjoy fishing for behemoth catfish and bass, swimming, and scuba diving.

Atop the six-mile Amistad Dam is a bridge that connects the United States to Mexico. Its center is marked by a pair of eagle statues, one on each side of the official border.

(Left) *An overlook reveals the dazzling Pecos River below.*

National Cowboy & Western Heritage Museum

When the founders of the National Cowboy & Western Heritage Museum put their heads together back in 1955, they envisioned creating a tribute to cowboys and people living on the frontier. Today the museum's mission statement, adopted in 1997, is "to preserve and interpret the heritage of the American West for the enrichment of the public."

It took a decade to find a site, construct the building, and amass a collection befitting the museum's mission. In 1965, the facility, located on top of Persimmon Hill in Oklahoma City, opened its doors. By 2005, the museum had evolved into a world-class, 200,000-square-foot complex showcasing one of the United States' top collections of Western art, with works by such legends of the genre as Charles Russell and Albert Bierstadt. "Canyon Princess" is one of the famous sculptures on display at the museum. The 16,000-pound white marble cougar by sculptor Gerald Balciar guards the entrance to the Gaylord Exhibition Wing.

In addition to the incomparable art, the museum has also fulfilled its mission with a re-created early-1900s cattle town, a research center, and galleries dedicated to firearms, Western performers, cowboys, and rodeos.

The statue titled "The End of the Trail" was put on display at the museum in 1994. It was created in 1915 and stood outside in Visalia, California's Mooney Grove Park, for 50 years before the museum acquired it.

Roswell

On July 4, 1947, many residents of the sleepy agricultural town of Roswell, New Mexico, reported seeing an unidentified flying object streaking across the night sky. Other locals reported a loud explosion.

The next week, the local newspaper, the *Roswell Daily Record*, reported that the authorities at Roswell Army Air Field had found the remains of a flying saucer that crash-landed in the vicinity. The story was based on the only military or federal disclosure of a possible UFO in history. The facts, however, quickly shifted: Officials recanted the initial account within days and said it was a weather-balloon experiment gone awry.

Nevertheless, the events of July 4, 1947, have been hotly debated ever since, with scads of conspiracy theorists and skeptics dissecting the facts and eyewitness accounts. Conspiracy buffs have cried that this was a government cover-up, alleging that the spacecraft and the bodies of its extraterrestrial passengers were taken to Area 51 in Nevada for top-secret research and experimentation. The skeptics, on the other hand, say the whole thing is hooey and that the UFO in question was indeed a weather balloon. Visitors flock to Roswell's International UFO Museum and Research Center to judge for themselves.

(Above) *The Roswell Museum features New Mexico art and provides studio classes.*

(Right) *The International UFO Museum and Research Center at Roswell is dedicated to collecting and preserving materials and information relevant to the 1947 Roswell incident and other unexplained phenomena.*

New Mexico Missions

In 1598, Spanish conquistador Don Juan de Oñate crossed the Rio Grande near the city limits of modern-day El Paso, Texas. De Oñate led his party north past Franciscan missionaries along the Rio Grande's banks to its intersection with the Chama River. Here he established the San Gabriel Mission, New Mexico's second Spanish capital, in 1600—a full seven years before the English settled in Jamestown, Virginia.

This first Spanish mission in modern-day New Mexico set the stage for many more to come. Many of the state's 17th-century churches are still standing, and active, to this day. In 1610, the Spanish capital moved to Santa Fe, where San Miguel Mission, now considered the oldest operational church in the United States, was established. Another nicely preserved church from this early era is the Mission of San José at Laguna Pueblo (1699), 45 miles west of Albuquerque. About 25 miles to the southwest is the Mission of San Esteban del Rey at Acoma Pueblo, perched majestically on a 367-foot sandstone mesa since 1626. To the southeast are the ruins of four more 17th-century missions that were abandoned before 1700 and now comprise Salinas Pueblo Missions National Monument.

(Above) *Builders carried the stones and beams up the 367-foot mesa to construct San Esteban del Rey (side view shown here).*

> ## Quick Fact
>
> ### Acoma Pueblo
>
> Nicknamed "Sky City" for its lofty locale atop a sandstone mesa that rises 367 feet above the surrounding desert, Acoma Pueblo is the oldest continuously inhabited city in the United States. It was established prior to 900 A.D.
>
> The 70-acre site was chosen because of its defensible location. Regardless, Sky City was battered during the Spanish colonial period in the 1500s. In fact, Acoma Pueblo was nearly destroyed in 1598 when Don Juan de Oñate led a group of 70 men up the sheer sandstone and took vengeance on the Acomans for an earlier quarrel.
>
> The Spanish took control of the Pueblo and organized mass Catholic conversions and the construction of the Mission of San Esteban del Rey between 1629 and 1640. Less than 50 Acomans live year-round in the pueblo today; about 3,000 more live in nearby villages.

(Right) *San Esteban del Rey was the mission built from 1629 to 1640 at Acoma Pueblo.*

Santa Fe Plaza

The Santa Fe Plaza has been a bustling outdoor market since the early 1600s. This bazaar featuring all things Southwestern is an amazing place where history, chic, and kitsch comfortably coexist.

When the Spanish came to Santa Fe in 1607, they adopted the native Pueblo's concept of building a central plaza surrounded by walls that could be defended easily. But what was designed for defense was also a good fit for commerce. Intercultural trading began soon after construction started. Because the southeast corner of the plaza was the official endpoint of the heavily traveled Santa Fe Trail (a conduit to and from the Old World), it soon became a thriving market. The original Santa Fe Plaza was more than twice its current size.

Dominating the north side of the Santa Fe Plaza is the Palace of the Governors, the oldest government building in the United States. Merchants display their wares in front of the hotels, shops, and restaurants now occupying the surrounding structures. The central area is open, and what once was used for town meetings and livestock grazing is now ideal for people-watching. Today the architecture of the plaza's buildings represents its diverse history as a crossroads of Pueblo and Spanish culture.

The marble obelisk in the central plaza has been a source of controversy: It commemorates the Confederate occupation of the city in 1862 and the city's defenses against American Indians.

Taos

The Taos Valley, cradled amidst the 14,000-foot peaks of the Sangre de Cristo (Spanish for "Blood of Christ") Mountains, has a rich and fascinating history. The first permanent settlement here was a pueblo built in the 10th century, and the present village of Taos was developed in the 14th century. In the 1600s, the Spanish came and built missions, converting as many natives as they could.

But it was an accidental visit in 1898 that shaped modern-day Taos perhaps more than the Franciscan missionaries did. Artists Bert Phillips and Ernest Blumenschein came to town to have a wagon wheel repaired; they became enchanted by the surroundings and ended up settling in Taos. They invited other artists to the valley, and word of its beauty spread quickly. By the 1920s, Taos was one of

Taos Pueblo is made from adobe—a mix of sun-dried earth and straw.

the world's most vibrant and renowned artist communities.

In 1955, the Taos Ski Valley opened, marking another seminal moment in Taos's history. Today people come to Taos for its history, culture, galleries, and slopes.

Carlsbad Caverns National Park

Carlsbad Caverns National Park was established in 1930 to protect Carlsbad Cavern and more than 100 other caves inside a Permian-age fossil reef. The park offers a glimpse into the delicate subterranean plumbing that creates a limestone cavern.

The winged wildlife is a prime attraction at Carlsbad. Every nightfall between May and October, as many as 250,000 Mexican free-tailed bats emerge from the caverns to dive-bomb insects at speeds up to 25 miles per hour. The bats have inhabited the caverns for

Tiny stalactites called soda straws form Dolls Theater, part of the Big Room in Carlsbad Cavern.

Quick Facts

Spelunker's Glossary

Many beautiful and delicate geological formations can be found in the limestone caves of Carlsbad Caverns.

columns—formed when a stalactite and stalagmite join.

helictites—curving formations that curl, sometimes appearing to defy gravity. They are very delicate, and geologists are unsure of what causes them to curl.

soda straws—hollow mineral tubes formed when water leeches through cracks in the rocks.

stalactites—deposits of calcium carbonate resembling icicles that form when water drips from the ceiling.

stalagmites—deposits of calcium carbonate formed by water that drips onto the floor.

---

the past 5,000 years. However, DDT (an agricultural pesticide that was banned in the United States in the 1970s because of adverse environmental effects) nearly crushed the park's bat population; in 2005 it was about 10 percent of what it had been in 1930.

Carlsbad Caverns National Park includes Carlsbad Cavern, which is highly accessible to visitors, as well as the United States' deepest limestone cavern, Lechuguilla Cave, which snakes down to 1,567 feet below the New Mexican desert. Spelunkers must take extreme care: Many of the park's "living" features have been irrevocably damaged by human hands.

Canyon de Chelly National Monument

Canyon de Chelly in northeastern Arizona blends archaeology, history, and geology.

The canyon was carved by eons of runoff from spring storms and has been inhabited by humans for about 2,000 years. The cliff dwellings are spectacular structures with perfectly preserved specimens and ruins set in deep caves at the base of vivid red and yellow sandstone walls. The caves are surrounded by an incredible vista of cottonwood trees, green pastures, and fields of maize.

But unlike most of the national parks in the United States, Canyon de Chelly is also part of the Navajo Nation and home to a living community of people who consider the canyon sacred ground. Likewise, visitors to Canyon de Chelly should treat the canyon as such and tread lightly on its floor.

The red sandstone monolith Spider Rock towers 800 feet above the floor of Canyon de Chelly.

Quick Fact

Spider Rock

One of the most striking attractions in Canyon de Chelly is Spider Rock.

According to Diné (Navajo) lore, Spider Woman made her home perched at the top of the rock. She was an important and revered deity and is said to have taught the Diné the art of weaving on a loom.

Children were often told if they did not behave, Spider Woman would scurry down her web ladder, snatch them up, and bring them back to the top to devour them. Some said that the top of Spider Rock was white from the bleached bones of Diné children who had misbehaved.

Grand Canyon National Park

The Great Wall of China, the Great Pyramids of Cheops, the Grand Canyon—all are places only superlatives serve to name.

More than four million visitors come to Arizona's Grand Canyon each year. They explore the canyon by helicopter, raft, mule, car, bus, or boat. Why are so many drawn to this place? What makes it so compelling? Perhaps it was best expressed by John Wesley Powell, the first explorer to navigate the Colorado River through the great canyon, who said, "The wonders of the Grand Canyon cannot be adequately represented in symbols of speech, nor by speech itself."

So there it is—awe. You must go see it for yourself. If you still aren't convinced, you might want to know the Grand Canyon has been named one of the Seven Natural Wonders of the World, and it's the only one in the United States. Take a moment to imagine the Grand Canyon: Most tourists view the canyon from the South Rim's Grand Canyon Village Historic District, where the canyon extends ten miles across and one mile down (though if you're hiking from rim to river, the trail is seven miles long). The Grand Canyon trails descend as much as 800 feet in places, and the canyon itself stretches as much as 18 miles wide. That is some serious real estate!

Apart from its sheer size, Powell noted another aspect of the profound beauty of the Grand Canyon: Its geology displays sequences of Kaibab limestone, thick Coconino sandstone, Hermit shale, and Supai formation shales and sandstones, creating a sense of order on an almost unimaginable scale.

The path of the Colorado River through the Grand Canyon is 277 miles long. The canyon is not the deepest in the world (Hells Canyon in Idaho, for instance, at 8,000 feet deep is nearly ten times deeper), but it is an immense natural spectacle deserving of its name. The Grand Canyon is the crown jewel of the Colorado River, whose labors also created Arches National Park, Canyonlands National Park, and Lake Powell in the Glen

Wind and water eroded the canyon's rocky landscape, revealing colorful layers of limestone, sandstone, and shale.

Canyon National Recreation Area (all of which are located in Utah). The canyon borders the Havasupai, Navajo, and Hualapai Indian reservations.

There are countless spectacular spots for gazing across the canyon or peering into the riverbed below, and each view will seem more amazing than the last. Visitors choose from four park entrances, and a trip from the rim to the riverbed is an overnight hike from any entrance. To get to the park, most take the route north from regional hub Flagstaff, Arizona, to the South Rim and view the canyon from the popular Mather Point overlook or from Hermit Road. Or they take the nearby east entrance, home to the dramatic 70-foot-high stone Watchtower at Desert View. To the north of the South Rim, some enter through the Hualapai Indian Reservation. Adventurous tourists enter the park from the remote North Rim, which is 1,000 feet higher than the South Rim. Roads

Views from the Grand Canyon's overlooks reveal the multihued, sculpted chasms.

leading to the North Rim are closed by heavy snows from late October to mid-May.

There are no words to adequately describe the canyon, and even one visit is not enough to truly grasp it. As Powell said, "You cannot see the Grand Canyon in one view, as if it were a changeless spectacle from which a curtain might be lifted."

Sedona

At the base of the Mogollon Rim and its lofty formations of vibrant red sandstone lies Sedona, Arizona. While only 110 miles north of Phoenix, it seems a world away. Sedona is a small town of just over 10,000 residents, but its brilliant scenery and lively culture attract more than four million tourists each year.

Atop the Mogollon Rim, many of the wondrous sandstone formations that tower over Sedona are named after objects they appear to mimic, such as Cathedral Rock, Coffeepot Rock, and even Snoopy Rock, named for the beloved beagle from the comic strip *Peanuts*.

Sedona is nestled beneath these dominating formations. Boutiques and art galleries are common along the cobblestone roads. And visitors can enjoy intimate restaurants, friendly local cafés, and quaint bed-and-breakfasts during their stay.

The view of Cathedral Rock from Red Rock Crossing at sunset is unforgettable.

Quick Fact

Beyond the dramatic natural surroundings, Sedona has attracted attention from the New Age community and UFO watchers. The area has become known as a hotspot for vortex meditation sites that are believed to aid spiritual development. This reputation has attracted an array of mystics, healers, yoga gurus, and other metaphysical specialists.

Sabino Canyon

The hiking trail leading up Sabino Canyon on the outskirts of Tucson, Arizona, is among the most beautiful in the United States. The steep red walls, dotted with saguaro, mesquite, and ocotillo, plummet to the canyon floor, where a paved trail beckons hikers and bikers. There is also a tram to deliver passengers to the top without breaking a sweat.

Due to rainy seasons in summer and winter, Sabino Canyon is surprisingly green for a desert, providing habitat for roadrunners, deer, rattlesnakes, mountain lions, and the collared peccaries known as javelinas. Seasonal storms replenish Sabino Creek, which runs down the canyon, and a number of pools that lie along the creek bed.

The 3.8-mile paved road through the canyon crosses nine stone bridges over Sabino Creek.

Beyond the paved trail taken by the tram, a more primitive trail leads to the spectacular terminus of Bear Canyon and the cold splash of water known as Seven Falls, which cuts through the untouched desert.

Taliesin West

The organic design of Taliesin West blends perfectly with the surrounding arid landscape.

Once the winter home of Frank Lloyd Wright, Taliesin West is a visionary architectural achievement. In the late 1930s, Wright designed and built the complex in Scottsdale, Arizona, as the winter counterpart to his original Taliesin in Spring Green, Wisconsin. Each site included his living quarters, studio, and campus for his schools of architecture.

Taliesin West covers 600 acres of rugged Sonoran Desert at the foot of McDowell Mountain. The landscape is an integral part of the site: Wright employed rocks and sand on the property as key ingredients in his masterpiece. He didn't limit himself to native materials, however; he also used plastics, canvas, and concrete in innovative ways.

Despite its historic status, Taliesin West is no museum. Since 1940, the vibrant complex has been the headquarters of the Frank Lloyd Wright Foundation. The foundation strives to preserve Wright's contributions to architecture and to promote organic architecture that blends with its natural environment, of which Taliesin West is a dazzling example.

Petrified Forest National Park

Some 225 million years ago, the arid desert of north-central Arizona was a lush, tropical forest dominated by towering conifers. This era ended when catastrophic floods devastated the area, uprooting tree after tree and casting them into the rivers. The rivers carried the forest trees to the middle of the floodplain and left them for dead.

Over millions and millions of years, layers of silt, mud, and volcanic ash covered the spent trees and slowed the process of decay. Silica from the ash gradually penetrated the wood and turned to quartz. Minerals streaked the former wood with every color of the rainbow, resulting in wet-looking "logs" spanning the spectrum from bright red to lime green, navy blue to deep purple.

These unearthly looking specimens proved alluring to pioneers, who shipped them back East where they fetched a high price. To protect the petrified wood in its natural environment, President Theodore Roosevelt created Petrified Forest National Monument in 1906; it became a national park in 1962. Beyond the magnificent petrified wood, the park also contains one of the best fossil records from the Late Triassic period, including aquatic phytosaurs, armored aetosaurs, sharp-toothed rauisuchians, and crocodylomorphs, the ancestors of today's crocodiles.

Over millions of years, ancient trees in Arizona were streaked with minerals and preserved as shimmering petrified wood.

Window Rock

Window Rock is both a community and a geological masterstroke. It is the capital of the Navajo Nation, the largest Native American government in the United States, and home to about 3,000 people. It is also a natural landmark—the city took its name from the wondrous pothole arch. Over millions of years, sunlight, wind, water, and chemical exfoliation formed the distinctive window. These elements slowly peeled away layer after layer of red sandstone, leaving a nearly perfect circular hole in its place.

Chemical and thermal exfoliation of Entrada sandstone created the astonishing arch known as Window Rock.

The formation is known as *Tséghághoodzání*, which in Navajo means Perforated Rock. Window Rock has long been a sacred place in the Water Way Ceremony, or *Tóhee*. The 200-foot formation has traditionally been one of four sources for the water Navajo medicine men use in the ceremony performed to ask the gods for rain.

Great Basin National Park

Nevada's second-tallest mountain, Wheeler Peak, reaches an elevation of 13,063 feet.

Amidst the lonely desert that unfolds between the Rockies and the Sierras, a rugged landscape rises into the beautiful blue sky of eastern Nevada. Cut by glaciers from a Pleistocene ice age, forested mountains tower a mile above the flatlands below. Great Basin has been a national park since 1986 and is defined by the Snake Range, which has 13 peaks more than 11,000 feet high and close to 100 valleys snaking among the soaring summits. Alpine lakes cascade into rollicking streams and rivers, and the bristlecone pine forest opens into lush meadows dotted with wildflowers. A labyrinth of limestone caverns winds underground.

Wheeler Peak is the centerpiece of the park. The main park road climbs to 10,000 feet above sea level; a trail leads the adventurous up an additional 3,063 feet to the peak. From this perch, hikers have plenty of space and fresh air to take in the incredible views of the ruggedly idyllic country.

Hoover Dam

In the Black Canyon of the Colorado River, just 30 miles south of fabulous Las Vegas, Nevada, sits the engineering marvel known as Hoover Dam. The dam was constructed between 1931 and 1935 and consists of 3.25 million cubic yards of concrete, enough to pave a road from New York to San Francisco. The dam widens the Colorado into the vast waters of Lake Mead, a year-round recreation destination that attracts millions of visitors each year for swimming, boating, water skiing, and fishing.

About 20,000 laborers built the Hoover Dam, which was the largest dam in the world when it was completed. While no longer the world's biggest, Hoover Dam stands as a symbol of the United States' progress during the adversity of the Great Depression. It is a National Historic Landmark and was named a Monument of the Millennium by the American Society of Civil Engineers.

Hoover Dam harnesses the power of the mighty Colorado River, generating power and providing water for millions in the Southwest.

Quick Facts

Hoover Dam

- Height—726.4 feet
- Weight—6.6 million tons
- Can store up to 9.2 trillion gallons of the Colorado River in its reservoir, Lake Meade. That's nearly two years of the average "flow" of the river.
- Has a power-generating capacity of 2.8 million kilowatts.
- Is part of a system that provides water to more than 25 million people in the southwest United States.

Pyramid Lake

Named for the distinctive 400-foot rock near its eastern shore, Pyramid Lake is a striking contrast to its rugged, arid surroundings in northwestern Nevada. The lake is one of the largest desert lakes in the world and is famous for its tufa rock formations. Its surface vacillates from turquoise to dark blue. Across the lake, views of the mountains, streaked with gray and pink, are unforgettable.

In 1844, John C. Fremont, said to be the first Anglo to gaze at the lake, put a fitting description to paper after this vast oasis punctuated his journey through the desert: "A defile between the mountains descended rapidly about two thousand feet; and, filling up all the lower space, was a sheet of green water, some twenty miles broad. It broke upon our eyes like the ocean."

Visitors can kayak across idyllic Pyramid Lake or swim or fish in its waters.

Located on the Paiute Indian Reservation, Pyramid Lake's warm, shallow waters are a magnet for anglers and swimmers. The world-record cutthroat trout—a 41-pound whopper—was pulled from these electric blue waters in 1925.

Chapter Six

The Rocky Mountains

The mere mention of the words "Rocky Mountains"

conjures images of wild terrain with snowcapped peaks.

This is one of the least-populated regions in the United

States—a place where the cities are few and far between

and natural wonders abound. In Montana, Wyoming,

Colorado, Utah, and Idaho, the landscape ebbs and flows

from vast grasslands to crisscrossing chasms. The Rocky

Mountains are the centerpiece of a diverse region of dense

conifer forests, arid deserts, striking badlands, powerful

rivers, and mountain peaks towering higher than

anywhere else in the continental United States.

A picturesque landscape of aquamarine lakes, lush evergreen forest, and
snow-dusted peaks covers Glacier National Park in Montana.

Pikes Peak

Lieutenant Zebulon Pike first spied this 14,110-foot mountain along Colorado's Front Range in November 1806. But his attempt to scale the mountain that now bears his name was foiled by heavy snow, and Pike said the rocky pinnacle would never be reached.

Never say never: In 1820, a party led by Major Stephen Long reached the top of Pikes Peak in two days. They were the first to see the commanding views from the mountaintop.

Today, more than half a million people make it to the summit house each year. Of course, nowadays reaching the peak of the mountain is less daunting. Visitors can hike the 13-mile trail to a height of 7,000 feet, or they can avoid breaking a sweat and take the cog railway (since 1889) or highway (since 1916) to the top. In fact, "America's Mountain" is the most visited mountain in North America. Only Japan's Mount Fuji has more visitors each year.

The snow-capped majesty of Pikes Peak looms over the red rock formations of Garden of Gods in Colorado Springs.

Pikes Peak plays host to several annual events, including celebratory fireworks displays, a marathon, and the second oldest car race in the United States: the Pikes Peak Hill Climb, featuring 156 twists and turns on its 12.4-mile route.

Telluride

Telluride is one of the most alluring towns in the West. This picture-perfect Western boomtown is nestled in a snug box canyon and surrounded by forested peaks and idyllic waterfalls. It is the perfect blend of ski resort and historic community. According to local legend, Telluride derived its name from a contraction of "to hell you ride," due to the difficulty of reaching the town in the 19th century.

Tucked among the snowcapped Rockies, Telluride is a skier's paradise.

Telluride's beginning years in the late 1800s were marked by ambition. The silver veins in the surrounding mountains proved exceptionally rich. The newfound wealth of the town lured outlaws such as Butch Cassidy and the Sundance Kid—Butch's first bank robbery was at the San Miguel Valley Bank in downtown Telluride. The town became one of the world's first electric communities, boasting electric lighting even before Paris, the "City of Lights."

But Telluride's mining economy faltered after World War I, beginning a long, slow period of decline. The United States Postal Service gave up on the town, and the population dropped to 600. Downtown lots sold for as little as $100, and many structures began to deteriorate. But in 1972, the Telluride Ski Resort was born, and the population of miners gave way to Bohemians. The town's destiny—which at one point appeared to be total abandonment—changed suddenly. The entire town has been a National Landmark Historic District since 1964, and this status has kept its lovely character intact.

Mesa Verde National Park

About 700 years ago people now called the Anasazi lived in communities clinging to the cliffsides of the American Southwest. The name Anasazi originally meant "enemy ancestors" in Navajo but has come to mean "ancient people" or "ancient ones." These ancient people were the ancestors of today's Pueblo Indians, about 20 tribes including the Hopi and Zuni. They left a most remarkable legacy in what is now Mesa Verde ("green table" in Spanish) National Park, which comprises more than 4,000 archeological sites, including 600 cliff dwellings.

Visitors can see a handful of the most spectacular of these uncanny ruins on tours led by park rangers, and trails to mesa tops are open to hikers. Some tourists balk at the regimentation of the guided tours, but regulation, or overregulation (as some believe), is the price today's travelers pay for the damage done by visitors before them. Pillaging Mesa Verde is nothing new: An 1889 "pottery sale" of stolen artifacts is a notable early example.

Still, Mesa Verde is spellbinding. An anonymous architect said it held "timeless forms and abiding mystery." Others such as author Evan

The nicely shaded cliff dwellings in Mesa Verde National Park were home to the Anasazi people, who abandoned them about 700 years ago.

S. Connell have written about the captivating shadows, sunlight, and transcendental aura of the ancient civilization.

The Mesa Verde cliff dwellings were abandoned for about 700 years. The area's Ute Indians refused to go near the Two-Story Cliff House, believing it was sacred and occupied by spirits of the dead. They were reluctant even to show the ruins to their white friends.

Despite modern amenities, visitors should make no mistake that the park is part of the rugged American West. Hiking at an altitude of 8,400 feet with next to no humidity is a great way to enjoy Mesa Verde —be sure to include lots of water, sunblock, and your best hiking boots.

If you're planning a scenic trip to Mesa Verde, first fly to Albuquerque, New Mexico, then drive north along US 550. Take your time visiting Pueblo ruins on the way at significant excavations such as Chaco Canyon, Hovenweep National Monument, Bandelier National Monument, Yucca House National Monument, and Aztec Ruins National Monument.

Many Mesa Verde visitors stay in nearby Cortez or Mancos, Colorado, or in Durango, which is about 20 miles east of the park and the site of the historic Strater, Rochester, and General Palmer hotels. On-site accommodations are available at the only hotel inside the park, the Far View Lodge, near the heart of the mysteries of the ancient ones.

The ruins of Mesa Verde are some of the best preserved archaeological sites in the Southwest.

Quick Fact

Magnificent Ruins

In 1874, explorer-photographer William Henry Jackson discovered Two-Story Cliff House and other small cliff dwellings in what is now Ute Mountain Tribal Park. In 1888, two ranchers searching for a stray herd discovered the greatest of all the cliff communities, the Cliff Palace complex, which has 150 individual rooms, 23 underground kivas (ceremonial rooms), and towers rising four stories high.

Mesa Verde's fame spread quickly to an astonished world. "The edge of the deep canyon in the opposite cliff sheltered by a huge, massive vault of rock...laid before their astonished eyes a whole town with towers and walls, rising out of a heap of ruins...ruins so magnificent that they surpass anything of the kind known in the United States," wrote Gustaf Nordenskiöld in *The Cliff Dwellers of the Mesa Verde* in 1893.

Great Sand Dunes National Park and Preserve

Stretching across 8,000 square miles at an average elevation of 7,500 feet, southwestern Colorado's vast San Luis Valley is the world's largest alpine valley. It's full of mysteries and surprises, from UFO lore to alligator farms to potato farms.

But the most incredible surprise here may be the Great Sand Dunes, sculpted by wind,

Masterworks of wind, water, and earth, the Great Sand Dunes reach heights of up to 750 feet.

water, and time. In the shadow of the Sangre de Cristo ("Blood of Christ") Mountains, these are the tallest dunes in North America, reaching as much as 750 feet in height.

The dunes have formed here because the wind blows abundantly from multiple directions. Winds from the southwest and northeast shake loose available sand, blowing it into one of three deposits in the valley: the densely packed sabkha (or salt flat), the outer sheet of fine sand, or the inner dune field—the domain

of the biggest dunes. Nearby creeks carry sand from the dune field's north and east borders back to where the wind can blow it into the heart of the dunes.

The scale is striking: The dunes contain nearly five billion cubic meters of sand. The best way to get a feel for this ever-changing landscape is to lace up your hiking boots and work your way up to the summit of High Dune—the view from the top gazing across the sandy dunes is sublime.

Red Rocks Park and Amphitheatre

The giant Creation Rock and Ship Rock frame Red Rocks Amphitheatre.

wasn't fully realized until decades later. In the 1920s, the city of Denver bought the land and enlisted the help of the federal government. Red Rocks Amphitheatre was completed in 1947; the venue's first annual Easter Sunrise Service, a tradition that continues to this day, occurred that first year.

A "Who's Who" of the music world has taken the stage here, including Willie Nelson, the Beatles, Jimi Hendrix, and the Grateful Dead. Concert industry trade journal *Pollstar* named Red Rocks its "Best Outdoor Venue" every year from 1989 to 1993 and its "Best Small Outdoor Venue" every year from 1995 to 1999. It then dropped the amphitheatre from consideration—and named the small outdoor venue award after Red Rocks.

The dramatic red rock formations that give the amphitheatre its name are both visually striking and accoustically ideal.

In Morrison, Colorado, Red Rocks Park and Amphitheatre is nestled in the stunning mountainside and natural red rocks. Its acoustics are superb, perhaps rivaled only by the beauty of its spectacular surroundings. The north and south sides of the amphitheatre are 300-foot geological masterstrokes named Creation Rock and Ship Rock, respectively.

The seats stretch across the steep slope between the two.

In the early 20th century, John Brisben Walker hatched a plan to develop a world-class performance venue here. He went as far as building a temporary platform where he staged numerous concerts featuring leading stars of the East Coast opera scene. But Walker's vision

Rocky Mountain National Park

Perched atop the Continental Divide, Colorado's Rocky Mountain National Park is archetypal high country, offering a jaw-dropping panorama of daunting summits and alpine tundra. There are 60 peaks in the park that reach 12,000 feet above sea level. The highest, Longs Peak, scrapes the sky 14,259 feet above sea level.

Based on these lofty numbers, it should come as no surprise that the park has the highest average elevation of any U.S. national park, including those in Alaska. It's even been nicknamed "America's Switzerland." A good portion of Rocky Mountain National Park is above the area's 11,500-foot timberline. A stretch of Trail Ridge Road, the highest continuous road in the United States, climbs above the timberline to a height of 12,183 feet. But the meadows below are starkly different from the harsh landscape of the mountaintops, especially after the wildflowers push through the ground in spring.

More than three million people visit the park each year. The drive along Trail Ridge Road from Estes Park on the east side to Grand Lake, its western gateway, reveals picturesque scenes. The park's bountiful backcountry is a world-class destination for climbing, fishing, hiking, and cross-country skiing.

Crystalline lakes refilled by annual snowmelt are nestled at the feet of Rocky Mountain National Park's awe-inspiring peaks.

The Great Stupa of Dharmakaya, Shambhala Mountain Center

Cradled in the pine-clad mountains near Red Feather Lakes, Colorado, the Great Stupa of Dharmakaya is the largest stupa (monument to a great Buddhist teacher) in the western hemisphere. It is also the largest and most elaborate example of Buddhist sacred architecture in North America.

The monument was built in honor of the great Buddhist teacher Chögyam Trungpa Rinpoche (1939–1987), the founder of the Shambhala movement and one of the key figures who helped introduce Tibetan Buddhism to the United States. He established more than 100-meditation centers across the United States and founded the first Buddhist-inspired university in the country, Naropa University in Boulder, Colorado. His skull is encased in the large statue of Buddha in the chamber at the stupa's base, called the heart center.

Construction on the Great Stupa of Dharmakaya began in 1988, and the monument was consecrated in 2001. The 108-foot masterpiece is a mesmerizing work of ornate art, laden with meaningful symbolism and built to last a millennium. (The engineers behind it used reinforced concrete to maximize the stupa's durability.) Stupas in the West have come to represent the contrast between modern and ancient world views. The interior of the Great Stupa of Dharmakaya is spacious. Its design and artwork reflect the connection between Japanese aesthetics and Shambhala teachings.

The largest stupa in the western hemisphere is a monument to Chögyam Trungpa Rinpoche, the founder of the Shambhala movement.

Yellowstone National Park

Yellowstone was not only the first national park in the United States—it was the first national park in the entire world. At 2.2 million acres, it is one of North America's largest areas of protected wilderness. These distinctions have preserved Yellowstone's wild nature and made it a model for other parks, whose managers have benefited from the lessons learned, and mistakes made, at Yellowstone.

One striking aspect of Yellowstone is the volcanic plumbing below Earth's surface that powers geothermal features including dramatic geysers such as Old Faithful, steaming fumaroles (holes in volcanic regions that issue vapors and hot gasses), bubbling hot pools, and belching mud pots. While strolling on the boardwalks that provide close-up views of these superheated attractions, keep in mind that Yellowstone is one of only two intact geyser basins on the planet. (The other, on the Kamchatka Peninsula in Russia, is much less accessible.) Dozens of others have been developed into spas, tapped for energy, or otherwise used and abused by humans.

Geysers are scattered throughout the park, and they dominate the landscape in the area near Old Faithful. A quarter of the world's geysers are located on the hillsides and riverbanks near the Upper, Midway, and Lower Geyser Basins.

Yellowstone's wildlife is every bit as astounding as its thermal features. The Lamar Valley, in the park's northeastern corner, is

Yellowstone is a natural patchwork of pine forests, glacial lakes, and imposing mountains.

known as "The Serengeti of North America." There are more large mammals here—deer, moose, elk, bison, bears, and wolves—than in any other ecosystem on the continent. During the spring, this diverse menagerie is on display as animals graze, scavenge, and hunt.

Yellowstone's wealth doesn't begin and end with the geysers and the animals. The park is a trove of aquatic wonders, especially Yellowstone Lake (the largest high-altitude lake in the continental United States, at 7,733 feet above sea level) and the spectacular geothermal theatrics on its shores at West Thumb. There is also the Grand Canyon of the Yellowstone River, a geological masterwork punctuated by two dramatic waterfalls, 109-foot Upper Falls and 308-foot Lower Falls.

The subtle yet striking beauty of Yellowstone is transitory. The volcanism that powers the geysers is close to Earth's surface under the caldera, which is the heart of the park. The Yel-

The lakeside thermal features at West Thumb are among the many spectacular sights in the park.

lowstone Caldera is still active and has erupted three times in the last two million years, at an average interval of once every 600,000 years. The last eruption—whose force was equivalent to about 10,000 times that of the 1980 Mount St. Helens eruption—occurred about 600,000 years ago. Do the math: The result is a reminder that nature's masterworks are constant works in progress, and some are more temporary than others.

Cody

The terrain around Cody, Wyoming, is remarkably varied, running the gamut from rolling hills to red rocks to evergreen-laden mountains.

Named for its founder, William "Buffalo Bill" Cody, this is one town in the country where the West lives on. Cody, Wyoming, is a bit of a bug in amber, with wooden boardwalks fronting its historic storefronts on Sheridan Avenue, the city's main drag. Sure, minivans have replaced horse-drawn wagons, and modern development has not passed over Cody entirely, but the culture here still smacks of the Old West in many ways. The city bills itself as the "Rodeo Capital of the World," and it's tough to argue. It's the only city in the country that has a rodeo every night of the week, all summer long: the Cody Nite Rodeo.

With a population of about 9,000 people, Cody is not a big city by any means, but it shines in comparison with its similarly sized peers. The 300,000-square-foot Buffalo Bill Historical Center, for instance, is a world-class museum with five distinct wings dedicated to Native Americans, natural history, Western art, firearms, and "Buffalo Bill" Cody himself. Outdoor recreation is also big in these parts. The Shoshone River runs right through town, and there are mountainous destinations in its backyard, including Yellowstone National Park just 52 miles to the west.

Grand Teton National Park

The beauty of the Teton Range in northwestern Wyoming is rapturous. It's difficult to take a picture in Grand Teton National Park without capturing these awe-inspiring peaks. The summit of Grand Teton, perhaps the most recognizable mountain in the United States, is 13,770 feet above sea level, and it shoots a mile-and-a-half straight up from the valley floor below. This precipitous rise is nothing short of breathtaking.

Grand Teton National Park is situated in Jackson Hole, the famed valley bounded by Yellowstone to the north and the Tetons to the west. Grand Teton, Mount Owen, and Teewinot are collectively known as the Cathedral Group, and the view of these mountains from the northeast is astounding. Atop the Tetons, the granite is more than three billion years old, making it some of the oldest rock on the continent. The mountains themselves, however, are among the youngest in the Rockies—they formed about ten million years ago.

Farther north, the colossal 12,605-foot Mount Moran rises alone beyond Jackson Lake, the largest of seven crystalline lakes at the foot of the mountain. From there, one can see the Snake River. It follows a 30-mile course through the park, a scenic stretch of wilderness favored by moose, cutthroat trout, and bald eagles.

Looming above Jackson Hole, the Cathedral Group of the Grand Tetons comprises Grand Teton, Mount Owen, and Teewinot.

Devils Tower National Monument

The igneous spire now known as Devils Tower, which in 1906 became the United States' first national monument, had many other names before earning its current moniker. Long before the United States was a country, the Lakota people called the tower *Mato Tipila*, or "bear lodge." The Cheyenne dubbed it *Na Kovea*, meaning "bear's tepee." Both tribes hold it sacred to this day.

The origins of Devils Tower date back 60 million years, when columns of molten magma cooled underground, a full mile-and-a-half below Earth's crust. After eons of erosion, the soft sedimentary layers that once covered the spire disappeared, and the tower now reaches 867 feet from its base into the sky. Its honeycombed columns, cracked on the south side and smooth on the north (due to the sun), are nothing short of bewildering.

Wildlife is abundant near the tower: More than 100 species of birds circle in the sky, chipmunks scurry on the tower, and the forested base is alive with rabbits, deer, and porcupines. Above, the sky holds the promise of unidentified flying objects: Like the Lakota and the Cheyenne, sci-fi fans have long held Devils Tower sacred, thanks to its star turn as the setting for the climactic scene of Steven Spielberg's *Close Encounters of the Third Kind*.

The pillar of igneous rock that is now Devils Tower was buried until wind and water swept away the layers of sedimentary rock millions of years ago, revealing the columnar tower.

Cheyenne Frontier Days

Cheyenne Frontier Days is the world's largest outdoor rodeo, earning the nickname "The Daddy of 'em All." But it's not just a rodeo, not by a long shot. It's a midsummer celebration of Western heritage, food, art, and music. There's even a carnival midway and much, much more.

The main event, of course, is the rodeo. Bronco riding, steer roping, wild-horse racing, team roping, and barrel racing are standards—but bull riding is the main attraction and grand finale. The appeal and lofty status of bull riding in the rodeo world today is due in large part to Cheyenne Frontier Days. The bulls weren't reliably ornery until livestock contractors bred a Brahma bull from India into the mix for the event in the 1920s. These beasts weighed more than 1,500 pounds each and were perfectly angry and ferocious buckers, making way for their widespread acceptance in the sport ever since.

The first Frontier Days was staged in 1897. The event began as a plan hatched to revitalize the economy after the silver bust of 1893. Since its beginning, Frontier Days has been a volunteer operation, and its success is due to the thousands of hospitable Wyoming residents who make the event possible each year. In fact, they feed more than 30,000 rodeo fans a free pancake breakfast every year.

(Right) *Beyond its myriad rodeos and stock shows, Cheyenne Frontier Days features concerts and a carnival midway.*

(Above) *The "Daddy of 'em All" features a cattle drive to the fairgrounds.*

Medicine Wheel National Historic Landmark

Wyoming's Medicine Wheel is located in a remote area of the Bighorn National Forest at an elevation of 9,642 feet on Medicine Mountain. It is one of the oldest active religious sites on the planet: For 7,000 years, this mountain has been sacred.

Medicine Wheel is part of a larger system of interrelated religious sites, altars, sweat lodge

Measuring 75 feet across, Medicine Wheel in northern Wyoming has been an active religious site for thousands of years.

sites, and other ceremonial venues, and it is still in use. In recent years, members of dozens of Indian nations have held ceremonies here, including the Arapaho, Cheyenne, and Crow.

The lasting artifact at the site is the actual Medicine Wheel, which is 75 feet in diameter and composed of 28 "spokes" of rocks intersecting in a central rocky cairn. Originally built several hundred years ago, it is now a National Historic Landmark enclosed by a simple fence of rope. It is considered one of the best-preserved sites of its kind.

Zion National Park

The Colorado Plateau, the Great Basin, and the Mojave Desert converge in Zion National Park. The name Zion, which was given by Mormon pioneers, is Hebrew for "sanctuary." While the park was established in 1909 as Mukuntuweap National Monument, it became Zion National Park in 1919.

The sheer, vibrantly colored cliff and canyon landscape of Zion stretches across 229 square miles in southwestern Utah. Nine distinct layers of rock can be found throughout the park. The colors of the rocks are accented by traces of iron, creating an array of reds, pinks, whites, and yellows as well as flashes of black, green, and purple.

More than 200 million years ago, the land here was a sea basin, but tectonic forces thrust the land up, and rivers and wind carved the winding canyons. Fossils of seashells, fish, trees, snails, and bones have been found embedded in the rocks. The highest point in the park, atop Horse Ranch Mountain, reaches 8,726 feet. Along the north fork of the Virgin River is a spectacular gorge where the walls of the canyon rise 2,000 to 3,000 feet.

Zion has the richest diversity of plants in all of Utah—in all there are more than 800 plant species including larkspurs, junipers, pinyon pines, sand buttercups, violets, columbine, asters, and sunflowers. Wildlife is abundant, and you may even catch a rare glimpse of a mountain lion or ring-tailed cat.

There's much more to do at the park than just sight-see: Outdoor activities such as biking, backpacking, hiking, camping, climbing, horseback riding, and swimming are readily available. And bold travelers may even choose to brave the famous Narrows Trail, a 15-mile hike that involves wading upstream through a river, providing breathtaking views of the canyon walls that jut 2,500 feet into the sky.

The entrance to Zion National Park is a gateway to some of the most visually stunning geological formations on the planet.

Arches National Park

Arches National Park in eastern Utah defies the imagination. Sandstone has eroded and been whittled into an astonishing landscape of color, shape, and texture. The definitive features in the park are, of course, the arches of its namesake. The park is home to the densest concentration of these rocky masterworks on the entire planet—there are over 2,000 in all.

The size of the park's arches range from three feet in diameter to the massive 306-foot Landscape Arch (the world's longest arch).

This arch is one of eight along the two-mile-long Devils Garden Trail. The park's best known attraction is Delicate Arch, which stands picturesque against a dazzling panorama of infinite sandstone.

While these dramatic sandstone portals are the stars of the park, Arches is home to a rich and unusual ecosystem. It sits atop the Colorado Plateau, a high desert region that unfolds from western Colorado into Utah, New Mexico, and Arizona. Other geological wonders are found throughout the park, including balanced rocks, spires, slick-looking domes, and "Park Avenue," a series of bright red fins that loom over the vivid desert like Manhattan skyscrapers.

This rocky, arid landscape is surprisingly rife with flora and fauna. Arches' soil is actually

Utah's Arches National Park has more natural arches than any other tract of land on Earth—there are more than 2,000 total.

(Left) *Delicate Arch is a natural masterpiece of sculpted red sandstone.*

hunter-gatherers started frequenting the vicinity of the modern park at the end of the last ice age, about 10,000 years ago. Up until about 700 years ago, the Fremont and Pueblo people inhabited the region, and they were followed by the Ute, Paiute, and Shoshone, who still lived in the region when Europeans began exploring it in the 18th and 19th centuries.

Quick Fact

A Geological Primer

The sandstone here was adjacent to a great inland sea hundreds of millions of years ago. Over time the sea vanished and left behind a salt bed thousands of feet thick in places. Wind carried dust from the adjacent coastal plain, which buried the salt under layers of sediment that compacted into rock over time. This sandstone crust was once more than a mile thick, but it cracked and buckled as the salt gave way under the rock's immense weight. This era left behind a landscape of domes and vertical cracks and set the stage for the formation of the arches seen today.

Water flooded the gaps in the sandstone and, along with the wind, it wore away layers of rock. This left behind a series of "fins" that were further wracked when ice formed on their walls. Sometimes ice would expand in indentations during cold periods and create openings that would allow daylight, wind, and water through. Many of the fins collapsed, but others had the perfect symmetrical blend of durability and steadiness to survive—as arches.

spots. In spring, the sandy red washes come alive with wildflowers.

Many animals such as lizards, kangaroo rats, bobcats, mountain lions, and owls live in the park. Rainwater collects in natural basins in the sandstone (better known as "potholes") that support seasonal populations of hardy amphibians and insects.

Arches National Park also has numerous petroglyphs and tool-making sites, signs of a long and storied human history. Nomadic

alive: Much of the park is sheathed in a groundcover of multicolored lichens that support an array of desert plant life. Yucca and cacti thrive year-round, and there are pockets of willows and ferns in the park's few soggy

(Above) *Beyond the park's namesake arches is a diverse array of stunning geology, including Balanced Rock in the Windows area.*

Temple Square

(Above) *The stunning spires of the Salt Lake Temple are the result of four decades of labor.*
(Inset) *Temple Square is home to the world-renowned Mormon Tabernacle Choir and the site of one of the largest pipe organs in the world.*

Temple Square is the most visited site in Utah. The striking Salt Lake Temple is at its center. This architectural wonder is a living legacy to 40 years of hard work and perseverance.

Work on the Salt Lake Temple began in 1853, six years after Brigham Young led thousands of Mormons to the Great Salt Lake to escape persecution in Nauvoo, Illinois. During the next four decades, workers painstakingly carved granite blocks from the walls of Little Cottonwood Canyon—now the home of two renowned ski resorts—about 20 miles southeast of Temple Square. Weighing in excess of a ton and sometimes as much as 5,600 pounds, each block was transported by ox-drawn wagon or railroad to the construction site. Master stonecutters then fit the blocks perfectly into place, without the aid of mortar.

Brigham Young did not live to see the Temple's completion in 1893. But he certainly would have approved of the majestic building, capped with six towering spires, which he directed to be built to last an eternity.

Great Salt Lake

Utah's Great Salt Lake is the largest lake in the United States west of the Mississippi. It covers about 1,700 square miles in the shadows of the grand Wasatch Range. The lake is a remnant of a prehistoric inland sea called Lake Bonneville that was at one time ten times as big as it is now.

The water of the Great Salt Lake is much saltier than the ocean. Because of the high salinity, the lake supports no fish, but provides habitat for brine shrimp, brine flies, and flocks of migratory birds. Early European explorers believed that the lake was the tip of a Pacific fjord or fed by a river from the ocean.

(Right) *The rocky shoreline of the Great Salt Lake contrasts with the water's still surface and the surrounding salt flats.*

(Left) *The remnant of a once-vast inland sea, the Great Salt Lake has a higher salinity than the Pacific Ocean.*

Today people boat and swim in its waters and sunbathe on white sand beaches. If you're planning to boat, nonmotorized crafts such as kayaks or sailboats are a better choice—the salty water is corrosive to metal. There are also trails for hiking and mountain biking on Antelope Island, a Utah State Park, as well as other stretches of shoreline. A luminescent sunset over the Great Salt Lake—clouds and sky streaked with vivid hues of orange and red—is unforgettable.

Monument Valley

Mythic-looking monoliths of red sandstone loom over the sandy desert floor of Monument Valley in Utah and Arizona. Monument Valley is a Navajo Nation Tribal Park. It offers some of the most enduring images in the West. The valley's striking formations have been photographed countless times for Hollywood Westerns, postcards, and advertisements of all kinds—for good reason.

Little has changed since John Ford directed John Wayne here in *Stagecoach* in 1939. Many of the formations in Monument Valley (known as *Tsé Bii'Ndzisgaii* in Navajo, or "Valley of the Rocks") straddle the Utah–Arizona border. They were pushed through Earth's surface by geological upheaval, then carved by wind and rivers. The rock is stratified in three principal layers, with siltstone atop sandstone atop shale.

Two of the most recognizable formations in Monument Valley are the aptly named East Mitten and West Mitten buttes.

Among the most recognizable formations in Monument Valley are the 300-foot-tall, precariously narrow Totem Pole; the arch known as Ear of the Wind; and the East Mitten and West Mitten buttes.

Canyonlands National Park

The wide-open wilderness of sandstone canyons in Canyonlands National Park is the remarkable product of millions of years of rushing water. The Colorado and the Green rivers have shaped this landscape of precipitous chasms and vividly painted mesas, pinnacles, and buttes.

Writer Edward Abbey described Canyonlands as a savage, barren region of Utah. He downplayed the elegance and intense beauty of this rugged land to try to keep people away and preserve its undisturbed wonder.

At the amazing confluence in the heart of Canyonlands, the rivers meet, merge, and divide the park into four distinct sections. In the north is the Island in the Sky, a mesa that rises more than 1,000 feet above the rivers. East of the confluence is the Needles, a landscape of grassy valleys dominated by banded pinnacles. The isolated western area of the park is The Maze, so named for its labyrinth of canyons. The final section, Horseshoe Canyon, is known for its rock art and spring wildflowers. And the rivers themselves provide a habitat that is in many ways the polar opposite of the surrounding arid desert.

The Y-shape confluence of the Colorado and Green rivers is the heart of Canyonlands National Park.

Lake Powell

With a labyrinth shoreline totalling almost 2,000 miles, Lake Powell is a boating and fishing paradise.

Beyond the Glen Canyon Dam, the Colorado River widens into Lake Powell. The lake stretches from Lee's Ferry in Arizona to Utah's Orange Cliffs. There are two sides to the story of the reservoir—it has been beloved by some and reviled by others.

Lake Powell is a mecca for outdoors buffs of every stripe, from anglers and boaters to hikers and mountain bikers. The spectacular 187-mile body of water is vast and nestled in the blissful surroundings of red rock. Many vacationers spend their entire trip on the water itself in a rented houseboat. Lake Powell's shoreline stretches nearly 2,000 miles, which is longer than that of the entire Pacific Coast of the contiguous United States.

The construction of Glen Canyon Dam in the 1950s and 1960s remains controversial to this day. Many people opposed building the dam and the submersion of Glen Canyon. After it was built, the dam became a rallying point for environmentalists, who in recent years have called for draining Lake Powell and restoring Glen Canyon.

Bryce Canyon National Park

Bryce Canyon is a spectacular display of geological formations in southern Utah. It is the sculpted side of the Paunsaugunt Plateau that is now a fantasyland covered by thousands of red and orange hoodoos (rock columns). These sandstone towers were left behind when layers of the surrounding rock eroded.

The seeds for Bryce Canyon's dense forest of hoodoos were planted 60 million years ago, when inland seas and lakes covered southwestern Utah. Over eons, sediment collected on the lake's floor and congealed into rock. Later movements in the Earth's crust pushed the Paunsaugunt Plateau skyward, leaving its eastern edge exposed to the ravages of wind and water. The resulting multihued hoodoos are awe-inspiring.

Bryce Canyon is dynamic. The Colorado River whittles Bryce's rim away at a rate of two to four feet every 100 years—amazingly fast by geological standards.

An intricately carved collection of vibrantly colored hoodoos populates the unforgettable landscape of Bryce Canyon National Park.

Capitol Reef National Park

Capitol Reef is not actually a reef, but an area of towering limestone that was indeed underwater millions of years ago. It is actually a monoclinal, what geologists call a wrinkle in Earth's crust.

This wrinkle is known as the Waterpocket Fold, which rises in ridges for 100 miles across southern Utah. Capitol Reef, with sheer cliffs rising 1,000 feet in some places, is the most scenic segment of the fold. The 19th-century pioneers who named it were inspired by the white domes of sandstone that crown it, resembling stately rotundas from afar.

Capitol Reef was known to the native Navajo as "The Land of the Sleeping Rainbow" due to the broad color spectrum adorning the rock walls. It is home to numerous unique formations, including the looming Castle.

Capitol Reef is the most photogenic stretch of the Waterpocket Fold, a 100-mile-long wrinkle in the earth of southern Utah.

The Temple of the Sun and the Temple of the Moon are opposing twin monoliths in the spectacular Cathedral Valley near the park's northern border. These sandstone giants were carved by erosion.

Little Bighorn Battlefield National Monument

As the U.S. government encouraged westward expansion after the Civil War, rapid development threatened the way of life of the Cheyenne and Lakota peoples. In the early 1870s, violence between native warriors and U.S. soldiers escalated, and Lieutenant Colonel George Custer was dispatched to lead 12 companies of the 7th Cavalry in defense of national interests in the Wild West.

At a ridge above the Little Bighorn River near Hardin, Montana, Custer's party was taken by surprise and overwhelmed by a far larger Sioux and Cheyenne war party on June 25 and 26, 1876, during what is now known as "Custer's Last Stand." Custer and more than 200 soldiers under his command perished in the battle, as did at least 60 Cheyenne and Lakota (the exact number is unknown). Despite the outcome, Custer's Last Stand marked the end for the Cheyenne and Lakota peoples' nomadic way of life in the West.

In 1879, the battlefield became a national cemetery for the fallen U.S. Army soldiers. In 2003, a corresponding Indian Memorial— a striking sculpture garden named "Peace Through Unity"—was dedicated. These memorials honor all who fought here, whether for their country, for land, or to preserve their way of life. The solemnity of the battlefield inspires quiet reverence.

The memorial on Last Stand Hill was built over the mass grave of 7th Cavalry soldiers, U.S. Indian scouts, and others who died here.

Glacier National Park

Etched over eons, the perfect geometry scoring the sides of the canyons, valleys, cirques, and mountains of Montana's Glacier National Park is the majestic work of nearly extinct glaciers. Over the last 60 million years, these glaciers have melted, contracted, receded, and shaped vast areas of rock and earth.

Nearly parallel grooves worn into the rocks are a timeless testament to the dogged power of the ice that was once massive enough to pulverize mountainsides and move boulders. Glaciers once dominated the landscape, but after creating the perfectly etched lines on the canyon walls, many melted and became long, deep blue lakes. Smaller glaciers can be seen on north-facing walls and other cool alcoves shaded from sunlight.

But this is still a land of water, wind, and ice, with a long, determined winter. Six hundred and fifty-three lakes and 1,000 miles of rivers and streams are shoehorned into roughly 1,600 square miles (about the size of Delaware). Cutting over Logan Pass through some of North America's most sublime scenery is Going-to-the-Sun Road, completed in 1932. The trail system covering the rugged terrain is a hiker's paradise.

The creation of Glacier and all of its perfect lines boggles the mind. Renowned naturalist John Muir dubbed it "the best care-killing scenery on the continent." Considering the amount of time and slow, stubborn power required to carve the park's unmistakable scenery makes day-to-day calendars and troubles seem small, short-lived, and self-centered—which for many is a good thing.

The origins of this geological masterpiece are the Lewis and Livingston Mountain Ranges that are at the park's heart. Most of the telltale glacial scars marking the park's scenery follow parallel lines down mountain slopes where

The park's glaciers are the source of water for countless scenic waterfalls.

Quick Fact

Flathead Lake

Flathead Lake, which lies just southwest of Glacier National Park, is the largest natural freshwater lake west of the Mississippi River. It is the defining feature of the valley of the same name and a prime habitat for a wide range of wildlife. It is 28 miles long and 15 miles across at its widest point.

Flathead Lake is surrounded by forested mountains. It contains Wild Horse Island, one of the largest inland islands in the entire United States, which is home to wildlife including bighorn sheep, black bears, and bald eagles. Legend has it that the island's name comes from the Salish-Kootnai Indians, who kept their horses on the island to prevent them from being stolen.

Many visitors come to fish in the lake, which is known for its trophy trout. Scenic cruises are also popular. There are plenty of cultural amenities near the shore, including the theater and restaurants in the charming village of Bigfork and the Mission Mountain Winery on the southwestern lakefront.

Flathead Lake is 370 feet deep at its deepest point, which has helped fuel legends of a prehistoric sea creature lurking in its depths. Sightings of a whalelike beast have been reported for more than a century.

bears and grizzly bears, which were driven to the high country when their natural habitat of the plains was developed for agriculture.

The glaciers here are receding quickly. With global temperatures on the rise, the number of ice shelves has dwindled from historical highs by 50 percent in recent years, and climatologists believe the glaciers might be gone in the next century. Regardless of their fate, the glaciers of northwestern Montana have left a lasting mark on the land—come wintertime, snow beautifully frosts the thousands of hypnotic grooves one by one.

Just southwest of Glacier National Park, Flathead Lake is another terrific Montana destination—and allegedly home to a secretive monster.

gravity pulled the glaciers across the rock. Then there are occasional lines that avert from the parallel slant, where the rock withstood the ice, causing the glacier to veer off course, slightly changing its trajectory though never stopping or reversing it.

Viewed from the plains east of Glacier National Park, the Rocky Mountains are stunning. They abruptly rise from 4,000 feet in elevation to over 10,000 atop the highest peaks, then just as precipitously drop off to about 3,000 feet at Lake McDonald in the park's southwestern quarter. To the north, Glacier connects with Waterton National Park in Alberta, Canada, and the two make up International Peace Park, a World Heritage Site.

Atop Glacier's alpine passes, bighorns munch on the hardy plants that speckle the rocky cliffs. This is also the domain of black

Museum of the Rockies

Long before grizzlies and bighorn sheep roamed the Rockies, Montana's claim to fame was wildlife of a different kind—dinosaurs. About 60 million years ago, the region was tropical. Local dinosaurs included the *Tyrannosaurus rex*, *Apatosaurus*, and *Triceratops*, all of which thrived until a shift in climate wiped them out.

This rich prehistory is told at Bozeman's Museum of the Rockies, home to the largest collection of American dinosaur bones in the world, nearly all of which were discovered in Montana. Under the umbrella of Montana State University, the museum gives insight into a world-class dinosaur research center. The museum is in large part the brainchild of Dr. Jack Horner, a celebrated paleontologist and consultant to the *Jurassic Park* films.

(Above) *The world-class dinosaur exhibits at the Museum of the Rockies in Bozeman, Montana, include the skull of a* T. rex—*and its jagged smile.*

Outside the museum, a living-history farm offers a peek back in time into the lives of the Gallatin Valley's pioneers.

Visitors begin with a crash course on the history of the Rockies, starting with the Big Bang theory. Then they explore the dinosaur exhibits. Some displays showcase casts, and others hold real fossils, including the largest dinosaur skull in the world (a nine-foot Torosaurus noggin) and a *T. rex* femur that amazingly revealed soft tissues that had been preserved inside for 68 million years. The Museum of the Rockies provides comprehensive displays that go well beyond the typical dusty collection of giant skeletons. The exhibits dig into dinosaur biology and behavior, as well as the science and research that goes into fossil recovery and paleontology.

Makoshika State Park

The bleak but beautiful badlands of Makoshika State Park in Glendive, Montana, sit in stark contrast to the surrounding plains.

Some 65 million years ago, the plains in eastern Montana were vast, lush, and green. For a geological split second, dinosaurs thrived in the area. Then they became extinct, the sea receded, the mud dried, and the first of several ice ages hit. After the last ice age 11,000 years ago, the ancient glacial marks left here were buried under layers of silt.

But wind and weather wore the silt away, revealing layers of red sandstone atop layers of gray mudstone atop layers of dark shale; hoodoos, caprocks, and other geological anomalies; and an otherworldly badlands landscape the Lakota dubbed Makoshika, or "bad earth."

Besides exposing Makoshika's rugged beauty, erosion also helped unearth fossils hundreds of millions of years old, including a remarkable triceratops skull, excavated in 1991. It, along with other fossils discovered here, is now on display in the park's visitor center. There is also an exhibit on one prehistoric area resident that didn't go the way of the dinosaur: the paddlefish, which still swims in the depths of the nearby Yellowstone River.

Craters of the Moon
National Monument and Preserve

The eerie landscape of Craters of the Moon National Monument and Preserve does not look like it belongs in southern Idaho. In fact, it doesn't even look like it belongs on this planet—thus the lunar moniker.

The area owes its mysterious appearance to its volcanic past. The craters are actually pocks

(Above right) *The otherworldly landscape is a result of a violent volcanic epoch that lasted from 15,000 years ago to 2,000 years ago.*

(Above left) *Unusual igneous rock formations dot the varied landscape at Craters of the Moon National Monument.*

in several lava fields dotted with sagebrush and cinder cones. The eruptions that created the terrain took place between 15,000 and 2,000 years ago, leaving behind a sheet of hardened lava 60 miles wide and more than 10,000 feet deep at its deepest point.

Craters of the Moon is home to all sorts of interesting features forged by once red-hot magma, such as unusual-looking splatter cones and cavelike lava tubes. The tallest cinder cone, Big Cinder Butte, rises more than 700 feet above the surrounding plain; and there are 19 others at least 100 feet high. Many scientists think the volcanic zone—called the Great Rift—that created the monument is due for another explosion in the next few centuries.

Hells Canyon of the Snake River

A huge lake once covered the area now bisected by the Oregon–Idaho state line. The rocky bulge of the Owyhee Mountains kept the Snake and Columbia rivers separate until giving way roughly a million years ago. Then the Snake rapidly cut its way through as much

The view of the Snake River from the rim of Hells Canyon is nothing short of spectacular.

as ten miles of igneous rock to join with the Columbia, chiseling out the chasm now known as the Hells Canyon of the Snake River.

Today, Hells Canyon is one of the continent's most dramatic landscapes. The adjacent mountain ridges rise an average of more than a mile above the canyon floor, towering over the white water below. The pinnacle of He Devil Mountain is almost 8,000 feet higher than

the river, making for the deepest gorge in the United States.

The oldest rocks in the canyon originated from underwater volcanoes when Hells Canyon was part of a Pacific island chain. Rivers eroded some of the lava, carrying it downstream, and the Seven Devils and Eagle Cap Mountains were pushed skyward. The result is the spectacular Hells Canyon.

Chapter Seven

The Pacific

California is the most populous of the 50 states and

possibly the most diverse. The terrain is extreme, from

the peaks of the Sierra Nevada Range to the depths of

Death Valley, from the remote beaches of the northern and

central coasts to the bustling cities of Los Angeles and

San Francisco. California and its neighboring states to the

north and the west share one common thread—the Pacific

Ocean. The Pacific waters that flow beneath the Golden

Gate Bridge lap at Washington's Puget Sound and the

mouth of the Columbia River in Oregon, not to mention

Alaska's ice-laden Glacier Bay and the amazing

volcanic Hawaiian Islands.

*Hulking El Capitán and Glacier Point, reflected in the
shimmering Merced River, frame Yosemite Valley in California.*

Redwood National and State Parks

Near remote stretches of California's ocean-front, the water, soil, and sun blend perfectly for redwood growth. The results are the redwood forests, which are nothing short of astounding. Walking through the old-growth redwood forest may make you feel as though you've ingested the same potion Alice swallowed after she tumbled down the rabbit's hole into Wonderland.

More than 100,000 acres of soul-stirring forest are protected under the auspices of Redwood National and State Parks, but the ecosystem has been threatened by the logging industry for years. These kings of the conifers once grew elsewhere in North America, but this is the last spot where they thrive in such size and number. Beyond the towering trees, the cool coastal climate is ideal for hiking and taking in the Jurassic-looking scene.

Imagine this: The tallest redwood in the parks is more than twice as tall as the Statue of Liberty. The parks' tallest trees, located in the aptly named Tall Trees Grove, measure about 360 feet from base to treetop, heights that have taken more than 600 years to attain. The first branches of these trees begin 100 to 200 feet above the spongy forest floor, a result of higher branches blocking sunlight as their pinnacles inched skyward.

The number of trees growing today is a mere fraction of those that once blanketed the

The forest is on a larger scale than any other, affording visitors a brand-new perspective.

region. In the late 1700s, the redwood forest in California and Oregon covered an estimated two million acres. A century later, loggers had pushed into the region and decimated mile after mile of pristine, primeval forests.

By 1965, the redwood forest had been whittled down to 300,000 acres, and Congress passed legislation in 1968 for about 60,000 acres of it to be protected in national and state parks. In 1978, Congress added another 48,000 acres, including 39,000 logged acres that one park official described as resembling an active war zone. Today, the clear-cut area has been reclaimed for redwood trees, but officials estimate that it will take 50 years for the logging scars to disappear and another 250 years for the new redwoods to grow to modest size.

Despite the redwood's dominance over the scenery, the complex ecosystem of the forest relies on much more than just the trees. The cycles of tree growth and rot supply nutrients to a host of plants and fungi. The lush greenery makes a great habitat for small creatures, such as voles and banana slugs, and large animals, including a sizable elk herd. Marine mammals, including gray whales during their annual migrations, are also visible near the park in the Pacific Ocean.

Fallen redwoods become the base for all sorts of new vegetation in the damp climate.

Many also believe this area to be the home of the legendary Sasquatch, and hiking through the dense forest and its oversize underbrush makes the existence of Bigfoot seem possible. In these rugged, nearly impenetrable woods, it's conceivable that an entire species could remain hidden for as long as it wished—provided the trees remain protected from the logger's ax.

Point Reyes National Seashore

The peaceful, pastoral Point Reyes Peninsula is a world apart from San Francisco, just 22 miles to the south. From its eastern boundary, Inverness Ridge, to the Pacific Ocean, the peninsula is a land of windswept beaches, grasslands, and forest. It's the windiest spot on the West Coast.

The entire Point Reyes Peninsula is in perpetual motion—it's moving northwest at approximately two inches a year. The peninsula lies on the Pacific Plate along the San Andreas Fault. Along the fault, pressure builds up gradually when the plates shift, and the fault eventually gives way—in other words, an earthquake occurs. The biggest earthquake was in 1906, when the entire peninsula shot 20 feet northwest in an instant.

Point Reyes National Seashore is rich with human history, dating back to the Coastal Miwok Indians, who inhabited the peninsula circa 3000 B.C. It is currently a mixed-use unit of the National Park Service, complete with active dairy operations, an oyster farm, and a historic lighthouse.

Bordered on three sides by the Pacific Ocean, the picturesque Point Reyes has recorded more than 490 bird species.

Napa Valley Vineyards

Napa Valley is only five miles across at its widest point and 30 miles long, but its reputation stretches around the world. Located 50 miles north of San Francisco, the valley is home to 110,000 people, five incorporated cities, and 200 wineries.

In the late 1800s, there were more than 600 wineries in the valley. The longstanding success of the local wine industry is a result of the climate and soil, which are ideal for growing grapes. The soil is especially diverse: Fully half of the varieties of soil on the planet are found within the confines of Napa Valley. Stringent county policies limit development outside the cities in Napa Valley, leaving the agricultural land wide open and pastoral.

Napa Valley was carved by the Napa River, which flows directly into San Francisco Bay

In Napa, it's all about quality, not quantity. The verdant 30-mile-long valley contributes only a fraction of California's total wine production.

and attracts anglers and paddlers. But most visitors come for fresh air, good food, and, of course, great wine. The "crush" that accompanies the fall harvest is one of the valley's busiest times.

Golden Gate Bridge

The Golden Gate Bridge does for the West Coast what the Statue of Liberty does for the East: It welcomes newcomers while proclaiming the strength, determination, and promise of the United States.

The Golden Gate Bridge also introduces visitors to the sumptuous San Francisco Bay Area. According to Mayor Gavin Newsom, "San Franciscans know we live in the most beautiful city in the world, a jewel on the edge of the Golden Gate."

The bridge opened in 1937 with a celebration in which 200,000 jubilant pedestrians crossed it. During its 50th-anniversary celebration, 300,000 pedestrians walked across, which is one terrific way to visit the bridge if you're in shape.

The Golden Gate Bridge, which is painted orange vermilion (more commonly called "international orange"), is golden in every other respect.

The Golden Gate's vibrant color and 4,200-foot span make it one of the most distinctive bridges on the planet.

The bridge was named not for its color but because it spans the Golden Gate Strait, named by explorer John C. Fremont. In 1919, architect Irving Morrow wrote, the strait "is loveliest at the cool end of the day when, for a few breathless moments, faint afterglows transfigure the gray line of hills." Years later, Morrow was responsible for the bridge's stylized Art Deco embellishments as well as its famous color. Some opponents argued that only steel gray or carbon black paint could protect the bridge; the U.S. Navy wanted it painted yellow with black stripes. Morrow insisted paint could be invented to protect and burnish the bridge's graceful, sinewy architecture as well as increase its visibility in fog while blending with its natural surroundings. He was right: The bridge didn't require an overall repainting for 27 years.

Quick Fact

Alcatraz Island

Legendary tales of convicts' daring escape attempts surround Alcatraz Island, also known as "The Rock." One of the first escape attempts occurred on January 13, 1939. Five prisoners attempted to flee the island, but they were all captured or killed in the process. The spot now called Barker Beach marks where Arthur "Doc" Barker was shot dead during this prison break.

Alcatraz was an official federal penitentiary from 1934 through 1963, though military prison materials date from 1859 to 1934. While it was initially a military fort built to protect San Francisco Bay, its isolation made Alcatraz the perfect sentencing spot for dangerous convicts. In its years as a prison, no one ever escaped The Rock.

(Left) *Motorists are prohibited from changing tires on the Golden Gate Bridge.*

The Golden Gate Bridge saved San Francisco from its isolation on a peninsula. The bridge—which, at 4,200 feet from tower to tower, reigned as the world's longest suspension bridge for 27 years—heralded an era in which suspension bridges defined modernism. So striking and beautiful is its sculptural design, the bridge forged the way for a generation of graceful, buoyant Art Deco architecture in the midst of the Great Depression.

The beautiful bridge is also the centerpiece of the Golden Gate National Recreation Area (though the bridge and recreation area are managed by different agencies). Golden Gate is one of the most popular destinations in the national parks system, with more than 14 million visitors each year. The 74,000-acre expanse includes favorite destinations such as China Beach, Muir Beach, Fort Mason, and Alcatraz Island. It also includes the Presidio of San Francisco, which was established by the Spanish in 1776 and has become the oldest continuously operating U.S. military base.

The park provides panoramas of the Golden Gate Bridge that have been made famous over the years, mainly by Hollywood. The memorable scene in Hitchcock's *Vertigo*, which emphasized the bridge's overwhelming scale and sweep, was filmed under it, on the San Francisco side near Fort Point. It's definitely a view to see firsthand. From across the bay, check out the bridge's magnificence from Fort Baker, located in Marin County. You can find another picture-perfect vantage point across the bridge on its northern side at Marin Headlands, best reached by bus or car. The views from high on the San Francisco side are breathtaking as well, and don't forget the bracing scene from Alcatraz Island!

Chinatown and Chinese New Year

For 15 days during Chinese New Year, San Francisco's Chinatown neighborhood bustles with sound and color—even more than it usually does. This is the largest Chinatown on the continent, and it pulls out all the stops for the annual festivities. The Chinese New Year begins on the first day of the first moon of the lunar calendar, which usually falls between late January and mid February.

The Chinese New Year Parade (a San Francisco tradition since just after the 1849 Gold Rush) is now the biggest illuminated nighttime parade in North America. In fact, it's the largest event of its kind on any continent except Asia. Participants take the year's theme and run with it, crafting gorgeous floats that range from purely aesthetic to political. Dancers and stilt-walkers entertain the crowds, and others light firecrackers, pass out "funny money," and do their best to bring good luck to the New Year. The parade culminates with Gum Lung, the Golden Dragon—an ornate, human-powered 200-foot silk, gauze, and velvet beast with a bamboo skeleton.

Year-round, Chinatown is one of the Bay Area's most visited tourist hotspots, with plenty of eateries, bars, and shops. But it also serves as an authentic neighborhood where people live, work, and play.

San Francisco's vibrant Chinatown is the most populous neighborhood of its kind in North America and a must-see stop on any visit to the City by the Bay.

Winchester Mystery House

CUPID FOUNTAIN

In 1884, Sarah Winchester, heiress to the Winchester Rifle Company, visited a soothsayer after the death of her husband and baby daughter. The medium told her that her fate was tied to her house: Continuous building would appease the evil spirits and help her attain eternal life. Winchester took the premonition very seriously. She continued building her San José mansion for the ensuing 38 years, spending the bulk of her multimillion-dollar inheritance in the process.

Sarah Winchester's superstitions resulted in an oddity of a mansion that was under continuous construction for almost four decades.

When the hammering finally stopped after Winchester's passing in 1922, there were 160 rooms. But there's more than just sheer size at work here: Winchester chose designs to ward off the evil spirits that she believed plagued her every move. Some stairways and doors lead nowhere, and the stained glass seems to be inspired by a disturbing spider web. A plethora of features are tied to a certain number. The number of palms lining the driveway? The number of hooks in the séance room? The number of lights in the chandeliers? The answer to all three questions is 13, a further sign of Sarah Winchester's superstitions.

Yosemite Valley

The bearded father of the conservation movement, John Muir, loved Yosemite Valley. One glimpse and it's easy to see why: The unmistakable panorama reveals a dazzling wonderland of granite sculpted over eons by ice, wind, and water. Waterfalls cascade down the granite cliffs, the most famous of which is Yosemite Falls, at 2,425 feet the tallest waterfall in North America—the equivalent of 13 Niagaras. And that's just scratching the surface.

Yosemite Valley is bookended by two famous geologic masterworks. These hulking, distinct formations are known worldwide: Half Dome rises 4,800 feet above the eastern end of the valley, while the 3,600-foot El Capitán (Spanish for "the captain") stands sentry at the western entrance, fronted by one of the sheerest cliffs in the world. As any visitor to Yosemite quickly learns, it's difficult to take a photograph in Yosemite Valley without framing this handsome pair.

Yosemite Valley is undoubtedly one of nature's most awe-inspiring creations, and Muir eloquently described its wonders time

The 2,425-foot ribbon of water known as Yosemite Falls is just one of many superlative sites visitors gawk at from the valley floor.

and time again. "Nearly all the upper basin of the Merced was displayed, with its sublime domes and cañons, dark upsweeping forests, and glorious array of white peaks deep in the sky, every feature glowing, radiating beauty that pours into our flesh and bones like heat rays from fire," he wrote of a view he enjoyed from Yosemite's high country. "Never before had I seen so glorious a landscape, so boundless an affluence of sublime mountain beauty."

The peaks and meadows of today's landscape in Yosemite Valley are the work of glaciers. The slow-moving sheets of ice carved this masterpiece over the course of the last three million years, expanding and contracting and tearing granite asunder.

Another valley lies to the north: Hetch Hetchy is Yosemite's counterpart in both scale and aesthetics. But in 1913, Congress passed legislation to dam the Tuolumne River, flooding Hetch Hetchy. Muir led the fight against this action, but Congress sided with the city of San Francisco, whose sudden growth called for more and more water.

The transcendent scenery, sheer beauty, and untamed nature of Yosemite Valley draw a crowd. With more than three million visitors each year, the summer traffic can get quite thick. At times, the valley's population exceeds 20,000, making it the center of activity for the entire Sierra Nevada region. Crowds form at the developed areas, the hotels, and the various eateries throughout the valley, but there's still plenty of room to roam. Yosemite National Park is about 750,000 acres in all. And though Yosemite Valley is a mere fraction of that total, even John Muir couldn't investigate every last nook and cranny in his 76 years.

The landmark granite formation Half Dome was once considered impossible to climb.

Monterey Bay Aquarium

One of the finest aquariums in the United States—and quite possibly the world—the Monterey Bay Aquarium attracts almost two million visitors a year, and it's easy to see why.

The aquarium is located in the converted former Hovden Cannery, which canned squid and sardines until the early 1970s on Monterey's legendary Cannery Row. The aquarium opened in 1984 after seven years of planning and construction. In the 1990s, an expansion doubled its size. Today, the aquarium is home to more than 30,000 aquatic creatures, with everything from jellyfish to sharks. The many residents range from large (dolphins, sea turtles, sea otters, sharks) to small (anchovies, barnacles, zooplankton).

The aquarium's exhibits are fed by water that comes directly from Monterey Bay, which hosts one of the most diverse marine ecosystems on the planet. The mudflats, kelp forests, and nutrient-rich water support all sorts of sea life in the confines of the bay.

Monterey Bay Aquarium is home to a diverse population of sea creatures, including the leopard shark (top right) *and pelagic sting ray* (bottom right). (Above) *A diver swims to the depths of the aquarium's three-story kelp forest.*

Death Valley National Park

Generally accepted as the hottest, driest, and lowest place in North America, Death Valley is a land of extremes. It is known for its precipitous peaks surrounded by the ever-shifting dune fields.

A brutally beautiful land of extremes, Death Valley holds the record for the highest temperature ever recorded in the western hemisphere—134 degrees Fahrenheit. The average annual rainfall is less than two inches, making Death Valley the driest spot on the continent. It also contains the lowest point in the hemisphere—near Badwater, the surface is 282 feet below sea level. But the park ventures to other extremes as well, such as Telescope Peak, with an elevation of 11,049 feet and plenty of snow in wintertime. Pacific storms occasionally roar in, causing flash floods that wash out roads, trails, and campgrounds.

At 3.3 million acres, Death Valley is the largest U.S. national park outside Alaska. The vast and varied landscape includes seemingly endless salt and alkaline flats, swaths of ever-shifting sand dunes, and colorful rock cliffs and ridges. The park also includes its share of human history: The Timbisha Shoshone people have called the region home for thousands of years, and a few members still live in the park year-round.

Hearst Castle

Today, Hearst Castle is a popular tourist attraction on the Golden State's central coast. It remains a tribute to wealth and power beyond almost anybody's wildest dreams.

Over the course of nearly three decades, newspaper baron William Randolph Hearst built this luxurious and legendary home on the 250,000-acre San Simeon ranch he inherited in 1919. An opulent example of Mediterranean Revival architecture, the estate's prime attraction is Casa Grande, the 60,645-square-foot main house. Its more than 100 rooms are the setting for Hearst's priceless collection of European art and antiques. The estate includes a trio of guest abodes (smaller than Casa Grande but still over-the-top and oozing with luxury) and some of the most magnificent swimming pools in all of California, including the stunning marble Neptune Pool.

Providing inspiration for Orson Welles' Xanadu in *Citizen Kane*, Hearst Castle is now property of the California State Park system (the Hearst Corporation donated it to the state in the 1950s). It is one of the largest historic house museums in the United States. Visitors can choose from five different tours, each revealing sections of the estate from the upper floors and library to the north wing and guest rooms to the gardens and wine cellar.

Currently a state historical monument, the former domicile of newspaper baron William Randolph Hearst is one of the most opulent estates in the country.

Hollywood

Hollywood is not just a place. In certain contexts, Hollywood is shorthand for America's film industry. In others, it's the destination for every aspiring actor, director, or screenwriter. It's also the setting for so many legends and rumors it's hard to keep them straight.

Regardless, Hollywood is amazing. The rolling Hollywood Hills, clad in a lush layer of greenery, cradle neighborhoods of all kinds and feature the one-of-a-kind American icon, the Hollywood sign. At first, the sign was a real-estate promotion that read "Hollywoodland." But by 1973, it was in tatters—one O had toppled, and a vandal had set an *L* on fire. This led to its $250,000 reconstruction in 1978.

Down below, on Hollywood Boulevard, the sidewalk sports 2,000 terrazzo-and-brass stars that immortalize giants of the entertainment industry. The street is a colorful spot for people-watching and is the address of Mann's Chinese Theatre, perhaps the most famous cinema in the world. The unmistakable theater has two enormous red columns out front, a bronze roof, and authentic furnishings imported from China. Cast in the cement of the forecourt are the footprints, handprints, and hoofprints of past and present movie stars.

Nine 50-foot letters comprise one of the most recognizable signs in the world.

Venice Beach

The Los Angeles neighborhood of Venice and its fabulous beach were once home to Ocean Park, a Coney Island-like amusement pier that attracted throngs of fun-seekers. While the park went out of business in the 1960s, Venice Beach has remained a magnet for people from all walks of life.

Venice was founded in the 20th century and was named and modeled after Italy's Venice. Its three-mile beach is in many ways an afterthought. A few people come for the sand and surf, but many more come to shop, talk, or just wander and people-watch. The beach's boardwalk is the heart and soul of California cool, with merchants hocking an array

(Above) *Developers modeled the area after Venice, Italy—canals crisscross the residential neighborhoods in the area around Venice Beach.*

of eclectic art, cheap sunglasses, souvenir T-shirts, and much, much more. Venice Beach has been called the "Roller Skating Capital of the World"; it's fronted by a skating and bicycling path that runs along California's coastline, uninterrupted for 22 miles. There's also Gold's Gym, the famous outdoor weightlifting hotspot commonly called "Muscle Beach."

Perhaps Mike Bonin, a staff member for the Los Angeles City Council, put it best: "There's lots special about Venice. It is internationally recognized as a place of free expression, diversity, tolerance, and incredible artistic talent. Not to mention funky weirdness."

Venice Beach is the epicenter of California cool; visitors are drawn to its lively, carefree shores.

La Brea Tar Pits

Rancho La Brea is in the heart of urban Los Angeles, thick with traffic and skyscrapers. It's hard to imagine that millions of years ago it was submerged in the ocean, teeming with sea life. When the Pacific Ocean receded about 100,000 years ago, sediment sheathed the area and fossil fuels formed below the surface.

About 40,000 years ago, oil began to seep through the labyrinth of fissures and permeable rock, creating what are now known as the La Brea Tar Pits. Back then, dire wolves, saber-

An anomaly in downtown Los Angeles, the La Brea Tar Pits remain an archaeological treasure trove of fossils from thousands of years ago.

tooth tigers, mastodons, mammoths, and giant sloths (all of which are now extinct) roamed across what would become Los Angeles. The tar pits were an especially dangerous place for these animals. Called "asphalt seeps" by geologists, the oily pits captured and trapped many animals one by one.

Today, these animals' unfortunate fate translates into an exceptional fossil record preserved in the pits. Archaeologists have unearthed an entire prehistoric ecosystem here, from plants to insects to camels and bison. Today, the La Brea Tar Pits remain an active archaeological site and research facility. Pit 91, the most active area, is excavated during a few months each year in the summer. More than 1,000 fossil samples are discovered here each year.

Tournament of Roses Parade

In the late 1880s, Pasadena's Valley Hunt Club hatched a plan. The club's members (transplants from points east) wanted to flaunt the balmy Southern California climate. "In New York, people are buried in snow," said Professor Charles Holder at one of the club's meetings. "Here our flowers are blooming and our oranges are about to bear. Let's hold a festival to tell the world about our paradise."

The floats in the Tournament of Roses Parade are ornate—albeit temporary—works of movable art.

With that, the first Tournament of Roses Parade hit the streets of Pasadena on New Year's Day 1890. Flower-adorned carriages cruised down the street in front of a crowd of some 2,000 onlookers. Polo matches, footraces, and tug-of-war contests followed the parade. The event grew more elaborate each year. In 1902, the first Rose Bowl was held. It was the first postseason collegiate football game and is now known as "The Grandaddy of Them All." The modern Tournament of Roses Parade features multimillion-dollar floats, every last square inch of which must be covered in flowers, seeds, bark, or other plant material.

San Diego Zoo

On 100 acres in Balboa Park, just north of downtown San Diego, is a community with 4,000 full-time residents. Some are quiet and some noisy; others keep to themselves. Some rise at the break of dawn, and some are night

The African black rhino is one of the 800 animal species that call the San Diego Zoo home.

owls—literally. There are meat-eaters, vegetarians, and still others who aren't picky at all.

These residents have one thing in common: None of them are human. These animals represent the 800 non-*Homo sapiens* species that make their home in the San Diego Zoo. Among the most famous residents are the giant pandas on loan from the Chinese government, but

the entire animal kingdom is well represented, from honeybees to California condors, koalas to Komodo dragons.

The zoo has won many awards for its innovative enclosures and conservation efforts since its founding in 1916. Beyond the animals, the zoo's breathtaking gardens include an amazing 700,000 plants.

Pioneer Courthouse Square

Pioneer Courthouse Square in Portland, Oregon, is nicknamed "Portland's Living Room." And like every good living room, the square offers entertainment and plenty of seating. The two amphitheaters host more than 300 events each year, including concerts and cultural festivals. Those with a flare for art enjoy the fountain, pillars, sculptures, and an astounding Weather Machine, an innovative creation with three symbols that each represent an element of Portland's climate. There's even a signpost that shows how far it is to places as distant as Red Square in Russia.

The square has taken on many forms throughout history. A shoemaker named Elijah Hill bought the block for $24 and a pair of boots in 1849, two years before the city of Portland was officially established. James Field sold it to the fledgling Portland School Board less than a decade later, and they built a schoolhouse on the spot. In 1883, the schoolhouse was relocated to make way for the ritzy Portland Hotel, which remained open until 1951. The spot became a two-level parking structure for about 30 years, until the city acquired the land and transformed it into one of the nation's most vibrant public commons. Today, the square attracts millions of people each year to its special events, including the annual midsummer Festival of Flowers.

Now serving as "Portland's Living Room," Pioneer Courthouse Square is decorated with colorful swashes and greenery.

Crater Lake National Park

The intense blue of Crater Lake is striking. The vivid color is due in part to the depth of this freshwater lake. At its deepest, the lake's floor plunges 1,932 feet below the surface, making it the deepest lake in the United States.

The lake was created centuries ago when rain and snowmelt filled a caldera, a huge bowl that was the remnant of a volcano. During some years, the lake is replenished by wintertime snowfalls of 50 feet or more. Because no water flows through the lake, its water remains pure and tranquil.

Scientists have discovered evidence of hydrothermal vents near Crater Lake's floor, which may play an important role in the lake's ecology. Green algae grows at a record depth of 725 feet below the surface, indicating that sunlight may penetrate deeper into Crater Lake than any other body of water in the world.

In the lake, the remarkable Phantom Ship is an island created by cooled lava, with 160-foot-high ridges and peaks that resemble a ship. Wizard Island is a volcanic cone that rises 700 feet above the impossibly blue surface.

The vivid blue, perfectly still surface of Crater Lake hides the deepest lake in the United States, which bottoms out nearly 2,000 feet below.

Mount Hood

Picture-perfect Mount Hood is a visual reminder to Portland's city dwellers that the great outdoors is just a short drive away—47 miles east, to be exact. At 11,239 feet above sea level, the peak is the fourth highest in the Cascade Range.

Like all of its Cascade brethren, Mount Hood is a volcano, and an active one at that. It erupted twice in the mid-1800s and has had at least four eruptive periods in the last 15,000 years. The volcanic cone atop the mountain is dominated by snow and ice, with glaciers and snowfields shrouding it year-round.

Mount Hood is a recreational paradise, with popular ski resorts, hiking routes, and backcountry trails. The historic Timberline Lodge is perched at 6,000 feet above sea level and fills to capacity during ski season—which sometimes lasts all year long.

Oregon's Mount Hood is one of the few mountains where skiers can hit the slopes in the middle of summer.

Newberry National Volcanic Monument

In the heart of central Oregon's Deschutes National Forest, Newberry National Volcanic Monument sits atop an active geothermal hotspot. The crux of this hotspot is Newberry Volcano, one of the most massive volcanoes in the United States. Newberry's last eruption, about 1,300 years ago, created a devastatingly beautiful caldera. Located at the summit of the volcano nearly 8,000 feet above sea level, the nearly 20-square-mile Newberry Caldera has two idyllic alpine lakes, one of which drains into a magnificent waterfall.

The volcano's hardened lava flanks are dotted by hundreds of cinder cones and fissure vents. One especially massive cinder cone, Lava Butte, rises 500 feet above its surroundings and was the source of the lava that flowed over this entire area 7,000 years ago. Today, the once-red-hot landscape can be explored via the Trail of the Molten Land.

The striking boundary between spared forest and volcanic devastation in Newberry National Monument is unmistakable.

Multnomah Falls

Ancient Multnomah Falls is a sight to behold. Cascading from its origin on Larch Mountain, it highlights the picturesque Columbia River Gorge in central Oregon. At 620 feet, some claim it's the second-tallest year-round waterfall in the nation. The falls are fed by an underground spring that provides a continuous flow of crystal-clear water that's enhanced by seasonal snowmelt and spring rainstorms. On rare occasions, unusually frosty weather rolls into the gorge and transforms Multnomah Falls into a massive icicle, and the flow of water slows to a slight trickle.

Many visitors take the foot trail up to Benson Bridge (built in 1914 under the direction of Simon Benson). Some believe it's the best spot to view the falls: Look up to see the thin ribbon of the upper falls, or peer down to see the powerful lower cascade as it empties into the Columbia River. From the bridge, a mile-long trail leads to Larch Mountain Lookout at the top of the upper falls, providing a commanding view of the Columbia River Gorge.

Beyond the scenic highway that leads to Multnomah Falls, the gorge is full of beautiful overlooks, excellent hiking trails, and pristine wilderness areas. There are numerous waterfalls beyond Multnomah; the trail to its mouth connects to a network that provides views of eight others nearby.

At 620 feet tall, Multnomah Falls is one of the scenic highlights of the Columbia River Gorge in Oregon's heartland.

Astoria–Megler Bridge

Critics call it "The Bridge to Nowhere," and the Astoria–Megler Bridge in northwestern Oregon often appears as just that: a bridge snaking into a soggy fogbank, with miles of water on all sides. It spans four miles across the mouth of the Columbia near where it empties into the Pacific Ocean.

The bridge connects Astoria, Oregon, to Point Ellice, Washington. Constructed in 1966, it replaced the congested ferry system that had previously linked the communities. Despite the "Bridge to Nowhere" nickname, the Astoria–Megler Bridge has been a success. It carried a quarter-million vehicles in its first full year and was the last link in US Highway 101 connecting Mexico to Canada.

The Astoria–Megler Bridge is the world's longest continuous truss bridge. It was built to withstand some of the most treacherous conditions on the Pacific Coast. The concrete piers that support the bridge can survive wind gusts up to 150 miles per hour and raging floodwaters that can uproot trees and reach a velocity of nine miles per hour.

The Astoria–Megler Bridge spans the four-mile mouth of the Columbia River.

Seattle Space Needle

Seattle's Space Needle is the most popular tourist attraction in the city, receiving more than a million visitors each year. Originally built for the 1962 World's Fair and still the defining feature on this Emerald City's skyline, the 605-foot Space Needle was the tallest building west of the Mississippi when it was completed in late 1961.

The futuristic blueprints for the Space Needle evolved from artist Edward E. Carlson's visionary doodle on a placemat. Collaboration with architect John Graham resulted in a prototype space age design that looks a bit like a flying saucer balanced on three giant supports.

But appearances can be deceiving—the Space Needle isn't going anywhere. Anchored to its foundation by dozens of 30-foot bolts, the structure was built to withstand winds of up to 200 miles per hour. Wind does cause the needle to sway, but the top house has only closed once—for an hour and a half in 1993 due to 90-mile-per-hour winds.

The elevators travel at about ten miles per hour, making the trip from the ground to the observation deck in 41 seconds. Once you're at the top, take in the unbeatable views of Seattle and Puget Sound, then partake in a drink at the bar or a meal in the world's second-oldest revolving restaurant.

Seattle's most recognizable structure is the futuristic Seattle Space Needle. It was the premier attraction at the 1962 World's Fair, whose theme was Century 21.

Olympic National Park

Olympic National Park, in northwestern Washington, is home to one of the most lush, impenetrable rainforests on the planet. Climate conditions are perfect for the forest to thrive. Moisture is plentiful and the temperature mild, thanks to the Pacific Ocean. Some areas in the park get up to 167 inches of rain a year—more than any other spot in the continental United States. The rain supports a land-

scape covered by moss, lichen, and fern, giving the forest a vibrant green glow.

But the beauty of Olympic National Park doesn't end with the rainforest. It is one of the most diverse national parks in the United States. The untouched Pacific coastline is

ruggedly beautiful, and the majestic Olympic Mountains rise from the heart of the peninsula. While the western side of the park is deluged by rain, the eastern side is just the opposite—it's one of the most parched spots on the West Coast north of Los Angeles.

Remarkably diverse, Olympic National Park is home to isolated beaches (below) *and dense rainforests* (right).

Mount Rainier National Park

The world of snow and ice atop Mount Rainier, 14,410 feet above sea level, never thaws. At times, the annual snowfall exceeds 90 feet on the mountain's slopes.

But below Mount Rainier's frosty covering, conditions are the polar opposite: Inside, the mountain is an active volcano. Mount Rainier is the tallest mountain in the volcanic Cascade Range. This range also includes Mount St. Helens, which last erupted in 1980 but has shown signs of activity since 2004, and Lassen Peak in California, which blew its top numerous times between 1914 and 1921.

Mount Rainier last erupted in the mid-19th century, leaving a small crater near the peak. While the mountain has been quiet for more

Exceeding 14,000 feet, Mount Rainier is a majestic peak with an icy coat and fiery interior.

than a century, many scientists believe Mount Rainier is due for an eruption any day now—give or take a few thousand years. Mudflows from past eruptions snaked right through what is now downtown Seattle.

Mount Rainier is about one million years old, which is much younger than the mountains over which it towers. (The surrounding mountains, with peaks about 6,000 feet above sea level, are nearly 12 million years old.) Its abrupt growth is a result of its volcanic activity. In its infancy, Rainier was just a volcanic vent atop a slab of solidified lava; thousands of eruptions created the immense mountain.

The frigid climate at Rainier's peak fuels a number of glaciers. In winter, snow and ice accumulate, and the summer warmth then melts some of the ice. The glaciers currently cover 36 square miles on Mount Rainier, amounting to about a cubic mile of ice and snow. It has more glacier cover than any other mountain in the continental United States.

Like the magma below the surface, Mount Rainier's glaciers are a dynamic phenomenon. During the last ice age, about 20,000 years ago, glaciers covered most of the park, whereas today that figure is about 10 percent.

More recently, until about 1850, many of the glaciers on Mount Rainier experienced gains in mass during a 500-year period known as the Little Ice Age. During the Little Ice Age, Rainier's Nisqually Glacier advanced 150 feet, and other glaciers grew, merged, and began to retake land lost in warmer years.

Between the apex of the Little Ice Age and 1950, Mount Rainier's glaciers lost about 25 percent of their length, with melting accelerating significantly after 1920. Then, from 1950 through the early 1980s, most of the gla-ciers grew again, thanks to a mid-century cold spell and heavy snowfall. In the early 1980s, however, the climate shifted, and the glaciers receded once again.

All of this water feeds the vibrant wildflowers. Come summertime, Rainier's subalpine meadows explode with color as lupines, monkeyflowers, asters, and myriad other species bloom. The kaleidoscope of multihued flora is a startling contrast to the stark blue and white of the looming peak.

About 70 miles away from Seattle, Mount Rainier is a distant but singular symbol of the world beyond the city. The mountain is either "out," meaning not obscured by clouds, or it isn't. Most days it isn't, but on clear, summer days the perfect majesty of Rainier beckons the entire city to the great outdoors.

Mount Rainier's glaciers melt during the warmer months, fueling a labyrinthine network of rivers and streams that flow down the mountain in every direction.

Mount St. Helens

Washington's Mount St. Helens is perhaps the most famous volcano in the United States. It earned its reputation the morning of May 18, 1980. The mountain shook, and its north face cascaded into a debris avalanche, which created a towering mushroom column of ash that blotted out the sun and drifted into Idaho and beyond. The eruption continued through the evening, lasting about nine hours.

Two years later, President Ronald Reagan signed a bill making Mount St. Helens a National Volcanic Monument, allowing the ecosystem to respond naturally to the eruption. Mount St. Helens National Volcanic

The infamous North American volcano Mount St. Helens showed signs of activity starting in 2004 after a mostly quiet quarter-century.

Monument attracts scientists who use it as a living laboratory as well as hikers and other outdoors buffs.

The volcano is part of the Cascade Range, which also includes Mount Rainier and Lassen Peak. In recent years, Mount St. Helens has shown new signs of activity, with a lava dome growing under the crater left from the 1980 eruption.

Museum of Glass

Tacoma's Museum of Glass is a work of architectural art adorning the waterfront.

The Museum of Glass is Tacoma, Washington's splashy contribution to the contemporary art world. Its wide array of works in different media have one thing in common: They all incorporate glass. The museum opened in 2002 and has been an architectural landmark along the city's waterfront ever since.

Inside the museum, visitors can browse permanent and temporary exhibitions of all kinds of contemporary glass art. The museum's Visiting Artist Collection is permanent, featuring works created on-site in the Hot Shop Amphitheater. The Hot Shop has hot and cold glass studios and seating for 138 visitors.

The Chihuly Bridge of Glass connects the museum to downtown Tacoma. The 500-foot steel-and-glass pedestrian bridge is adorned with colorful glass spires. It serves as not only a walkway but as a display providing a preview of the stunning glass art masterworks in the museum.

Pike Place Market

Seattle's Pike Place Market is legendary. The nine-acre spot in downtown Seattle has served as a prime place of commerce since the early 20th century.

Pike Place Market came about because of a 1,000 percent spike in the price of onions in 1906 and 1907. Seattle City Councilman Thomas Revelle offered a solution: a public street market that would cut out greedy inter-mediaries and allow citizens to buy their pro-duce directly from farmers. The next summer, Pike Place Market opened to the public at the corner of Pike Street and First Avenue. Thou-sands of customers crowded the corner: They cleared out the eight attending farmers in a matter of a few hours.

From that early success, the market snow-balled into its modern incarnation: the fore-

The goods at the bustling Pike Place Fish Market are fresh from the water.

most farmer's market in the United States. It now has space for 120 farmers and even more craftspeople, as well as 200 other year-round businesses. There are also street performers and the occasional flying salmon—launched by the boisterous staff of Pike Place Fish.

Glacier Bay National Park and Preserve

Glacier Bay is Alaska's southernmost national park. It is also a living laboratory where scientists study glacial recession. The ice in and around Glacier Bay is melting at a remarkable pace; in fact, the phenomenon is the fastest glacial retreat on record.

When Captain George Vancouver first charted these waters in 1794, what is now the bay was little more than an indention in a vast sheet of ice that extended for hundreds of miles. Over the next 200 years, the glaciers receded more than 60 miles, revealing the islands and shorelines visible today and creating a masterpiece of rock, ice, and water.

Today, 16 massive glaciers and majestic mountains, some of which have peaks 15,000 feet above sea level, ring Glacier Bay. The bay is also a critical wildlife habitat, sustaining humpback whales, orcas, porpoises, seals, and sea otters in its waters and moose, black bears, brown bears, wolves, and deer on the surrounding shore.

Ringed by massive cliffs of cracked rock and ice, Glacier Bay is home to 16 glaciers that are retreating at a rate faster than any other glaciers on record.

Denali National Park and Preserve

Denali means "The High One" in the native Athabascan tongue. It's an apt moniker, considering that the 20,320-foot-tall mountain—also known as Mount McKinley—is North America's highest peak. It's also one of the most striking mountains in the world—when it's visible from the surrounding subarctic plateau. Due to clouds, visitors are generally more likely to see a grizzly bear on the plateau than they are to see the top of the mountain. The clouds cooperate about half the time in summer, and when they do, Denali is an awe-inspiring sight. The mountain's sheer bulk, not to mention the precipitous rise of its eternally frosted summit, is overwhelming. At 18,000 feet from base to summit, Denali is home to some of the longest mountainsides in the world.

Because the park is so far north—about 240 miles north of Anchorage—its mountains are not forested like the Rockies and the Sierra Nevada. The timberline falls between 2,000 and 3,000 feet at Denali's northern latitude. Below the rugged high country are tundra-

The staggering beauty of Denali on a clear day is a rarity: Clouds usualy obscure its peak, 20,320 feet above sea level.

> ## Quick Fact
>
> ### A Sweet Mountaintop Picnic
> The first successful expedition up Denali's 19,470-foot North Peak was accomplished by a group of local residents in 1910. Amazingly, they enjoyed hot chocolate and donuts at the summit.

Denali National Park is not just the centerpiece peak—it also includes the surrounding subarctic plateau, an area larger than some states.

covered lowlands. Immense glaciers connect the two, creeping down Denali and the neighboring peaks.

The park that encompasses Denali and the adjacent mountains of the Alaska Range is a vast, pristine wilderness larger than Massachusetts. Possibly more of a lure than the actual mountain, wild animals attract many of the park's visitors. Denali has earned the nickname "The Subarctic Serengeti" for its thriving wildlife population. Denali's "big five" mammals are grizzly bears, gray wolves, caribou, Dall's sheep, and moose. Peregrine falcons, golden eagles, and other birds soar above; but there are no reptiles in the park, and only one amphibian, the wood frog.

More than 300,000 people visit Denali each year, making it Alaska's most popular park. Compared to other national parks in the state such as Katmai, Kobuk Valley, and Lake Clark, it is more civilized and more easily accessible. The Anchorage–Fairbanks Highway runs right up to the park's eastern border, and the Alaska Railroad makes regular stops at Denali station.

Denali National Park is free of traffic problems; there's just one 90-mile gravel road in its boundaries, and only park buses are allowed to drive to its interior endpoint at Wonder Lake. The absence of cars allows the wild animals to behave more naturally. And, unlike their brethren in Yellowstone and Glacier National Parks, Denali's grizzlies aren't conditioned by the constant flow of traffic.

Visitors naturally tend to focus their wildlife watching near this one road. En route to Wonder Lake, it crosses five river valleys and four mountain passes—in other words, plenty of great habitat for the aforementioned "big five." More ambitious park-goers get off the bus to hike and backpack through the rugged terrain. The primary route into these mountains is Muldrow Glacier, which is literally a river of ice fed by several other glaciers.

Saxman Native Totem Park

This is the world's largest totem park, consisting of two dozen ornate totem poles in Saxman, near Ketchikan in southeast Alaska. Most of the poles are not dated and were reclaimed from abandoned Tlingit villages in the 1930s by the Civilian Conservation Corps and the United States Forest Service. The poles were relocated to Saxman from villages on Cape Fox and Tongass, Cat, and Pennock islands.

Each totem pole at Saxman Native Totem Park is unique. The colorful carvings share the stories of their makers and the stories of the villages where they once stood.

Among the fascinating totems in the park are the "Sea-Bear Pole," which has a bear-figure base capped by the long fin of a killer whale; a memorial pole to a man who died while fishing for octopus, which has an eagle at its top and a rock oyster at its bottom; and a totem that relates to the Tlingit legend "The Princess and the Frog Clan People." Master carvers create new poles for museums, corporations, and private collectors on-site using traditional techniques.

This totem is one of more than 20 ornately carved and painted poles on display at Saxman Native Totem Park.

Quick Fact

The Low Man on the Totem Pole

While the expression "the low man on the totem pole" has been interpreted as the least important person, it's actually incorrect. On true totems, the lowest figure (which could be a man, woman, animal, or supernatural being) was actually the *most* important.

Totems were carved to help remember and share stories. Often a chief carver and several apprentices would together carve one totem. The chief would personally carve the lower ten feet of the pole, so that the part that was eye level with viewers was the most intricate. Less experienced apprentices carved the top portion, where the story thinned out.

Iditarod

"The Last Great Race on Earth," the Iditarod is the equivalent of the Super Bowl, World Series, and Kentucky Derby wrapped into one for the world of dogsledding.

Since 1973, mushers have led teams of 12 to 16 sled dogs from Anchorage to Nome beginning the first Saturday of March. They usually cross the finish line a little more than a week later—but sometimes the race takes nearly a month. On the way to Nome, par-

ticipants cross two mountain ranges on alternating routes that follow the Yukon River and then cross the frozen Norton Sound. The distance covered is more than 1,000 miles, through some of North America's most spectacular terrain.

The race grew out of Alaska's rich history: In the 19th century, dogsled teams brought mail and supplies to the interior mining camps and took gold out to Anchorage. After a pair

Starting in Anchorage and ending in Nome, the Iditarod is among the most grueling competitions for both dogs and humans.

of 25-mile commemorative races in the 1960s, the first full-fledged Iditarod—a native word for "clear water" or "distant place"— took place in 1973. Nearly 100 teams typically enter the modern race, making for more than 1,200 dogs.

Mauna Loa

Part of Hawaiian Volcanoes National Park, Mauna Loa (meaning "Long Mountain") rises 13,677 feet above the blue surface of the Pacific Ocean. It is second in height (in Hawaii) only to Mauna Kea, a quieter volcano. While many mountain peaks rise higher than Mauna Loa, its actual size is nothing short of astonishing. Measured from its base, which is 18,000 feet underwater, Mauna Loa exceeds even Mount Everest in height—by a full 2,000 feet. And the sea floor, compressed by the sheer bulk of the mountain, has sunk nearly another 30,000 feet. This makes Mauna Loa the world's most massive single mountain, with a bulk more than 100 times that of Washington's Mount Rainier.

Atop the summit of Mauna Loa, a caldera called Mokuaweoweo features a number of craters that have previously erupted. The caldera floor is covered with lava contorted into

Predictable eruptions of Mauna Loa draw crowds to view the impressive fireworks display.

otherworldly formations, daunting pits, and towering cinder cones. Current-day eruptions within the crater of the volcano are relatively harmless. Volcanologists have been able to reliably predict activity. Because of this, an impending eruption typically draws thousands of people to the crater's rim.

Haleakala National Park

As legend has it, a long time ago the god Maui captured the sun in a great mountain's summit basin on a Hawaiian island. The mountain came to be known as Haleakala, Hawaiian for "House of the Sun."

Haleakala is actually an enormous volcano that—while dormant since 1790—is a striking reminder of the power seething below the Earth's surface. Impressive cinder cones and lava sculptures on the upper slopes of Haleakala are lasting remnants of furious, tumultuous moments in its past.

The massive crater on Haleakala is not, however, a child of all this volcanism. A climactic shift led to massive rainfall here long ago, and the cascading water eroded the moun-

While Haleakala is a dormant volcano, the otherworldly valley at its peak was shaped by a flood of water, not lava.

tainsides into valleys. The crater was created when two valleys became one as the floodwaters wore away the ridge between them.

At the base of Haleakala, the lush, green Kipahulu Valley unravels to the coast. This tropical ecosystem is a distant memory from the volcano's 10,000-foot summit: Guava trees and ferns below give way to yellow brush known as mamane and the silversword plant, unique to the volcano.

Hanakapi'ai Falls

Named for a Hawaiian princess, Hanakapi'ai Falls on the northwestern side of the island of Kauai is the picture of tropical paradise. The beautiful, 300-foot ribbon of water delicately cascades down a rugged volcanic wall, tumbling into an idyllic pool. There are many waterfalls and pools on Kauai, but this is perhaps the most sublime; perfect for swimming, and set amidst a thick rain forest that's teeming with life.

The falls are a popular destination for experienced hikers. The Kalalua Trail, which leads to the falls, begins at Ke'e Beach. This strenuous hike is about four miles long. Be prepared to spend a full day hiking to the falls and back, and be sure to wear sturdy hiking boots and to bring water, food, insect repellent, and sunscreen.

From Ke'e Beach, follow the trail upslope to the Hanakapi'ai Valley, a lush cradle of greenery dotted with a vibrant array of wildflowers. From there the trail continues down to the secluded Hanakapi'ai Beach and the start of the final two-mile leg to Hanakapi'ai Falls. The first leg of the trail from Ke'e Beach is a necessity—the only other ways to get to Hanakapi'ai Falls involve parachutes or boats. But once you reach the falls, you'll be rewarded with breathtaking views and a relaxing swim in its tranquil pools.

A perfect tropical paradise, Hanakapi'ai Falls is a popular day destination for swimmers and hikers on the Hawaiian island of Kauai.

USS *Arizona* Memorial

On the morning of December 7, 1941, the quiet of Honolulu's Pearl Harbor was shattered by the sounds of gunfire and bombs exploding. The surprise air attack by the Imperial Japanese Navy left the United States' Pacific Fleet

The solemn memorial spans the middle of the sunken USS Arizona, *commemorating the lives lost when the ship sank on December 7, 1941.*

in tatters and claimed the lives 2,390 Americans. Of those victims, 1,177 died on the USS *Arizona*, the battleship that sank to the harbor floor less than nine minutes after it was hit by an armor-piercing bomb.

Twenty years later, the memorial now spanning the middle of the USS *Arizona* was finished. It was dedicated in 1962 to honor those killed during the attack. The memorial

is divided into three areas: the first is the entry and assembly rooms, the central section is for ceremonies, and then there's a shrine with the names of all 1,177 victims engraved on the walls. The memorial can be accessed only by boat. Its location in the heart of the harbor provides a serene setting to honor those who died there during the attack that spurred the United States' entry into World War II.

Chapter Eight

Mexico and Canada

The sun-soaked mesas and ancient ruins of Mexico and the snowcapped mountains, alpine valleys, and pristine lakes of Canada provide stunning playgrounds for North American travelers. In Mexico, take in the colorful, elaborate homes, buildings, and churches of Guadalajara's Spanish colonial-influenced architecture. Explore the sprawling sun-seared Copper Canyon. Or cheer on the matadors of Mexico City's Plaza de Toros Monumental, one of the world's largest bullfighting rings. In Canada, the influence of the French colonial period is still prevalent on the cliffs of Old Québec City and in the forts of Old Montreal. Enjoy the serenity of turquoise Lake Louise. Or relive the Old West with the rodeo cowboys at the Calgary Exhibition & Stampede. Sites across these countries are vivid, evocative, and stunning.

On the border of New York and Canada, water cascades over Niagara Falls, spraying the air with a delicate mist.

Los Cabos

The southernmost tip of Mexico's 1,000-mile-long Baja Peninsula is called *finisterra*, which translates into "the end of the Earth." The striking finality of the rocky desert isthmus, set against a vast, open backdrop of saltwater and sun, is punctuated by El Arco, "The Arch." Towering 200 feet above the azure waters, the

El Arco juts into the calm turquoise waters of the Pacific, drawing tourists to finisterra, *Latin for "the end of the Earth."*

magnificent granite arch is the most spectacular rock formation on the west coast of Mexico. This picturesque landmark is commonly used on postcards to represent Los Cabos.

El Arco is an enduring image to those going out to sea, as well as those coming in. Visitors can boat past it, swim and snorkel under it, or even walk under it at low tide. Climbing the rock, however, is against the law.

Surrounding the striking arch are the equally striking sands of La Playa del Amor,

or "Lover's Beach," which is accessed primarily by water taxis. (Some tour boats even sail right through El Arco.) The Sea of Cortez lies along the east side of the beach, which features an idyllic cove that is popular for snorkeling and swimming. The sea is also home to a diverse ecosystem of aquatic plants, birds, and even sea lions. The Pacific side of the peninsula beach, nicknamed "Divorce Beach" by locals, is considerably rougher, pummeled by the perpetual surf of the ocean.

dorado—became legendary, as did the tequila-fueled nightlife.

In 1973, the Transpeninsula Highway linking Tijuana and Los Cabos was completed, paving the way for further development along the Baja Peninsula, especially at its tropical tip. Luxurious hotels and condos, retirement homes, and golf courses are now common just outside the city limits. November through February is prime tourist season in Los Cabos, so plan accordingly.

(Above) *The balmy, palm-laden paradise of southern Baja is dotted with exclusive resorts, picturesque marinas, and idyllic beaches.*

The nearby resort town of Los Cabos has become a tourist hotspot and is now the seventh most popular tourist destination in Mexico. In the 1940s, entrepreneurs built upscale hotels for the rich and famous. Because there was no highway at that time, celebrities and wealthy tourists came by yacht or private plane, making for one of the most exclusive resort towns in the world. Its sport fishing—and tales of enormous tuna, marlin, and

(Right) *Many starry-eyed couples take water taxis to the romantic sand known as La Playa del Amor, or "Lover's Beach."*

Quick Fact

Some of the first Europeans to see El Arco, also known as the Arch of Poseidon (the Greek god of the sea), were pirates. They often hid their ships behind the arch to ambush merchant ships. Perhaps the most infamous of these pirates was Thomas of Cavendish, the Briton who sacked the supposedly unsinkable Spanish galleon *Santa Anna* off the coast of Cabo San Lucas in 1587.

Cozumel

Cozumel is the island pearl of the Mexican Caribbean. This magnet for sun worshippers and scuba divers lies just 12 miles off the coast of Mexico, not far from the gaudy resort of Cancún. Only about 5 percent of the island is developed.

The island is a world apart, especially for travelers preferring a more relaxed atmosphere than the mainland resorts offer. Cozumel hides countless coves, anonymous beaches,

Cozumel is a trove of natural and historic treasures, including ancient Mayan ruins.

and secret reefs waiting to be explored. Diving, deep-sea fishing, snorkeling, and kayaking are favorite activities. The beaches along the eastern shore are excellent for surfing and swimming, while the land along the west is more developed, and the water is calm for snorkeling or scuba diving.

Chankanaab National Park is among Mexico's oldest marine parks. It features a lagoon, a Mayan cenoté (or well), a pond that links to the ocean through underwater caves, peerless coral reefs, and replicas of Mayan buildings. At the center of the island, you can view real Mayan ruins amidst the jungle and swampy lagoons. Cozumel's San Gervasio is an extensive complex of ruins dating from 100 B.C. to A.D. 1600, when Spanish explorers arrived.

Guadalajara

At an altitude of almost a mile high, Guadalajara is a city of monuments, parks, and historic tree-lined streets. The city has been dubbed the "City of Roses," Mexico's Pearl of the West. The height of Spanish colonial art and architecture is evident throughout the city. Sterling examples include the University of Guadalajara, founded in 1792, and the historic district. At the city's heart is its Centro Histórico, where visitors can get acquainted with local history and colonial architecture. There's also the Catédral Metropolitana de Guadalajara, the city's Metropolitan Cathedral. Begun in 1561 and completed more than a century later, the cathedral is capped by distinctive twin yellow-tiled steeples. Nearby is Plaza Tapatía, Guadalajara's largest plaza, which covers seven square blocks. It's best traveled by foot or *calandria*, traditional horse-drawn touring carriages.

While Guadalajara is not a resort town, there is plenty of golf, tennis, shopping, and restaurants for tourists to enjoy. There's also a zoo, a children's amusement park (Selva Mágica), bullfights at Plaza de Toros Nuevo Progresso, and rodeos at Lienzo Charro de Jalisco. The city is blessed with a mild mountain climate, and its culture and history draw people from all over the world. Guadalajara is also known by some as the birthplace of mariachi music and the Mexican hat dance.

The "City of Roses" is built around Centro Histórico, which features the striking colonial architecture of landmarks such as Catédral Metropolitana de Guadalajara.

Chichén Itzá

Chichén Itzá is the largest and most-restored archeological site in Mexico. It lies 75 miles from Mérida, Mexico, which was probably the most important Mayan city in its time. The ancient relics are anything but ordinary, and many visitors take day-long bus tours to see the ancient cities that make up Chichén Itzá.

The cenotés, or wells, are a highlight of the tour. Some of these wells still yield skeletal remains. Visitors today are told lurid tales of the sacrifices of virgins, children, and the elderly tossed down the wells. These tales are true, though scholars say human sacrifices

probably numbered far fewer than some people believe.

Chichén Itzá's four-plus square miles consist of three regions. The Toltecs made the area their capital in the late tenth century A.D. They continued building the stone city until the twelfth century, when it declined and the local residents stopped building great structures.

The central wonder of Chichén Itzá is the Kukulcán Pyramid, called El Castillo del Serpiente Emplumada, which means "The Castle of the Feathered Snake." The astonishing city unfolds at the base of the pyramid. Near the

The amazing Kukulcán Pyramid is the defining feature of Chichén Itzá.

Temple of the Warriors is the Group of the Thousand Columns, a forest of columns that proceeds into the jungle. Then there's the Temple of the Jaguar complex and Caracol, known as the Mayan Observatory.

About one football field's distance from the Kukulcán Pyramid is the Great Ballcourt of Chichén Itzá. It is 545 feet long and 225 feet wide, open to the sky, and a whisper at one end can be heard clearly at the other. This is

where the Mayans played their sacred game of *pok ta pok*, in which teams tried to put a natural rubber ball through a stone hoop without the use of their hands. The losing captain was sacrificed, either by decapitation or removing the heart.

Before you go, take into consideration that Mayan prophecy holds that on December 22, 2012, Kukulcán will rise from the ground beneath the Great Ballcourt and destroy the world. So you might want to plan around that.

Reclining amid a forest of columns, this statue of the Toltec god Chaac-Mool atop the Temple of the Warrior was the altar on which ritual sacrifices were placed.

Sierra Tarahumara

The Sierra Tarahumara is an immense area of linked canyons and forested plateaus. The extensive canyon system is the largest in North America and is nearly four times the size of the Grand Canyon. There are six major canyons that wind through the region. Of these, four are about as deep as the Grand Canyon: Urique Canyon is 6,136 feet deep, Sinforosa and Batopilas canyons are each more than 5,900 feet deep, and Copper Canyon is almost 5,800 feet deep.

The canyons are known to be a hiker's paradise and paradox. Most trails are not marked or mapped, and novice hikers are advised to stay near the outskirts or hire local guides. The climate is temperate along the mile-high canyon rims, with cold winters and mild summers. Summer is the rainy season, and wildflowers flourish from the end of September through October. Rivers wind along the bottom of the canyons: Many are impassable due to great boulders and massive waterfalls. The climate is tropical along the bottoms of the canyons, providing a habitat for many threatened animal species, including jaguarundis, jaguars, and ocelots.

The area is home to Mexico's Tarahumara Indians. They call themselves Rarámuri, which translates to "the Runners," and are known for their supreme endurance when chasing game and traveling throughout the canyons. The Tarahumara have maintained many tribal customs and traditions living in remote parts of the Sierra Tarahumara.

"Overwhelming. That is perhaps the word that best describes the impact on one's senses, on seeing the Sierra Tarahumara for the first time..."

—*Bernard L. Fontana*, Tarahumara: Where Night Is the Day of the Moon

The Copper Canyon of the Sierra Tarahumara is one of four Grand Canyon–size crevasses in the area, bottoming out almost 5,800 feet below the rims.

Plaza de Toros Monumental and Estadio Azteca

Mexico City is as sports-crazed as many cities in the United States. However, the sports that have endured here are bullfighting and *fútbol* (or soccer, if you prefer).

Bullfighting is one of the few remaining bloodsports, and fights in Mexico City combine ritual and pageantry. The height of the bullfighting season is November through March. Brave matadors duel 1,800-pound bulls in Plaza de Toros Monumental. This is possibly the largest bullring in the world (some argue that the bullring in Madrid is larger), with seating for 41,262 and a capacity of 45,000, including standing room. The stadium opened in 1946 and was acclaimed from the start for its monumental architecture, spectator comfort, and exhibitions of bullfighting talent.

Mexico City's other world-class stadium is the three-tiered, 144,600-seat Estadio Azteca. It is the only stadium to host two World Cup finals (1970 and 1986), and it has also hosted the Olympic games (1968). The stadium is positioned so that as the sun passes overhead from east to west, it isn't a disadvantage for either team. The name of the stadium is an homage to the ancient Aztecs, who once inhabited the land where Mexico City now stands.

Mexico City's two landmark stadiums, Estadio Azteca (top) *and Plaza de Toros Monumental* (bottom), *can together seat nearly 200,000 people.*

Quick Fact

Corrida de Toros

An afternoon at the Plaza de Toros Monumental in Mexico City may be shocking for some. The ritual and drama of a *corrida de toros*, or bullfight, have long been a tradition in Mexican culture.

At the fight, three matadors will each fight two bulls. When each bull is released, the bullfighter's assistant, or *torero*, will take a few passes of the bull with his cape. Then the *picadores*, or horse riders armed with lances, enter the ring and jab the bull to weaken it. Next, the matador proceeds to dominate the bull through precise movements of his cape. At the opportune moment, the matador kills the bull. The traditional and ritualistic way to do this is by plunging the sword deep into the bull's back. If the move is not executed perfectly, great shame is brought to the matador.

Banff

Banff, Alberta, is about 80 miles from Calgary. Perched at the gateway to the Canadian Rockies, the little town of Banff (population 8,200) is known to some as the hiking, horseback riding, skiing, mineral springs–soaking, snowboarding capital of Canada. At an elevation of 4,537 feet, Banff is the highest town in Canada. The spectacular region rewards visitors with ice walks, snowshoeing, snowmobiling, dogsledding, and sleigh rides in the winter and hiking and rafting in the summer. The pleasing alpine village is crisscrossed with trails (about 1,000 miles in all in the region) and provides opportunities to spot local wildlife and view the stunning peaks of Mount Rundle and Cascade Mountain.

The town marks the entry to Banff National Park, Canada's first national park.

Banff, Alberta, is known as a gateway to the majestic Canadian Rockies, where myriad picturesque mountain lakes are nestled in glacial valleys.

Quick Fact

Lake Louise

The stunning and serene waters of Lake Louise are just 35 miles from Banff. Sometimes called the "Diamond in the Wilderness," it was first named Emerald Lake for its turquoise-hued waters. The panorama of the lake and sweeping views of Mount Temple, Mount Whyte, and Mount Niblock are breathtaking.

One of the gems of Lake Louise is the Fairmont Château Lake Louise, a spectacular five-star resort hotel nestled in this unique wilderness. The neon nightlife and celebrity glitz common at some mountain resorts are absent from the nearby village of Lake Louise, where the scenery, wildlife, and skiing take center stage.

The remarkably reflective surface of Lake Louise offers a second chance to see the beautiful mountain scenery, or at least its mirror image.

Mount Forbes is a spectacle here, reaching 11,850 feet into the sky. More than four million people visit each year: The mild summers make July and August prime time for tourists. In the northwest corner of Banff is Castle Guard Cave, part of the longest cave system in Canada.

Banff National Park is a UNESCO (United Nations Educational, Scientific, and Cultural Organization) World Heritage site. It is also home to the legendary Fairmont Banff Springs Hotel, which rises like a Gothic fortress out of a landscape of boundless mountain forests. Here you can enjoy fine food, golf, skiing, a wine bar, and a spa.

Vancouver

Vancouver—Canada's third largest city—is the urban cornerstone of British Columbia and the nation's gateway to the Pacific Rim. The city glistens where the mountains seem to vanish into the coastline and then rise again on Bowen and Vancouver islands. From a distance,

Known as one of the most progressive cities on the continent, Vancouver is considered a model city by urban planners around the world.

the city can look like a diamond cluster rising from the Strait of Georgia to the rolling Coast Mountains and the Fraser Valley beyond.

As Canada's west coast counterculture capital, Vancouver is an urban explosion with an environmental-minded style. The metro area has more than two million residents. The city is also known for its urbane thrills, its acceptance of alternative lifestyles, and a vigorous club scene.

Great green forests surrounding Vancouver lead to getaways up the fjords and rivers to adventures in Pemberton, up the Chilliwack River, in Cypress Provincial Park, and in the Skagit Valley Recreation Area. There are three ski resorts within a half-hour drive of downtown—Mount Seymour, Grouse Mountain, and Cypress Mountain. And the Capilano River, Seymour River, and Lynn Creek provide white-water thrills come spring meltdown.

Toronto

Toronto is Canada's largest city, with about five million people in its metropolitan area. The name Toronto actually comes from the Huron Indian word for "meeting place," and it rings true in this multicultural city. It is one of the most diverse cities in North America, with people from more than 100 cultures speaking more than 100 languages and dialects. After the official languages of French and English, the five most-spoken languages are Chinese, Italian, Portuguese, Punjabi, and Tamil. The ethnic neighborhoods of Greektown, Little Italy, and Chinatown are a special treat.

A must-see is the CN Tower; at 1,815 feet, it's the second-tallest freestanding structure above water in the world. The St. Lawrence Market in historic Old Town Toronto is one of the world's top 25 food markets. Tourists can explore Eaton Centre, a premier shopping destination with more than 320 shops, restaurants, and cinemas. And there's the Toronto Zoo, which at 710 acres is one of the largest in the world. More than 5,000 animals representing 450-plus species inhabit the zoo, and six miles of trails wind among the exhibits.

(Right) *Toronto's CN Tower is the second-tallest free-standing structure in the world.* (Inset) *Casa Loma is a lavish, 98-room mansion built for Sir Henry Pellatt in the 1910s.*

Yukon

The population of the Yukon Territory is 30,000, give or take a few hardy souls. More than 23,000 of those people live in the capital city of Whitehorse, which was known as a prospector's paradise during the Klondike gold rush of the late 19th century. While once the source for legends and lore, Whitehorse is now home to the SS *Klondike*, the preserved sternwheeler boat that once ferried goods and people along the Yukon River.

Dawson City is a town of just 2,000 people, but nearly 60,000 visitors come each year to see the literary shrines, including the cabins of Jack London and Robert Service. London wrote more than 50 books based on his experiences in the Yukon, Alaska, California, and at sea. Service was the author of volumes of verse, such as *The Spell of the Yukon*. He wrote of the northern land where he found, "The snows that are older than history/The woods where the weird shadows slant/The stillness, the moonlight, the mystery."

The fabled high mountains, vast ice fields, and lush valleys of Kluane National Park and Reserve in southwest Yukon are astounding. The park has one of the most extensive non-polar ice fields in the world. It's also home to Canada's highest summit, Mount Logan, at 19,545 feet. Ivvavik National Park in the northwestern part of the territory is known for its migratory herds of porcupine caribou. The mountains there were never covered by glaciers, and V-shaped valleys and isolated conical hills are part of the frigid landscape.

The harsh climate has taken its toll on the Yukon; weathered remnants of the Klondike gold rush of the late 1800s dot the countryside.

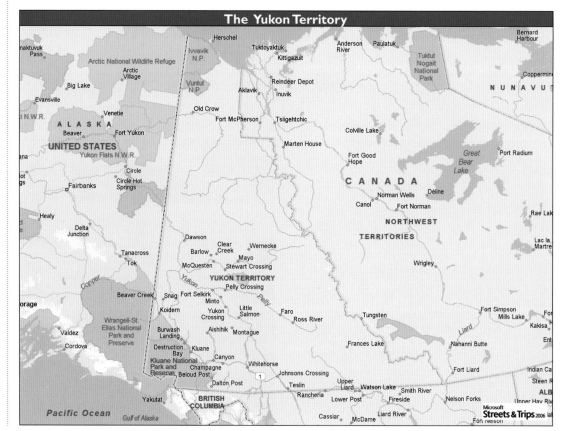

Montreal

Montreal is one of the largest French-speaking metropolises in the world. Following Québec's laws, all signs are posted in French, but services are available in English in the parts of the city most visited by tourists.

Many visitors start in Old Montreal, the Vieux-Port, which contains a collection of historic buildings that rival most cities in North America. The cobblestone streets lead to the great square, Place Jacques-Cartier. A promenade along quaint shops and fine restaurants takes you past Montreal City Hall. The Château Ramezay, built in the 1700s for the governor and now a museum, lies along rue Notre-Dame, the oldest street in the city. Nearby, don't miss the Place D'Armes square.

The Notre-Dame Basilica is one of the most stunning buildings in Montreal. The Neogothic-style church was built in 1829. The interior is lavishly beautiful, featuring stained glass windows, an elaborate altarpiece, a Casavant organ, and the largest bell on the continent, le Gros Bourdon.

Visitors seeking outdoor recreation are in luck. Montreal's Mount Royal Park sits on a dormant volcano. (The mountain is the origin for the city's name: Jacques Cartier referred to Mont Royal on his voyage there in 1535. At that time, *réal* was a variation of *royal*, and the contraction yielded Montreal.) At 761 feet, the overlook gives a dazzling view of the city.

The ornate altarpiece is a defining feature of the Notre-Dame Basilica in Montreal.

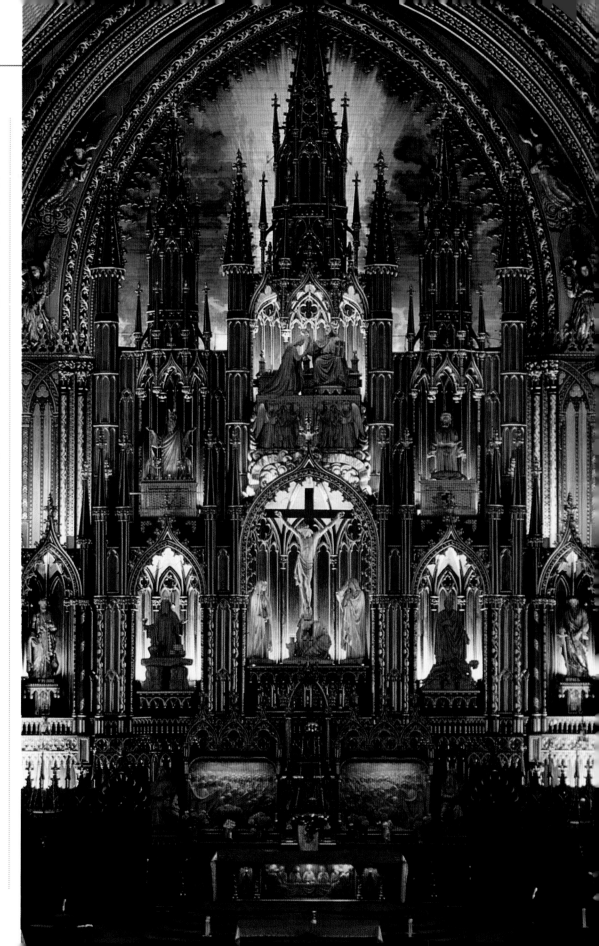

Québec City

Founded by Samuel de Champlain in 1608, Old Québec City is the cradle of French civilization in North America. The land was settled because of its strategic cliffs: The great stone city rises abruptly atop Cap Diamant. Fort Saint-Louis provided further protection.

Now the Old City offers a giant slice of history in a French-Canadian neighborhood replete with restaurants, bistros, bakeries, and bars. In Lower Town, the Place-Royale marketplace remains one of the most visited spots. Upper Town is the hotspot for fine dining and

Le Château Frontenac rises above the Victorian skyline of Upper Town in Québec City.

luxury hotels, most notably Le Château Frontenac. This historic hotel, which opened in 1893, overlooks the St. Lawrence River.

The Calgary Exhibition & Stampede

About 50 miles east of the Canadian Rocky Mountains, where prairie meets foothills, Calgary, Alberta, puts on one of the world's biggest Old West shows. The Calgary Exhibition & Stampede calls itself "The Greatest Outdoor Show on Earth"—and for good reason.

The Calgary Stampede was born back in 1912, when Guy Weadick, a cowboy from Rochester, New York, rode into town with a vision for a Wild West Extravaganza. Weadick talked the "Big Four" well-to-do Calgarians into ponying up $100,000 in all, and Calgary held its first Stampede—an immediate smash success, as it has been ever since.

For ten days each July, the city takes on the atmosphere of the Old West, as residents become cowboys, cowgirls, or lone gunslingers. Townsfolk decorate their homes and businesses in Western style, too. The Calgary Stampede gathers rodeo cowboys and Indians, calf ropers, and beauty queens. It features the Stampede Midway, the Stampede Indian Village, and the daily Grandstand Show, including the traditional Chuckwagon Races and live music acts, such as the famed Young Canadians. Spring sales and auctions (for example, the Calgary Bull Sale) lead up to animal and agricultural events, with contests including the World Championship Blacksmith Competition. More than one million Stampede attendees come to Calgary to soak up the rootin', tootin' action.

The Calgary Exhibition & Stampede sees all sorts of horseplay—even Canadian Mounties get in on the act.

Campobello Island

Campobello Island lies off the rugged northeast coast of Maine at the mouth of the Bay of Fundy. Discovered by French explorers around 1607, the island's main industry today is fishing. Locals harvest lobster, scallops, sea urchins, clams, herring, cod, mackerel, and pen-raised salmon.

The island has also enticed tourists. Beginning in the 1880s, Campobello Island was promoted as a summer resort and visited by many well-to-do families. In 1881, James Roosevelt and a group of New York and Boston businesspeople formed the Campobello Company, bought property on the island, and built luxury hotels. Roosevelt brought his wife, Sara, and infant son Franklin to Campobello in 1883.

Today the 2,800-acre Roosevelt Campobello International Park is administered by a joint U.S./Canadian Commission that welcomes more than 100,000 visitors each year. The Roosevelt summer home and four other historic summer cottages are on display. You can also enjoy walks along quiet trails through dazzling flower gardens, watch the harbor seals bask in the sun near the Mulholland Point Lighthouse, or stroll along the beaches at Herring Cove, Raccoon Beach, or Lower Duck Pond.

Originally a getaway for the Roosevelt family, Campobello Island is now an international park managed in concert by the United States and Canada.

Quick Fact

Sunrise at Campobello

Franklin D. Roosevelt became the 32nd president of the United States, but not before contracting polio at his family's "beloved island" at age 39. His struggles became the subject of an acclaimed play and movie, *Sunrise at Campobello*. In the public mind, the island became the scenic backdrop to an enduring story of personal and political courage.

Niagara Falls

Niagara Falls is the best-known group of waterfalls in North America, and quite possibly the world. Tourists have flocked here for more than a century, taking in the overpowering sights and sounds of water in motion as it courses over ancient rock.

Niagara Falls is where Lake Erie drains into the Niagara River, Lake Ontario, and beyond. The falls were born about 10,000 years ago when a slow-moving glacier dammed the river's route and forced it over the low point in the area, a north-facing cliff.

Niagara Falls actually consists of three splendid waterfalls on the Niagara River: Horseshoe Falls in southeastern Ontario (also called Canadian Falls), American Falls in northwestern New York, and Bridal Veil Falls, also in New York. Horseshoe Falls is the largest of the three, at about 177 feet in height. However, this doesn't make it all that tall of a waterfall—Yosemite Falls is more than 13 times taller. But Horseshoe Falls is notably wide—2,200 feet. In fact, more than six million cubic feet of water pour over these falls

American Falls (pictured) *and Bridal Veil Falls are in the United States, but the largest of Niagara's three waterfalls, Horseshoe Falls, is in Ontario, Canada.*

every minute, making for the most powerful group of waterfalls in North America.

Like all things, Niagara Falls is temporary. The falls have moved several miles southward over the last 200 years due to erosion, and a rockslide in 1954 altered the flow of the American Falls forever.

Resource Directory

Alabama
Vulcan Statue
Vulcan Park Foundation
205-933-1409
www.visitvulcan.com

Alaska
Denali National Park and Preserve
National Park Service
907-683-2294
www.nps.gov/dena

Glacier Bay National Park and Preserve
National Park Service
907-697-2230
www.nps.gov/glba

Iditarod
907-248-6874
www.iditarod.com

Arizona
Canyon de Chelly National Monument
National Park Service
928-674-5500
www.nps.gov/cach

Grand Canyon National Park
National Park Service
928-638-7888
www.nps.gov/grca

Petrified Forest National Park
National Park Service
928-524-6228
www.nps.gov/pefo

Sabino Canyon
Sabino Canyon Tours
520-749-2861
www.sabinocanyon.com

Sedona
Sedona Chamber of Commerce
  Tourism Bureau
800-288-7336
www.visitsedona.com

Taliesin West
The Frank Lloyd Wright Foundation
480-860-2700
www.franklloydwright.org

Arkansas
Blanchard Springs Caverns
USDA Forest Service
888-757-2246
www.fs.fed.us/oonf/ozark/recreation/
  caverns.html

Hot Springs National Park
National Park Service
501-624-2701
www.nps.gov/hosp

Ouachita National Forest
USDA Forest Service
501-321-5202
www.fs.fed.us/oonf/ouachita.htm

California
Alcatraz Island
National Park Service
415-561-4900
www.nps.gov/alcatraz

Chinatown and Chinese New Year
San Francisco Convention &
  Visitors Bureau
415-391-2000
www.onlysf.sfvisitor.org

Death Valley National Park
National Park Service
760-786-3200
www.nps.gov/deva

Golden Gate Bridge
Golden Gate Bridge, Highway, and
  Transportation District
415-921-5858
www.goldengatebridge.org

Hearst Castle
California State Parks
805-927-2020
www.hearstcastle.com

Hollywood
Hollywood Chamber of Commerce
323-469-8311
www.hollywoodchamber.net

La Brea Tar Pits
Page Museum at the La Brea Tar Pits
323-934-7243
www.tarpits.org

Mann's Chinese Theatre
Mann Theatres
818-784-6266
www.manntheatres.com

Monterey Bay Aquarium
831-648-4800
www.mbayaq.org

Napa Valley
The Napa Valley Conference
  & Visitors Bureau
707-226-7459
www.napavalley.org

Point Reyes National Seashore
National Park Service
415-464-5100
www.nps.gov/pore

Redwood National and State Parks
National Park Service
707-464-6101
www.nps.gov/redw

San Diego Zoo
Zoological Society of San Diego
619-231-1515
www.sandiegozoo.org

Tournament of Roses Parade
626-449-4100
www.tournamentofroses.com

Venice Beach Boardwalk
City of Los Angeles Department of
  Recreation and Parks
www.laparks.org/venice/venice.htm

Winchester Mystery House
408-247-2101
www.winchestermysteryhouse.com

Yosemite National Park
National Park Service
209-372-0200
www.nps.gov/yose

Colorado
Great Sand Dunes National Park
  and Preserve
National Park Service
719-378-6399
www.nps.gov/grsa

The Great Stupa of Dharmakaya
Shambhala Mountain Center
888-788-7221
www.shambhalamountain.org

Mesa Verde National Park
National Park Service
970-529-4465
www.nps.gov/meve

Pikes Peak
Pikes Peak Country Attractions Association
800-525-2250
www.pikes-peak.com

Red Rocks Amphitheatre and
  Visitor Center
303-295-4444
www.redrocksonline.com

Red Rocks Park
Colorado Tourism Office
800-265-6723
www.colorado.com

Rocky Mountain National Park
National Park Service
970-586-1206
www.nps.gov/romo

Telluride
Visit Telluride
888-605-2578
www.visittelluride.com

Connecticut
Mystic Seaport
888-973-2767
www.mysticseaport.org

Stonington Lighthouse
The Stonington Historical Society
860-535-1440
www.stoningtonhistory.org

Florida
Cape Canaveral, John F. Kennedy
  Space Center
NASA
321-449-4444
www.kennedyspacecenter.com/visitKSC

Castillo de San Marcos
National Park Service
904-829-6506 ext. 234
www.nps.gov/casa

Everglades National Park
National Park Service
305-242-7700
www.nps.gov/ever

Key West
Monroe County Tourist Development
  Council
www.fla-keys.com

Little Havana
Greater Miami Convention
  & Visitors Bureau
800-933-8448
www.gmcvb.com/visitors/little_havana.asp

Miami's South Beach
Greater Miami Convention
  & Visitors Bureau
800-933-8448
www.gmcvb.com/visitors/neighborhoods
  .asp#Sobe

Ringling Estate
The John and Mable Ringling Museum
  of Art
941-359-5700
www.ringling.org

Georgia
Amicalola Falls State Park and Lodge
Georgia State Parks
www.gastateparks.org/info/amicalola

Cumberland Island National Seashore
National Park Service
912-882-4336 ext. 254
www.nps.gov/cuis

The King Center
404-526-8900
www.thekingcenter.org

Jekyll Island
Jekyll Island Foundation
912-635-3636
www.jekyllisland.com

Martin Luther King, Jr., National
    Historic Site
National Park Service
404-331-5190
www.nps.gov/malu

Stone Mountain Park
Stone Mountain Memorial Association
800-401-2407
www.stonemountainpark.com

Tybee Island
www.tybeeisland.com

World of Coca-Cola
800-676-2653
www.woccatlanta.com

Hawaii
Haleakala National Park
National Park Service
808-572-4400
www.nps.gov/hale

Hanakapi'ai Falls
Hawaii Visitors & Convention Bureau
800-464-2924
www.gohawaii.com

Mauna Loa
Hawaii Visitors & Convention Bureau
800-464-2924
www.gohawaii.com

USS *Arizona* Memorial
National Park Service
808-422-0561
www.nps.gov/usar

Idaho
Craters of the Moon National
    Monument and Preserve
National Park Service
208-527-3257
www.nps.gov/crmo

Hells Canyon National Recreation Area
208-628-3916
www.fs.fed.us/hellscanyon

Illinois
Abraham Lincoln Presidential Library
    and Museum
800-610-2094
www.alplm.org

The Art Institute of Chicago
312-443-3600
www.artic.edu

Blue Chicago
312-642-6261
www.bluechicago.com

Chicago Blues Festival
Mayor's Office of Special Events
312-744-3315
www.cityofchicago.org/specialevents

The Magnificent Mile
The Greater North Michigan Avenue
    Association
312-642-3570
www.themagnificentmile.com

Millennium Park
Chicago Department of Cultural Affairs
312-742-1168
www.millenniumpark.org

Wrigley Field
The Chicago Cubs
773-404-2827
www.cubs.mlb.com

Indiana
The College Football Hall of Fame
800-440-3263
www.collegefootball.org

Indianapolis 500
Indianapolis Motor Speedway
www.indy500.com

Iowa
Amana Colonies
Amana Colonies Convention and Visitors
    Bureau
800-579-2294
www.amanacolonies.com

Iowa's Covered Bridges
Madison County Chamber of Commerce
800-298-6119
www.madisoncounty.com/bridge.html

Iowa State Fair
800-545-3247
www.iowastatefair.org

Kansas
Dodge City
Dodge City Convention and Visitors
    Bureau
800-653-9378
www.visitdodgecity.org

Kentucky
Kentucky Derby
Churchill Downs, Inc.
www.kentuckyderby.com

Mammoth Cave
National Park Service
270-758-2180
www.nps.gov/maca

Louisiana
Baton Rouge
Baton Rouge Area Convention and
    Visitors Bureau
800-527-6843
www.visitbatonrouge.com

Louisiana Old State Capitol
800-488-2968
www.sos.louisiana.gov/museums/osc/osc/
    osc-index.htm

Mardi Gras
http://mardigras.neworleans.com

Maine
Acadia National Park
National Park Service
207-288-3338
www.nps.gov/acad

Boothbay Harbor
The Boothbay Harbor Region Chamber
    of Commerce
207-633-2353
www.boothbayharbor.com

Penobscot Bay
The East Penobscot Bay Association
www.penobscotbay.com

Maryland
Assateague Island National Seashore
National Park Service
410-641-1441 (Maryland district)
757-366-6577 (Virginia district)
www.nps.gov/asis

Baltimore Inner Harbor
Baltimore Area Convention and
    Visitors Association
877-258-4673
www.baltimore.org/baltimore_inner_
    harbor.htm

Chesapeake Bay
The Chesapeake Bay Guide
www.thebayguide.com

National Aquarium, Baltimore
410-576-3800
www.aqua.org

Massachusetts
Boston Harborfest
617-227-1528
www.bostonharborfest.com

Boston Marathon
Boston Athletic Association
617-236-1652
www.bostonmarathon.org

Fenway Park
The Boston Red Sox
www.redsox.mlb.com

Freedom Trail
The Freedom Trail Foundation
617-357-8300
www.thefreedomtrail.org

Harvard Square
Harvard Square Business Association
617-491-3434
www.harvardsquare.com

Plymouth Rock, Pilgrim Memorial
    State Park
Massachusetts Department of
    Conservation and Recreation
508-866-2580
www.mass.gov/dcr/parks/southeast/
    plgm.htm

Walden Pond State Reservation
Massachusetts Department of
    Conservation and Recreation
978-369-3254
www.mass.gov/dcr/parks/northeast/
    wldn.htm

Michigan
Grand Hotel of Mackinac Island
800-334-7263
www.grandhotel.com

Isle Royale National Park
National Park Service
906-482-0984
www.nps.gov/isro

Mackinac Bridge
Mackinac Bridge Authority
www.mackinacbridge.org

Pictured Rocks National Lakeshore
National Park Service
906-387-3700
www.nps.gov/piro

Tulip Time Festival
800-822-2770
www.tuliptime.com

Minnesota
Boundary Waters Canoe Area Wilderness
877-550-6777
www.bwcaw.org

St. Paul Winter Carnival
St. Paul Festival and Heritage Foundation
651-223-4700
www.winter-carnival.com

Sculpture Garden and Walker Art Center
612-375-7600
http://garden.walkerart.org

Voyageurs National Park
National Park Service
218-283-9821
www.nps.gov/voya

Mississippi
Gulf Islands National Seashore
National Park Service
228-875-9057 (Mississippi)
850-934-2600 (Florida)
www.nps.gov/guis

Mississippi Delta Blues and
   Heritage Festival
Mississippi Action for Community
   Education, Inc.
888-812-5837
www.deltablues.org

Natchez Trace Parkway
National Park Service
800-305-7417
www.nps.gov/natr

Missouri
Branson Strip
Branson/Lakes Area Chamber
   of Commerce
www.bransonchamber.com

St. Louis Gateway Arch
The Gateway Arch Riverfront
877-982-1410
www.stlouisarch.com

St. Louis Gateway Arch, Jefferson National
   Expansion Memorial Park
National Park Service
314-655-1700
www.nps.gov/jeff

Montana
Flathead Lake
Montana Department of Commerce
406-841-2870
www.travelmontana.state.mt.us

Glacier National Park
National Park Service
406-888-7800
www.nps.gov/glac

Little Bighorn Battlefield National
   Monument
National Park Service
406-638-3204
www.nps.gov/libi

Makoshika Dinosaur Museum
406-377-1637
www.makoshika.com

Museum of the Rockies
Montana State University
406-994-3466
www.museumoftherockies.org

Nebraska
Carhenge
www.carhenge.com

Chimney Rock National Historic Site
National Park Service
308-586-2581
www.nps.gov/chro

Scotts Bluff National Monument
National Park Service
308-436-4340
www.nps.gov/scbl

Nevada
Great Basin National Park
National Park Service
775-234-7331
www.nps.gov/grba

Hoover Dam
U.S. Bureau of Reclamation
866-730-9097
www.usbr.gov/lc/hooverdam

Las Vegas Strip
Las Vegas Convention and Visitors
   Authority
877-847-4858
www.visitlasvegas.com

New Hampshire
Lake Winnipesaukee
www.winnipesaukee.com

White Mountain National Forest
USDA Forest Service
603-466-2713
www.fs.fed.us/r9/forests/white_mountain

New Jersey
Atlantic City Boardwalk
The Atlantic City Convention and
   Visitors Authority
888-228-4748
www.atlanticcitynj.com

Cape May
888-898-2997
www.capemay.com

Pine Barrens, Pinelands National Reserve
National Park Service
609-894-7300
www.nps.gov/pine

New Mexico
Carlsbad Caverns
Carlsbad Chamber of Commerce
760-931-8400
www.carlsbad.org

Carlsbad Caverns National Park
National Park Service
505-785-2232
www.nps.gov/cave

Roswell
Roswell Chamber of Commerce
505-623-5695
www.roswellnm.org

Taos
Taos County Chamber of Commerce
800-732-8267
www.taoschamber.com

New York
Central Park
Central Park Conservancy
212-310-6600
www.centralparknyc.org

Empire State Building
212-736-3100
www.esbnyc.com

Macy's Thanksgiving Day Parade
212-494-4495
www.macys.com

The Metropolitan Museum of Art
212-535-7710
www.metmuseum.org

National Baseball Hall of Fame and
   Museum
888-425-5633
www.baseballhalloffame.org

Rockefeller Center
212-332-6868
www.rockefellercenter.com

St. Patrick's Cathedral
The Archdiocese of New York
212-753-2261
www.ny-archdiocese.org

The Solomon R. Guggenheim Museum
Solomon R. Guggenheim Foundation
212-423-3500
www.guggenheim.org/new_york_
   index.shtml

Statue of Liberty
National Park Service
212-363-3200
www.nps.gov/stli

Times Square
Times Square Alliance
212-768-1560
www.timessquarenyc.org

United Nations
212-963-8687
www.un.org/tours

North Carolina
Biltmore Estate
800-624-1575
www.biltmore.com

Blue Ridge Parkway
National Park Service
828-298-0398
www.nps.gov/blri

Cape Hatteras National Seashore
National Park Service
252-472-2111
www.nps.gov/caha

Roanoke Island
Roanoke Island Festival Park
252-475-1500
www.roanokeisland.com

North Dakota
Fort Abraham Lincoln State Park
North Dakota Parks and
   Recreation Department
701-667-6340
www.ndparks.com/Parks/FLSP.htm

International Peace Garden
888-432-6733
www.peacegarden.com

North Dakota State Capitol
Bismarck-Mandan Convention and
   Visitors Bureau
800-767-3555
www.bismarckmandancvb.com

Theodore Roosevelt National Park
National Park Service
701-623-4466 (South Unit)
701-842-2333 (North Unit)
www.nps.gov/thro

Ohio
The Cincinnati Museum Center at
   Union Terminal
800-733-2077
www.cincymuseum.org

Cuyahoga Valley National Park
National Park Service
800-445-9667
www.nps.gov/cuva

Professional Football Hall of Fame
330-456-8207
www.profootballhof.com

Rock and Roll Hall of Fame and Museum
216-781-7625
www.rockhall.com

Serpent Mound
Adams County Travel and Visitors Bureau
877-232-6764
www.adamscountytravel.org

Serpent Mound
Independent Crop Circle Researchers'
Association (ICCRA)
734-891-2689
www.cropcirclenews.com

Oklahoma
National Cowboy & Western
Heritage Museum
405-478-2250
www.nationalcowboymuseum.org

Oklahoma City National Memorial
888-542-4673
www.oklahomacitynationalmemorial.org

Woody Guthrie Folk Festival
www.woodyguthrie.com

Oregon
Crater Lake National Park
National Park Service
541-594-3100
www.nps.gov/crla

Mount Hood
Mount Hood Area Chamber of Commerce
503-622-3017
www.mthood.org

Multnomah Falls
USDA Forest Service
503-695-2372
www.fs.fed.us/r6/columbia/millennium2/
information.htm

Newberry National Volcanic Monument
USDA Forest Service
541-593-2421
www.fs.fed.us/r6/centraloregon/
newberrynvm

Pioneer Courthouse Square
503-223-1613
www.pioneercourthousesquare.org

Pennsylvania
Fallingwater
Western Pennsylvania Conservancy
724-329-8501
www.paconserv.org/index-fw1.asp

Gettysburg
Gettysburg Convention and
Visitor's Bureau
717-334-2100
www.gettysburg.com

Groundhog Day
Punxsutawney Groundhog Club
www.groundhog.org

Independence National Historic Park
National Park Service
215-965-2305
www.nps.gov/inde

Mount Washington
Greater Pittsburgh Convention and
Visitors Bureau
877-568-3744
www.visitpittsburgh.com

Philadelphia's Old City
Old City Civic Association
215-440-7000
www.oldcity.org

Rhode Island
Benefit Street, "Mile of History"
The Rhode Island Historical Society
401-273-7507
www.rihs.org/tours.html

Block Island
Block Island Chamber of Commerce
800-383-2474
www.blockislandchamber.com

Newport Mansions
The Preservation Society of Newport
County
401-847-1000
www.newportmansions.org

South Carolina
Fort Sumter National Monument
The National Park Service
843-883-3123
www.nps.gov/fosu

Hilton Head Island
Hilton Head Island, Bluffton Chamber
of Commerce
843-785-3673
www.hiltonheadisland.org

Myrtle Beach
Myrtle Beach Area Convention and
Visitors Bureau
800-356-3016
www.mbchamber.com

South Dakota
Badlands National Park
National Park Service
605-433-5361
www.nps.gov/badl

Crazy Horse Memorial
605-673-4681
www.crazyhorsememorial.org

Mount Rushmore National Memorial
National Park Service
605-574-3171
www.nps.gov/moru

Sturgis Motorcycle Rally
605-720-0800
www.sturgismotorcyclerally.com

Tennessee
Beale Street
www.bealestreet.com

Graceland
Elvis Presley Enterprises
800-238-2000
www.elvis.com/graceland

Grand Ole Opry
800-733-6779
www.opry.com

Great Smoky Mountains National Park
National Park Service
865-436-1200
www.nps.gov/grsm

Texas
The Alamo
210-225-1391
www.thealamo.org

Amistad National Recreation Area
National Park Service
830-775-7491
www.nps.gov/amis

Austin
Austin Convention & Visitors Bureau
866-462-8784
www.austintexas.org

Big Bend National Park
National Park Service
432-477-2251
www.nps.gov/bibe

Big Thicket National Preserve
National Park Service
409-951-6725
www.nps.gov/bith

Corpus Christi
The Corpus Christi Convention
& Visitors Bureau
800-766-2322
www.corpuschristicvb.com

Guadalupe Mountains National Park
National Park Service
915-828-3251
www.nps.gov/gumo

Houston Livestock Show and Rodeo
832-667-1000
www.hlsr.com

San Antonio Riverwalk
The Paseo del Rio Association
210-227-4262
http://thesanantonioriverwalk.com

Space Center Houston
281-244-2100
www.spacecenter.org

South Padre Island
South Padre Island Convention
& Visitors Bureau
800-767-2373
www.sopadre.com

Utah
Arches National Park
National Park Service
435-719-2299
www.nps.gov/arch

Bryce Canyon National Park
National Park Service
435-834-5322
www.nps.gov/brca

Canyonlands National Park
National Park Service
435-719-2313
www.nps.gov/cany

Capitol Reef National Park
National Park Service
435-425-3791 ext. 111
www.nps.gov/care

Lake Powell in the Glen Canyon National
Recreation Area
National Park Service
928-608-6200
www.nps.gov/glca

Monument Valley Navajo Tribal Park
Navajo Parks and Recreation Department
435-727-5874
www.navajonationparks.org/htm/
monumentvalley.htm

Salt Lake City
Salt Lake Convention & Visitors Bureau
801-521-2822
www.visitsaltlake.com

Zion National Park
National Park Service
435-772-3256
www.nps.gov/zion

Vermont
Green Mountain National Forest
USDA Forest Service
802-747-6700
www.fs.fed.us/r9/gmfl

Lake Champlain
The Lake Champlain Regional Chamber
of Commerce
877-686-5253
www.vermont.org

Acknowledgments

Page 40: Verses from "The Bridge," from *Complete Poems of Hart Crane*, by Hart Crane, edited by Marc Simon. Copyright © 1933, 1958, 1966 by Liveright Publishing Corporation. Copyright © 1986 by Marc Simon. Reprinted by permission of Liveright Publishing Corporation.

Page 167: Quote by Carhenge creator Jim Reinders, from an interview with author Eric Peterson. Copyright © Eric Peterson. Reprinted by permission.

Page 173: Quote by Sturgis Motorcycle Rally attendee. Copyright © 2005 Sturgis Motorcycle Rally. Reprinted by permission.

Page 191: The Mission Statement for the National Cowboy & Western Heritage Museum. Copyright © 1997 the National Cowboy & Western Heritage Museum. Reprinted by permission.

Page 193: Memorial Mission Statement, the Oklahoma City National Memorial & Museum. Copyright © 1996 Oklahoma City National Memorial Foundation. Text and image reprinted by permission.

Trademark Acknowledgments

The brand-name products mentioned in this publication are trademarks or service marks of their respective companies. The mention of any product in this publication does not constitute an endorsement by the respective proprietors of Publications International, Ltd., nor does it constitute an endorsement by any of these companies that their products should be used in the manner represented in this publication.

AMC Gremlin® is a registered trademark of the American Motors Corp.; American Institute of Architects is a collective membership mark of the American Institute of Architects; Andy Warhol Museum® is a registered service mark of Carnegie Institute; Barney® is a registered trademark of Lyons Partnership, LP composed of Rhenclid, Inc.; Beanie Babies® is a registered trademark of Ty, Inc.; Bellagio® is a registered service mark of Bellagio, LLC, Ltd.; Belmont Stakes® is a registered service mark of the New York Racing Association; Biltmore Estate® is a registered service mark of Biltmore Co.; Bloomingdale's® is a registered trademark of Federated Department Stores; Bob Dylan® is a registered trademark of Bob Dylan; Boston Athletic Association® is a registered trademark and service mark of the Boston Athletic Association; Boston Marathon® is a registered trademark and service mark of the Boston Athletic Association; Boston Pops® is a registered service mark of the Boston Symphony Orchestra, Inc.; Boston Red Sox® is a registered trademark of the Boston Red Sox Baseball Club, LP; Cadillac® is a registered trademark of the General Motors Corp.; Camden Yards® is a registered service mark of The Maryland Stadium Authority; Chanel® is a registered trademark of Chanel, Inc.; Cheyenne Frontier Days® is a registered service mark of Cheyenne Frontier Days, Inc.; Chicago Cubs® is a registered trademark of the Chicago National League Ball Club, Inc.; Churchill Downs® is a registered service mark of CDIP, LLC, CDIP Holdings, LLC; Cinemascope® is a registered trademark and service mark of 20th Century Fox Film Corp.; Clifford the Big Red Dog™ is a trademark of Norman Bridwell; Club Coca-Cola® is a registered trademark of the Coca-Cola Co.; Coca-Cola® is a registered trademark of the Coca-Cola Co.; Colonial Williamsburg® is a registered service mark of the Colonial Williamsburg Foundation; Crisco® is a registered trademark of Procter and Gamble Co.; Daddy of 'em all® is a registered service mark of Cheyenne Frontier Days, Inc.; Empire State Building® is a registered service mark of the Empire State Building Co.; Fallingwater® is a registered trademark of the Western Pennsylvania Conservancy; Felix the Cat® is a registered trademark of Felix the Cat Productions, Inc.; Fenimore Art Museum® is a registered trademark and service mark of the New York State Historical Association; Fenway Park® is a registered trademark of the Boston Red Sox Baseball Club, LP; Ferrari® is a registered trademark of Ferrari SpA Joint Stock Co.; FIFA World Cup® is a registered trademark and service mark of Federation Internationale de Football Association Corp.; Fightin' Irish® is a registered trademark of the University of Notre Dame du Lac; Frank Lloyd Wright® is a registered trademark of the Frank Lloyd Wright Foundation; Freedom Trail® is a registered service mark of the Freedom Trail Foundation; Giorgio Armani® is a registered trademark of Giorgio Armani SpA Corp.; Gold's Gym® is a registered service mark of Gold's Gym Enterprises, Inc.; Graceland® is a registered trademark of Elvis Presley Enterprises, Inc.; Grand Hotel® is a registered service mark of the Grand Hotel Co.; Grand Ole Opry® is a registered trademark of Gaylord Entertainment Co.; Grateful Dead® is a registered trademark of Grateful Dead Productions; Green Bay Packers® is a registered trademark of Green Bay Packers, Inc.; Green Monster® is a registered service mark of the Boston Red Sox Baseball Club, LP and New England Sports Ventures, LLC; Gucci® is a registered trademark of Gucci America, Inc.; Hammacher, Schlemmer® is a registered service mark of Hammacher, Schlemmer & Co., Inc.; Harborplace® is a registered service mark of Harbor Place Associates, LP; Hearst Castle® is a registered trademark of the State of California Department of Parks and Recreation; Heinz® is a registered trademark of H.J. Heinz Co.; House of Blues® is a registered service mark of House of Blues Brands Corp.; Houston Livestock Show and Rodeo™ is a trademark of Houston Livestock Show and Rodeo, Inc.; Hugo Boss® is a registered trademark of HUGO BOSS Trade Mark Management GmbH & Co.; Iditarod® is a registered trademark of the Iditarod Trail Committee, Inc.; IMAX® is a registered trademark of IMAX Corp.; Indianapolis Motor Speedway® is a registered trademark and service mark of the Indianapolis Motor Speedway Corp.; Indy 500® is a registered trademark and service mark of the Indianapolis Motor Speedway Corp.; Indy Racing League® is a registered trademark and service mark of Brickyard Trademarks, Inc.; Jimi Hendrix® is a registered trademark of Experience Hendrix, LLC; John Wayne® is a registered trademark of Wayne Enterprises, LP; Jurassic Park® is a registered trademark of Amblin Entertainment, Inc. and Universal City Studios, Inc.; Keep Austin Weird® is a registered trademark of Nobonz, Inc.; Kentucky Derby® is a registered trademark of Churchill Downs, Inc.; Kingston Mines® is a registered service mark of Redfords Pub, Inc.; Lalique® is a registered trademark of Lalique Corp.; Lambeau Field® is a registered trademark and service mark of Green Bay Packers, Inc.; Louis Vuitton® is a registered trademark of Louis Vuitton Malletier Corp.; Macy's® is a registered trademark of Macy's, Inc.; Macy's Thanksgiving Day Parade® is a registered service mark of Federated Department Stores, Inc.; Mandalay Bay® is a registered service mark of Mandalay Bay Resort Corp.; Microsoft® is a registered trademark of Microsoft Corp.; Miss America Pageant® is a registered trademark of the Miss America Organization, The DBA Miss America Pageant; Monterey Bay Aquarium® is a registered trademark and service mark of the Monterey Bay Aquarium Foundation; Monticello® is a registered service mark of the Thomas Jefferson Foundation, Inc.; Mormon Tabernacle Choir® is a registered trademark and service mark of Intellectual Reserve, Inc.; Mount Vernon® is a registered trademark of the Mount Vernon Ladies' Association of the Union; Mystic Aquarium® is a registered service mark of Sea Research Foundation, Inc.; Mystic Seaport® is a registered service mark of Mystic Seaport Museum, Inc.; National Aquarium in Baltimore® is a registered service mark of the National Aquarium in Baltimore, Inc.; National Baseball Hall of Fame® is a registered service mark of the National Baseball Hall of Fame and Museum, Inc.; National Cathedral® is a registered trademark of the Protestant Episcopal Cathedral Foundation; National Cherry Blossom Festival® is a registered service mark of the National Cherry Blossom Festival, Inc.; National Cowboy Hall of Fame and Western Heritage Museum® is a registered service mark and collective membership mark of the National Cowboy Hall of Fame and Western Heritage Center; National Symphony Orchestra® is a registered trademark and service mark of the Trustees of the John F. Kennedy Center for the Performing Arts, a D.C. Trust; Neptune Festival® is a registered service mark of Virginia Beach Events Unlimited; Newport Jazz Festival® is a registered service mark of George Wein and Festival Productions; NFL® is a registered trademark of the National Football League; Nieman Marcus® is a registered service mark of NM Nevada Trust; OMNIMAX® is a registered trademark of IMAX® Corp.; Peanuts® is a registered trademark of United Feature Syndicate, Inc.; PNC Park® is a registered service mark of PNC Financial Services Group, Inc.; Porsche® is a registered trademark of Dr. Ing. h.c.F. Porsche AG; Port Discovery® is a registered service mark of The Baltimore Children's Museum; Preakness Stakes® is a registered service mark of the Maryland Jockey Club of Baltimore City, The Corporation Maryland Pimlico Race Course; Punxsutawney Phil® is a registered service mark of the Punxsutawney Groundhog Club, Inc.; Ralph Lauren® is a registered trademark of PRL USA Holdings, Inc.; Ringling Bros. and Barnum & Bailey® is a registered trademark and service mark of Ringling Bros. and Barnum & Bailey Combined Shows, Inc.; Rock and Roll Hall of Fame® is a registered trademark and service mark of the Rock and Roll Hall of Fame Foundation, Inc.; Rockefeller Center® is a registered service mark of Rockefeller Center, Inc.; Rose Bowl® is a registered service mark of the City of Pasadena; Rose Bowl Parade® is a registered trademark and service mark of the Pasadena Tournament of Roses Association; Rum Boogie Café® is a registered service mark of Creative Restaurants, Inc.; Ryman Auditorium® is a registered service mark of Gaylord Entertainment Co.; San Diego Zoo® is a registered service mark of the Zoological Society of San Diego, Inc.; Smithsonian Institution® is a registered service mark of the Smithsonian Institution Trust; Snoopy® is a registered trademark of United Feature Syndicate, Inc.; Space Needle® is a registered trademark of Space Needle Corp.; SPAM® is a registered trademark of Hormel Foods, Corp.; Sturgis® is a registered trademark and service mark of the Sturgis Area Chamber of Commerce; Sun Studio® is a registered service mark of Sun Studio, Inc.; Super Bowl® is a registered trademark of the National Football League; Taliesin® is a registered trademark of the Frank Lloyd Wright Foundation; Tall Ships® is a registered service mark of The American Sail Training Association; TelePrompTer® is a registered trademark of Teleprompter Corp.; Telluride® is a registered trademark of TSG Ski & Golf, LLC, Ltd.; The American Museum of Natural History® is a registered service mark of the American Museum of Natural History; The Beatles® is a registered trademark of Apple Corps Limited; The Chrysler Building® is a registered trademark of TST/TMW 405 Lexington; The Metropolitan Museum of Art® is a registered service mark of The Metropolitan Museum of Art; The Museum of Modern Art® is a registered service mark of the Museum of Modern Art; The Solomon R. Guggenheim Museum® is a registered trademark and service mark of the Solomon R. Guggenheim Foundation; The World of Coca-Cola® is a registered trademark and service mark of the Coca-Cola Co.; The World Series® is a registered trademark of the Office of the Commissioner of Baseball; Tiffany and Company® is a registered trademark of Tiffany (NJ), Inc.; Tournament of Roses® is a registered service mark of the Pasadena Tournament of Roses Association; Trump Taj Mahal Casino-Resort® is a registered service mark of Donald J. Trump; Twinkies® is a registered trademark of Interstate Brands Corp.; United States Postal Service® is a registered trademark of the United States Postal Service; University of Texas® is a registered service mark of the University of Texas System Board of Regents; Vlasic® is a registered trademark of Pinnacle Foods Corp.; Woody Guthrie® is a registered trademark of Woody Guthrie Publications, Inc.; World Trade Center® is a registered service mark of the World Trade Centers Association.